MUSIC AND THE FRENCH ENLIGHTENMENT

Music and the French Enlightenment

RECONSTRUCTION OF A DIALOGUE
1750–1764

CYNTHIA VERBA

CLARENDON PRESS · OXFORD

Oxford University Press, Walton Street, Oxford OX2 6DP
Oxford New York
Athens Auckland Bangkok Bombay
Calcutta Cape Town Dar es Salaam Delhi
Florence Hong Kong Istanbul Karachi
Kuala Lumpur Madras Madrid Melbourne
Mexico City Nairobi Paris Singapore
Taipei Tokyo Toronto
and associated companies in
Berlin Ibadan

Oxford is a trade mark of Oxford University Press

Published in the United States
by Oxford University Press Inc., New York

First published 1993

British Library Cataloguing in Publication Data
Data available

Library of Congress Cataloging in Publication Data
Verba, Cynthia.
Music and the French enlightenment: reconstruction of a dialogue,
1750–1764 / Cynthia Verba.
Includes bibliographical references and index.
1. Music—France—18th century—History and criticism.
2. Enlightenment.   3. Music—Philosophy and aesthetics.   I. Title.
ML270.3.V47   1993   780'.944'09033—dc20
ISBN 0–19–816281–2

3 5 7 9 10 8 6 4 2

Printed in Great Britain
on acid-free paper by
Antony Rowe Ltd
Chippenham, Wilts.

To
Sidney, Margy, Ericka, and Tina Verba,
and to Frieda Winston

ACKNOWLEDGEMENTS

THE evolution of this book has a long history, and a long list of people have influenced my thoughts throughout the years. Much of this influence has occurred through the process of informal dialogue—with family, friends, and colleagues. (The choice of 'dialogue' as subject-matter is by no means pure coincidence.)

Because of the informal nature of the discussions, as well as the long period of gestation, it is almost impossible to give credit to all the people who, knowingly or unknowingly, helped to shape my thoughts. It is easiest to begin with three of the more structured events that played a decisive role. The first was my doctoral dissertation, University of Chicago, written under the guidance of Philip Gossett. One of the most important things that I learned from Phil and from the dissertation experience itself is that research is never done. And indeed, some of my most important ideas about Rameau and the French Enlightenment occurred only after I had completed the study. What the dissertation did was to cement my strong kindred feelings about the spirit of the French Enlightenment, encouraging me to look beyond Rameau to the principal figures who embodied that spirit. Living in Paris for two years (with my spouse and three children) while I conducted my dissertation research could only enhance this sense of connectedness to that special era.

The second formal event was a seminar that I was invited to teach at Harvard University at Leverett House in 1978, as part of Harvard's programme in General Education. Entitled 'Eighteenth-century Opera and the French Enlightenment', the House seminar marked the actual beginning of the present book. I became aware while preparing the teaching materials for this course that there was very little available in English from the writings of the French Enlightenment philosophers on music. My original plan was simply to do a book of translations to remedy this situation. That goal was quickly overshadowed, however, once the idea took hold that there was an entire dialogue that needed reconstructing. For the opportunity to teach the seminar that led to this book, I would like to thank Kenneth and Caroline Andrews, who were then Master and Co-Master of Leverett House.

The third turning-point occurred when I became a Fellow at the Bunting Institute of Radcliffe College in 1987. With the opportunity to take time off from my administrative position at Harvard University, I was able to make great strides toward completion of the book. The Bunting opportunity also gave me something more precious than time.

Working side by side with so many accomplished women, and only women, gave me a sense of 'I can do it'. For this, I am particularly grateful to the Bunting Institute of Radcliffe College—may it thrive.

Now, on to the more difficult task of informal credits. No one has contributed more than my husband, Sidney Verba, who, although a professor of political science, surely deserves an honorary degree in musicology. As very close runners-up, my three daughters—Margy, Ericka, and Tina—have given a very special kind of support that only daughters can give. Even before they knew what the word meant, they were 'feminists' in the very best sense of the word—we are all so proud of one another. Speaking of pride, there is also my mother, who reads much of what I write and shows it to her friends, as if she were showing off the pictures of grandchildren (she does that too, of course).

Much of my writing took place in Mount Desert, Maine, to which we have returned each summer to renew ourselves for over a decade. In addition to the scenery, Maine has offered the further attraction of an established tradition of reunions every summer with our close friends, Janet Levy and Leonard Meyer, who have been long-standing participants in the dialogue process. On many a long hike, each of them has helped to clear up some thought about the book that was puzzling to me at the time, not to mention the overall encouragement that they have given me through the years.

The final stage of preparing the book took place in the Music Library of Harvard University. I would like to thank Mark Kagan, Music Department Administrator, for having provided comfortable working space. The final stage also introduced one new figure, Nick Nesbitt, a graduate student in Romance Languages at Harvard, who has worked as my assistant on some of the translations in the appendix.

Have I forgotten anyone? I know that I have, so this is a communal thank-you to all my friends and colleagues who have engaged in musical dialogue with me.

CONTENTS

ABBREVIATIONS

Assezat	*Œuvres complètes de Diderot*, ed. Jules Assézat and Maurice Tourneux, 10 vols. (Paris: Garnier, 1875–7)
CTW	*Jean-Philippe Rameau: Complete Theoretical Writings*, ed. Erwin R. Jacobi, 6 vols. (Rome: American Institute of Musicology, 1967–72, facsimile edn.)
Hermann	*Denis Diderot: Œuvres complètes, édition critique et annotée*, secretary-general Jean Varloot, 23 vols. to date (Paris: Hermann, 1975–). Each volume has its own editor, given at first reference to that volume.
JAMS	*Journal of the American Musicological Society*
Launay	Denise Launay (ed.), *La Querelle des Bouffons: texte des pamphlets avec introduction, commentaires et index*, 3 vols. (Geneva: Minkoff, 1973)

I

Introduction

AROUND the middle of the eighteenth century, some of the leading figures of the French Enlightenment became engaged in what was to be a prolonged series of writings and exchanges about music. Many of the discussions centred around the views of the composer-theorist Jean-Philippe Rameau, who was both a participant and increasingly a subject of controversy. The *philosophes* were reacting to, or were involved in, three different events which occurred fairly close to one another.

The first was Rameau's breakthrough in music theory with his formulation of the principle of the fundamental bass—a single principle that could explain the structure and behaviour of a multitude of chords and chord progressions used in eighteenth-century tonal practice.[1] The second was the prodigious undertaking of the *Encyclopédie*, with Diderot and d'Alembert as editors, and with Rousseau as principal contributor of articles on music, the first volume of which appeared in 1751. The third event was the eruption of the celebrated musical controversy of 1753, the 'Querelle des Bouffons', over the relative merits of Italian comic opera and French tragic opera.

Much of the writing which emanated from these three occasions took the form of a dialogue, as the principal participants—Rameau, Rousseau, Diderot, and d'Alembert—addressed their remarks to one another, or to others who entered into the discussion. Such exchanges were characteristic of the French Enlightenment. New ideas frequently emerged as the result of thrusts and parries, of rebuttals or further development of initial ideas. Thinking was almost a communal activity. Not only did they exchange thoughts in writing, they also conversed in person—at the salons and cafés that they frequented for just this purpose.[2]

What is noteworthy about this particular dialogue on music is its

---

[1] Rameau's first treatise, the *Traité de l'harmonie*, appeared in 1722. His theories, however, were still a lively subject of debate during the 1750s, especially since he continued to reformulate his ideas and produce new treatises during the intervening years.

[2] The following description, taken from Arthur M. Wilson's account of Diderot's early period in Paris during the 1740s, provides a vivid picture of the company that met: 'The power of Paris to draw to itself the talents of France is exemplified by the association around the table of the Panier Fleuri of these four young men—d'Alembert, the Parisian foundling; Condillac, the nobleman from Lyon; Rousseau, the plebeian from Genevä and Annecy; and Diderot, the bourgeois from Langres.' (Arthur M. Wilson, *Diderot* (New York: Oxford University Press, 1972), 66.)

thematic richness. The combined occasions of the launching of a new theory of music, a new *Encyclopédie* with thorough coverage of music, and a new operatic quarrel—all roughly at the same time—inspired musical discussions of extraordinary breadth. Music was treated as both an art and a science, making it almost inevitable that the discussions would deal with some of the most fundamental issues of the French Enlightenment: the nature of artistic expression, the nature of scientific inquiry, and the respective roles of reason and experience in art and science. The debate over these issues was a sustained one, pursued with intensity for over a decade.

The continuity of the dialogue was further strengthened by the fact that the principal participants played multiple and overlapping roles. Rameau was not only active as a music theorist, he was also the leading composer of French opera. As such, he was one of the principal defenders of the French in the 'Querelle des Bouffons', arguing chiefly against the *philosophes* who favoured the Italians.

Rousseau's prominence in the 'Querelle' was assured through his outspoken criticism of French opera in his *Lettre sur la musique française*. He had still further impact in the controversy through the success of his own comic opera, *Le Devin du village*, which was composed shortly before the outbreak of the 'Querelle'. In addition—as mentioned above—he was the author of most of the articles on music in the *Encyclopédie*, and they in turn drew heavily on the theoretical writings of Rameau. It should be noted that in his rejection of the French musical tradition Rousseau was more extreme or radical than any of the other *philosophes*. His views eventually brought him into conflict not only with the conservative Rameau, but with all his fellow *encylopédistes*.

D'Alembert contributed to music theory through his presentation of Rameau's theories in a simplified version, the *Elémens de musique théorique et pratique*, published in 1752. He also played a role as co-editor of the *Encyclopédie*, in which he had primary responsibility for articles on mathematics and related subjects. As a mathematician, he injected methodological rigour and objectivity into the theoretical debates. In addition, he played a mediating role in the 'Querelle', pointing to the relative merits of both sides.

Diderot was primarily occupied as chief editor of the *Encyclopédie*, but contributed as well to the 'Querelle' by introducing reasoned and conciliatory arguments into the otherwise heated exchanges of the pamphlet war. Also not to be overlooked was Diderot's strong interest in music as science. His 'Principes Généraux d'Acoustique', in his *Mémoires sur différens sujets de mathématiques*, published in 1748, summarizes the major recent findings in acoustics—of Sauveur, Euler, Taylor, and others—and presents a clear account of Rameau's principle of the 'sounding body' (the *corps sonore*) and its musical significance. Not only does Diderot draw very close to Rameau's position in this work, but according to contemporary testimony he played a direct role in the editing of Rameau's treatise, the *Démonstration du principe de l'harmonie*, published in 1750.[3]

Diderot's role in the musical dialogue, however, stands somewhat apart from the others. He was less directly involved in the immediate exchanges or quarrels—indeed, his harshest attacks against Rameau, as both opera composer and theorist, came mainly after the heated exchanges had subsided, in *Le Neveu de Rameau*, written in 1761. Through much of the debate, Diderot was largely attracted to the dialectical process itself. Each time he adopted a position, he was simultaneously aware of the complexities and inherent tensions in that position, pulling him onward to a new formulation. His views on music consequently underwent almost constant change—reflecting significant changes in his epistemology—with the important result that he carried many ideas further, and achieved a greater level of synthesis among opposing ideas than had been attained before. It is because of this synthesizing role that Diderot holds a special place in the present study.[4]

The continuity of the dialogue and close overlapping of musical activities among the principal participants was at its most intense during the years from about 1750 until the death of Rameau in 1764. During that time their writings tended to shift back and forth from one arena to another: from theoretical treatises, to the *Encyclopédie*, to literature of the 'Querelle'—as well as to letters, newspaper articles, and essays on the corresponding issues. Many of these shifts also involved a turn from aesthetic issues to scientific issues, and vice versa.

The abundance and rapidity with which new arguments appeared, further complicated by their changing forums and focal issues, presented little difficulty for the participants themselves in following the continuity of the dialogue. For the current scholar, however, this is a

[3] Strong evidence for this collaboration is presented by Anne-Marie Chouillet in 'Présupposés, contours et prolongements de la polémique autour des écrits théoriques de Jean-Philippe Rameau', in Jerome de la Gorce (ed.), *Jean-Philippe Rameau: Colloque international organisé par la Société Rameau: Dijon 21–24 septembre 1983* (Paris: Champion-Slatkine, 1987), 425–43. She cites among others the testimony of the Abbé Raynal, who discussed their collaboration in the *Correspondance littéraire*, a newsletter reporting on the literary and artistic scene in Paris. Further evidence is cited by Arthur Wilson in his biography of Diderot (*Diderot*, 89). Finally, a more precise view of Diderot's role is suggested by Thomas Christensen in his forthcoming book, *Jean-Philippe Rameau: The Science of Music Theory in the Enlightenment* (Cambridge University Press). His study of Rameau's original drafts of the *Demonstration* (in chs. 6 and 8) strongly points to the hand of Diderot in the Preface to the treatise.

[4] There were indeed others who made important contributions to the musical dialogue—notably the Barons Von Grimm and d'Holbach—but they had less sustained involvement in all three of the events cited above.

more serious problem. Some of the arguments appeared in unexpected places; others were never identified as part of an exchange.

If we are to understand the participants' writings on music more fully, then we must identify those portions that were part of a dialogue, and attempt to reconstruct all the connecting links in their arguments. The nature of the task becomes clearer if we consider just a few examples. The first concerns Rameau's essay, *Erreurs sur la musique dans l'Encyclopédie*, published in 1755. Contrary to the implication of the title, the essay is far more than an attack on the music articles in the *Encyclopédie*. Over a third of the text is devoted to Rousseau's doctrine of melodic supremacy, which posits that melody rather than harmony is the principal source of expression in music. This doctrine, however, was not yet present in the *Encyclopédie* articles, all of which were written around 1749. The concept appeared in 1753 in Rousseau's *Lettre sur la musique française*, where it became the centrepiece of his arguments against French opera. Rameau's *Erreurs*, then, should be viewed not only as an attack on specific articles in the *Encyclopédie*, but also as a response to Rousseau's *Lettre*. Unless the *Erreurs* is recognized as dealing with the larger issue of melodic supremacy, Rousseau's subsequent counter-arguments—including the development of a theoretical foundation for his position on melody—lose some of their meaning.[5]

Another example is d'Alembert's second edition of the *Elémens de musique théorique et pratique*, published in 1762. The production of a second edition of a work devoted to the theories of Rameau is in one sense a continued tribute to Rameau. The edition, however, includes a 'Discours préliminaire' and an appendix in which d'Alembert is strongly critical of the theorist. In particular, he objects to Rameau's extension of the harmonic principle and his claims for its applicability well beyond the domain of music. D'Alembert's remarks are actually culminating arguments in a series of exchanges with Rameau, and should be viewed in that context as well.

A third illustration—perhaps the most striking—is Rousseau's *Dictionnaire de musique*, published in 1768. Rousseau presented the *Dictionnaire* as a revised and expanded version of his earlier articles on music in the *Encyclopédie*. However, a large portion of the new material—distributed throughout numerous articles—consists of arguments,

---

[5] The most complete account of the debate between Rameau and the *encyclopédistes* is to be found in Alfred Oliver, *The encyclopédistes as Critics of Music* (New York: Columbia University Press, 1947; reprinted New York: AMS Press, Inc., 1966). This version, which has generally been accepted by scholars, fails to identify Rameau's responses to the *Lettre*—omitting not only his remarks in the *Erreurs*, but also Rameau's lengthy response in his principal aesthetic treatise, the *Observations sur notre instinct pour la musique* (Paris: Prault Fils, Lambert, Duchesne,1754) *CTW* iii. 255–330). It thereby loses a crucial link in the dialogue, one which will be dealt with at length in the present study.

counter-arguments and further development of ideas stemming from the *Lettre sur la musique française* and its aftermath. The *Dictionnaire*, then, was a major vehicle for Rousseau in expressing his views in the prolonged debate about music.

These examples indicate some of the difficulties in identifying the various arguments that were part of a fairly sustained musical dialogue. At the same time they underline the importance of doing so. In each case, the individual works might be regarded as self-contained, or as restricted to a given set of issues, when in reality they are intimately connected to a broad set of philosophical themes.

Still another problem confronts us as we try to view the dialogue after a time-lapse of several hundred years. The disagreements were aired in such a heated and noisy fashion—inevitably capturing our attention—that we tend to overlook the fact that there were extensive areas of agreement about music as well. The consensus applies not only to those who were on the same side, but also to Rameau and Rousseau, who were at the centre of the storm of dissension.[6]

Their quarrel over melodic versus harmonic supremacy in musical expression is well known—with Rameau an advocate of harmony, and Rousseau of melody. What is perhaps less well recognized is that they shared a commonly held belief in the neo-classical doctrine of imitation—a doctrine which in turn was inspired by Aristotle's *Poetics*. Both agreed that the doctrine applied to music as well as to the other arts—that music had to express something, that it had to have meaning. While there was disagreement about the means of musical expression, there was almost none about the view that music was an imitative art. As we shall see in greater detail in chapter 2, music generally meant music with text, principally opera; or, if without text, then expressive of the passions as if it had text or a subject to convey.

Another well-known disagreement—closely related to the harmony versus melody debate—was whether harmony was natural and subject to universal laws, as Rameau would have it, or simply a product of civilization and subject to change from culture to culture, as Rousseau described it in his later works. The remarkable area of agreement in this case was that, regardless of the universal or relative position, they held similar views of harmonic theory, essentially that it should be a search for simplifying underlying principles that could explain a multitude of harmonic events. They even agreed on many of the same underlying principles—still based on Rameau's theories, despite the growing dis-

---

[6] The common heritage of accepted ideas on musical expression will be examined in some detail in chapter 2. The importance of looking beyond the noisy quarrels—getting to the more essential views of the *philosophes* on music and aesthetics—is emphasized by Georges Snyders, *Le Goût musical en France aux XVIIe et XVIIIe siècles* (Paris: Librairie Philosophique J. Vrin, 1968).

agreements between the two. The more precise dispute—to be discussed in chapter 4—was over the degree of applicability of the underlying principles, or their status in relation to scientific law.

Just as it is important to view many of their writings on music in the context of the sustained dialogue of which they formed a part, so too is it important to view their disagreements in the context of the large areas of agreement that existed as well. Only by understanding the points at which their views converged can we appreciate more fully the fundamental aesthetic and scientific issues that drew them apart.

The quest in this study for a more accurate and complete reading of the views of the *philosophes* on music also has a bearing on a significant modernist debate over some of the same issues. In Jacques Derrida's analysis of Rousseau's *Essai sur l'origine des langues* and in Paul de Man's refutation of that analysis, both writers are concerned with self-contradictions in Rousseau's theory of imitation. Briefly, Rousseau posits an original stage in the evolution of language in which it is used to express feeling, conveyed through an inarticulate vocalization that unites language and melody. All subsequent stages of language and melody—including their evolution into what we normally think of as language and melody—are viewed by Rousseau as corruptions of their essential nature, reflecting a process of degeneration in society as well. Derrida questions how the process of degeneration of language and melody, which signifies a departure from their essential nature, can also be used to explain their essential nature; he questions how language and melody can become corrupt at the very moment when they acquire their defining qualities. Derrida concludes that Rousseau's self-contradictions lead to an inversion in his concept of imitation, inadvertently giving greater weight to the so-called corrupt forms of expression than to the pure language of feeling. De Man argues that Rousseau's ambivalence has to do less with self-contradictions in the concept of imitation than with the importance Rousseau assigns to a concept of music as an abstract system of relationships, a system in which imitation or expression is devoid of meaning. The present study recognizes ambivalences or tensions in Rousseau's thought—indeed, in the musical thought of the other *philosophes* as well—but finds that there is greater coherence and consistency in their views when they are properly placed within their dialogue context.[7]

A final point about this study has to do with its interdisciplinary

[7] Derrida in fact recognizes the musical debates as a factor in the genesis of Rousseau's theory of imitation, but focuses primarily on the issues of logic and continuity within Rousseau's own thought. For this modernist discussion see Jacques Derrida, *De la Grammatologie* (Paris: Minuit, 1967), and Paul de Man, 'The Rhetoric of Blindness: Jacques Derrida's Reading of Rousseau', in his *Blindness and Insight: Essays in the Rhetoric of Contemporary Criticism* (New York: Oxford University Press, 1971), 102–41.

nature. Music in the French Enlightenment, as we have already noted, was treated as both an art and a science. Many of the musical issues were discussed in scientific or technical terms. While all the dialogue participants were equipped with a knowledge of music theory—it was by no means the exclusive domain of Rameau or d'Alembert—contemporary scholarship is much more compartmentalized. Many specialists on Diderot or Rousseau, for example, who have closely followed their musical discussions, have done so mainly from the point of view of aesthetics; they have stopped short of entering the realm of music theory. Music specialists, on the other hand, have given relatively scant attention to the broader aesthetic or philosophical issues normally dealt with by Enlightenment scholars. The present study, although written by a music specialist, and with other music specialists in mind, is also aimed at a wider audience. In order to make some of the more technical portions more generally accessible, the presentation includes musical details that might be superfluous for the music specialist.

The volume is organized around the major themes of the dialogue and around the particular participants who gave the themes their essential shape. Each chapter not only attempts to re-establish the continuity among arguments that has been lost over time, but also to recapture the tenor and tone of the arguments. To this end, the use of direct quotations in the main body of the text is supplemented by an appendix containing lengthier passages that convey some of the salient arguments made by each of the dialogue participants. The passages are presented in translation, making most of them available in English for the first time.[8]

---

[8] With the goal of recapturing the original tenor and tone of the arguments in mind, the translations stay as close as possible to the original French wording, resorting to alternative solutions only when required for a clearer reading in English. A number of 18th cent. French terms do not have an exact equivalent in English, mainly because their meaning has changed over time. In such cases, the translations provide the closest approximations to the original meaning, guided by the context in which the expressions are used, and this is accompanied by the original expressions enclosed within square brackets.

2

Rameau and Rousseau Launch the Debate

IF we wish to become acquainted with the issues concerning music as expressive art in the prolonged dialogue on music, there is no better place to begin than Rousseau's provocative attack on French music in his *Lettre sur la musique française*, published in November 1753, and Rameau's response in the *Observations sur notre instinct pour la musique*, published four months later. Although the two texts can be considered as contributions to the 'Querelle des Bouffons', they stand apart from the main body of literature of the pamphlet war precisely because the authors deal with the larger issue about the nature of music as expressive art, rather than confining themselves to the more limited debate over the French–Italian musical rivalry.[1] Rousseau's critique of French music in the *Lettre*, while harsh and polemical in tone, is presented as part of a philosophical inquiry about the relationship between music and language. Rameau's defence is set within the context of a theoretical treatise which is concerned with the source of expression in music. Taken together, the two texts contain almost all the important issues on the nature of music that would be discussed for the next two decades and beyond.

At the time of Rameau's response in the *Observations*, the 70-year-old musician had reached the apex of his career as theorist and composer. In the realm of theory, he had already produced four major treatises— the *Traité de l'harmonie* (1722), the *Nouveau système de musique théorique* (1726), the *Génération harmonique* (1737), and the *Démonstration du principe de l'harmonie* (1750)—which had established his reputation as the leading theorist of his day.[2] Diderot and d'Alembert went beyond mere praise, and played a role in clarifying and disseminating his theories—not only through d'Alembert's *Elémens de musique théorique et pratique*, but also through the *Encyclopédie*, and other works.

---

[1] Rousseau's *Lettre* was published in a similar fashion to the other pamphlets of the 'Querelle'—as an unauthorized publication, without passing the censorship reviews that were standard at that time. Rameau's *Observations*, on the other hand, was approved by a representative of the King's Chancellor. It was published in Paris by Prault Fils, Lambert and Duchesne.

[2] Rameau's treatises are available in a facsimile edn. entitled *Jean-Philippe Rameau: Complete Theoretical Writings*, ed. Erwin R. Jacobi, 6 vols. (Rome: American Institute of Musicology, 1967–72) (*CTW*). The editor provides not only an extraordinary wealth of background information, but also additional reprints of related material. All references in the present study give the original pagination, accompanied by the pagination from *CTW*.

Rameau's operatic works had attained a similar success, leading to his ultimate triumph over his predecessor Lully, whose works had enjoyed a sustained popularity from the time of his founding of French opera under Louis XIV until well into the eighteenth century. Rameau's conquest over the more traditional works of Lully was assured by 1750, when Rameau's operas comprised a major portion of the repertory at the Opéra and his dominant position in Parisian musical life was widely recognized. Rameau's accomplishments in revitalizing French opera were acknowledged by the *philosophes*, even as their tastes turned toward Italian music in the ensuing rivalry of the 'Querelle des Bouffons'.[3] There is a certain irony in the fact that Rameau, who became the leading exponent of French opera in the face of the Italian challenge during the 'Querelle des Bouffons', was distinguished from Lully primarily through his incorporation of important features of Italian Baroque style—namely, an enriched harmonic vocabulary and a more complex contrapuntal texture—which helped to breathe new life into French opera.[4]

The abundant performances of Rameau's operas on the eve of the 'Querelle' included works in all the major forms of French opera. In addition to his four *tragédies en musique*—*Hippolyte et Aricie* (1733), *Castor et Pollux* (1737), *Dardanus* (1739) and *Zoroastre* (1749)—his operas included a large number of lighter works in the form of *opéra-ballets* and *pastorales héroïques*. He had also written a *comédie lyrique*, *Platée* (1745), which was particularly favoured by the *philosophes*. At this stage of his career, before his gradual rupture with the *philosophes*, Rameau was unmatched in his reputation as a composer and theorist.

Rousseau, at this same moment, was still a relative newcomer to the musical scene. His musical background was that of a self-taught amateur, with limited training and compositional skills. His knowledge of

---

[3] Grimm's *Lettre de M. Grimm sur Omphale*, for example, had the highest praise for Rameau's operas, even while proclaiming the virtues of Italian opera and attacking the deficiencies of Destouches's *Omphale*. This traditional French opera was first performed in 1701—with revivals that included a performance in 1752—and was closely associated with the older style of Lully. Paul-Marie Masson points out that Grimm's *Lettre sur Omphale*, which appeared in February 1752, before the successful season of the Bouffons, belongs to the older quarrel between the Lullists and the Ramists—contrary to the mistaken perception by a number of scholars that it launched the 'Querelle des Bouffons' (Paul-Marie Masson, 'La "Lettre sur Omphale"', *Revue de musicologie*, 27 (1945), 1–19).

[4] Rameau was nevertheless destined to be pitted against the Italian Bouffons because the style that he incorporated—closer to the Italian Baroque—was rapidly becoming outmoded, replaced by the newly emerging simpler *galant* style favoured by the *philosophes*. The influence of Italian music in France became a strong reality only after the death of Lully in 1687, the end of his monopoly control over French musical life being marked by a sharp increase in the flow of Italian music into France. Paul-Marie Masson, in his discussion of the quarrel between the Lullists and the Ramists, sees the influence of Italian style as an important factor in this quarrel—with the Lullists preferring the greater simplicity of Lully, and the Ramists favouring the Italian-inspired richness of Rameau (Masson, 'La "Lettre sur Omphale"').

harmony, ironically, was largely based on his earlier encounter with Rameau's *Traité*. Despite these limitations, Rousseau nevertheless at the age of 41 made a powerful adversary for Rameau. He succeeded in waging the war primarily on aesthetic and philosophical grounds, and he also managed to use his musical sensitivities to best advantage. By this time, he had already written the music articles for the *Encyclopédie* (drafted hastily in 1749, and heavily indebted to the theories of Rameau), which helped to establish his position as the intellectual leader of the *philosophes* on musical issues. His knowledge of Italian opera dated back to 1744 when, as Secretary to the French Ambassador in Venice, he first acquired a taste for Italian music. Before the 'Querelle des Bouffons', he had already written two letters to the Baron Von Grimm expressing his views on French and Italian opera. Interestingly enough, the earlier letter ('Lettre sur le drame musical en France et en Italie', unfinished and dating from around 1750 or earlier) was still very sympathetic to French opera, finding it more moving than Italian opera, and also criticizing the latter for its lack of choruses and for its uninspired harmonies and orchestration—and here he referred specifically to the contrasting example of Rameau.[5] By 1752, however, in Rousseau's second letter to Grimm (*Lettre à M. Grimm au sujet des remarques ajoutées à sa lettre sur Omphale*), he reversed himself—foreshadowing the anti-French position of the *Lettre sur la musique française*—by criticizing the monotony of Lully and his imitators on the one hand, and criticizing the contrapuntal complexity and the 'excess of learning' in Rameau's music on the other. He also criticized French opera for its failure to make a clear differentiation between recitative and aria.[6]

Rousseau had also engaged in two earlier exchanges with Rameau—in one case, a cordial interaction; in the other, a negative encounter that neither would forget. The first concerned the young Rousseau's new system of musical notation, which he presented in his 'Projet concernant de nouveaux signes pour la musique' in 1742. Although the system was considered to be impractical by Rameau and others, the exchange was conducted in a tone of mutual respect. The hostile encounter was the celebrated meeting in 1745, when Rousseau's *opéra-ballet*, *Les Muses galantes*, was performed at the home of La Poplinière, the wealthy and influential music patron and supporter of Rameau. During the performance Rameau was openly critical of the work, causing not only

---

[5] The letter was first published by Albert Jansen in his *Jean-Jacques Rousseau als Musiker* (Berlin: G. Reimer, 1884).

[6] For a discussion of the two letters see Eve Kisch, 'Rameau and Rousseau', *Music and Letters*, 22, 2 (1941), 97–115.

embarrassment to Rousseau, but the beginning of a personal animosity that grew increasingly bitter over the years and coloured all their subsequent encounters.

Rousseau's early humiliation as a composer was subsequently overshadowed by the prodigious success of his comic opera, *Le Devin du village*, which was first presented at Fontainebleau on 18 October 1752, and then premiered at the Paris Opéra on 1 March 1753, at the height of the 'Querelle des Bouffons'. Written in large part before the 1752 arrival of the Italian comic opera players—or 'Bouffons', as they were called—*Le Devin* nevertheless reflected Rousseau's earlier exposure to the Italians, and incorporated important features of Italian comic opera style (most noticeable in the Italian overture, the strong presence of conventional *buffa* melodic motives, and the use of recitative—as opposed to the French practice of spoken dialogue in musical comedies). The success of *Le Devin* had an enormous impact on French opera, sparking numerous imitations and a wave of compositional activity in which features of Italian comic opera were adapted and incorporated into the French genre.[7]

As further background to Rousseau's *Lettre sur la musique française* and the subsequent exchanges between Rameau and Rousseau, the 'Querelle des Bouffons' had been under way for close to a year, having begun with the triumphant performance at the Paris Opéra of Pergolesi's *La serva padrona* by the visiting troupe of Italian players on 1 August 1752. Widespread enthusiasm for Italian comic opera had quickly turned into a challenge to French opera, and especially to the grandiose musical tragedies of Rameau and others.[8]

To digress for a moment, it is important to review the essential features of French *tragédie lyrique* and Italian *opera buffa*, since the contrast between them had considerable bearing on the aesthetic issues that were taken up by Rameau and Rousseau and the other *philosophes*

---

[7] *Le Devin* was performed close to 400 times in Paris between its première and the close of the 18th cent. During that same period it was performed in almost every major city throughout Europe. It was also parodied by the French comic opera librettist Favart in a version which eventually was translated into German and set to music by the young Mozart as *Bastien und Bastienne* in 1768.

[8] *La serva* was first produced in Naples in 1733, and had already been staged in Paris at the Comédie Italienne in 1746. But it was only at this particular time that Italian comic opera met with such success and caused such commotion. The visiting troupe of Eustachio Bambini stayed from August 1752 until early 1754, when enthusiasm began to wane. During that time they produced 13 comic operas. They were called 'intermezzi' or 'intermède', referring back to the original practice, begun in Naples around 1710, of inserting comic episodes in between the three acts of Italian *opera seria*. Those that were performed in Paris in 1752–3 were actually *pasticcios*, since they consisted of popular arias by many different composers—a common practice in Italian opera in this period. The influence of the Italian genre was felt in French opera, transforming its very nature, well after the departure of the Bouffons.

as part of the prolonged dialogue on music. What they were faced with was a distinct choice between two alternative approaches to opera.[9]

French *tragédie lyrique* reflected the dignity and ornate splendour of the *ancien régime*, still following an operatic model established by Lully and his librettist Quinault during the reign of Louis XIV.[10] At the heart of the Lullian model are dramatic dialogue scenes, set mainly as recitative, and using a highly melodic recitative style that would remain a distinctive feature of the French genre. The setting, above all, highlights the text and dramatic situation. At the more impassioned moments in the dialogue the vocal line swells into brief lyrical passages called *petits airs*. The stylistic similarity between the melodic recitatives on the one hand, and the brief and simple arias on the other, maintains continuity in the dialogue, with the music flowing smoothly between recitative and *petit air*.[11] Continuity is further assured by the general avoidance of prolonged elaborate arias within the dialogue scenes—reserving more extended use of music for less intense dramatic moments.

As a balance to the musically austere dramatic dialogue scenes, French opera also contains lighter scenes of musical entertainment, known as *divertissements*. Drawing upon musical and theatrical ingredients traditionally favoured by the French, the *divertissements* are filled with choruses, ballet music, and lavish scenery and spectacle. The plots normally emphasize the magical effects of *le merveilleux* that were an equally beloved part of the French tradition. In the operas of Rameau the sensuous pleasure of such scenes was further heightened through the richness of his choral and orchestral writing—using an elaborate contrapuntal texture and a wide range of harmonies, plus a varied palate of orchestral colours in which the woodwinds featured prominently.[12]

The opera as a whole maintains a balance between the serious

[9] During the season of the Bouffons, audiences at the Opéra could in fact hear a performance of an Italian comic opera and a French musical tragedy on the same programme.

[10] Lully's primary role in establishing the model for French opera was assured through his obtaining the directorship of the Académie d'Opéra in 1672, and subsequently holding a monopoly control over French opera until his death in 1687. Even after that, his influence was maintained through the continued performance of his works well into the 18th cent., and through the continued use of the Lullian operatic model by subsequent composers. As has been noted, it was only in the 1750s that Lully's dominance was challenged by the growing popularity of Rameau. While the latter still closely followed the Lullian model, he was writing in a new musical style, reflecting Italian innovations that were finally heard in France once the monopoly control of Lully had ended.

[11] French recitative style, with its strong melodic contours, was closely derived from the stylized declamation used in the spoken tragedies of Corneille and Racine. The musical libretto, however, departed at times from the strict Alexandrines of spoken tragedy, employing instead the *vers inégaux* which better accommodated the supple nature of French music. Still another example of flexibility can be seen in the characteristic changing rhythmic metres of French recitative, which was one of the objects of criticism by Rousseau in his attacks on French opera.

[12] As we have already noted, this was in contrast to the simpler settings of Lully.

dramatic scenes and the lighter scenes of the *divertissements*. There is a customary happy ending, which invariably is achieved through the intervention of gods and goddesses mingling freely in the affairs of mortals.[13] The overall plan, in keeping with the general grandiose character, consists of five acts and an allegorical prologue paying tribute to the king. French opera, in sum, was an aristoctratic form of entertainment, carrying the audience into an artificial world of enchantment, or an equally extraordinary human world filled with noble or legendary characters moved by grand passions.

With this model in mind, the contrast presented by the Italian comic genre becomes quickly apparent. Pergolesi's *La serva padrona* is a more modest and popular form of entertainment, portraying ordinary people in everyday situations—a coquettish servant who tricks her ageing master into marriage, making her the mistress of his house. There are just two short acts, with a duet finale at the end of each act.[14]

The music and action move at a lively pace, clearly articulated through the use of brisk speech-like recitatives in the Italian *recitativo semplice* style, alternating with a series of tuneful arias written in the pre-classical *galant* style. Far from maintaining a continuous flow between recitatives and arias, the Italian opera sets them clearly apart from one another. The main focus of the music is on melody, with the aria accompaniment confined to extremely simple and even rudimentary part-writing, scored for four strings plus continuo. The Italian *opera buffa*, in sum, is the antithesis of French *tragédie lyrique* in virtually every respect: plot, character, structure, musical resources, staging, and especially in its use of the simple and popular style of the pre-classical *galant*.

Given this strong contrast, it is easy to appreciate why the popularity of the Italian players was seen as a challenge to French tradition. We can only speculate as to why French audiences turned with such interest to Italian comic opera at this particular time. When *La serva* was performed in Paris in 1746 it had relatively little impact. Some scholars have pointed to the political climate in pre-revolutionary France, noting that French opera was identified with privilege and authority, while Italian comic opera was considered anti-establishment and egalitarian (in *La serva*, the maid, after all, does become the mistress of the house). Rousseau's description of the rival factions in the

[13] As we shall see, French opera was criticized by strict neo-classicists such as Boileau, who objected to the *divertissement* scenes and other 'hedonistic' departures from the rules of classical tragedy.

[14] The duet or ensemble finale of comic opera was a far-reaching innovation in Italian opera, which had an impact on Italian *opera seria* as well. Another significant innovation of Italian comic opera was the use of varied aria forms, in contrast to the exclusive use of the *da capo* aria that characterized Italian serious opera at the time.

'Querelle', looking back upon it over a decade later in his *Confessions*, depicts the participants very much in political terms: 'All of Paris was divided into two camps, more heated than if it were a matter of an affair of state or religion. One, the more powerful and numerous, composed of the great, the rich, the ladies, supported French music; the other, with more vitality, pride, enthusiasm, was composed of true connoisseurs, people of talent, men of genius.'[15]

The close tie between music and politics was perhaps best summed up by d'Alembert, who explicitly identified the urge for musical change with a desire for political freedom:

I am astonished in a century where so many authors occupy themselves writing about freedom of trade, freedom of marriage, freedom of the press, and freedom in art, that nobody thus far has written about freedom in music. For all freedoms are bound together and are equally dangerous. Freedom in music implies freedom to feel, freedom to feel implies freedom to think, freedom to think implies freedom to act, and freedom to act is the ruin of nations. If we wish to preserve the kingdom, let us preserve opera as it is.[16]

In this political climate, could there be any doubt that an attack on French music served as an integral part of an overall attack on the *ancien régime*? Conversely, could there be any doubt that Rameau's eventual attack on the *Encyclopédie* would be considered as an attack on the cause of freedom?

Within the realm of music itself, there were indications that audiences were tiring of the aristocratic and artificial conventions of *tragédie lyrique*. One sign was the growing popularity of the Fair Theatres, or *Opéra-Comique*, which presented a popular form of entertainment called the *vaudeville-comédie*. These were spoken plays interspersed with familiar tunes to which new words were adapted. Still another form of entertainment was the *opéra-ballet*—a genre which was estab-

---

[15] Jean-Jacques Rousseau, *Œuvres complètes de J.-J. Rousseau*, ed. Bernard Gagnebin and Marcel Raymond, vol. i, *Confessions* (Paris: Bibliothèque de la Pléiade, Editions Gallimard, 1959), pt. 2, bk. 8, p. 384. As further evidence of the politicization of the 'Querelle', the supporters of Italian music gathered near the queen's box at the Paris Opéra—which became known as the *coin de la reine*—while the pro-French rallied near the king's box—called the *coin du roi*. For a thorough analysis of the political implications of Rousseau's writings on music see Robert Wokler, 'Rousseau on Rameau and Revolution', *Studies in the Eighteenth Century*, iv (1978), 251–83. One political result in particular that is observed by Wokler is that Rousseau's *Lettre sur la musique française* created so much agitation that it served as a distraction from serious political problems between the Paris *parlement* and the court—perhaps even averting a political revolt by the *parlement*, as Rousseau claimed it did in his *Confessions*. (The *Confessions* were written between 1764 and 1770, a period that he spent mainly in exile in Switzerland and England after his book *Émile* was condemned by the *parlement* of Paris in 1762.) A more general treatment of the *philosophes'* political agenda in their views on music is to be found in Snyders, *Le Goût musical*, 134–5.

[16] Jean le Rond d'Alembert, 'De la liberté de la musique', in *Mélanges de littérature, d'histoire, et de philosophie*, vol. iv, *De la liberté de la musique* (Amsterdam: Zacharie Chatelain et Fils, 1759), 396–7. A facsimile edn. of *De la liberté* is presented in *Launay, iii*. 2199–282.

lished with André Campra's *L'Europe galante* in 1697. It was a lighter form of opera, consisting of a series of separate acts or *entrées*, and having a primary emphasis on *divertissement* rather than serious dramatic scenes.[17]

The public's readiness for both musical and political change made a powerful combination, helping to explain the triumph of the Bouffons at this time and the heated pamphlet war that ensued. Contributors to the 'Querelle des Bouffons' were mainly journalists, critics, opera librettists, and musical amateurs.[18] Diderot also joined in, producing three pamphlets that injected a more conciliatory tone and greater objectivity into the heated quarrel, while still addressing the issue of the relative merits of French and Italian opera.[19]

When we reach Rousseau's *Lettre sur la musique française*, published in November 1753, we find a change in the subject of debate. Rousseau puts aside the narrower issue of the competing styles in favour of a broader philosophical inquiry. The question that he asks is not whether French music is better than Italian, but more basically whether French music exists at all: 'Before speaking of the excellence of our music, it would be perhaps good to assure ourselves of its existence . . .'.[20] Despite the provocative nature of this question and its clear anti-French bias, Rousseau nevertheless uses it as the occasion for a series of probing questions concerning the nature of music: What is the basis of musical

---

[17] The contrast between *opéra-ballet* and *tragédie lyrique* is emphasized by James Anthony. He observes that in the early experimental phase of the new genre—1697–1723—it avoided the mythological characters and deities of *tragédie lyrique*; it also introduced contemporary characters and settings and included some comic intrigue as well. (James Anthony, *French Baroque Music* (New York: W. W. Norton & Co., 1974), 132.)

[18] A more precise identification of the 'Querelle' participants, by social class and intellectual background, is presented in William Weber, 'Musical Taste in Eighteenth-Century France', *Past and Present*, 89 (1985), 58–85. The author notes that the arbiters of musical taste were not music specialists or musicians. Status as a 'learned' critic was less clear in music than in the other arts. In the latter, it meant having a knowledge of antiquity and the classics. In music, however, there were virtually no models from the past. Taste was fixed in the present, primarily determined by the 'honnêtes gens' of privileged society. Serious musical connoisseurs had some role, to be sure, but it was mainly to inform taste and not to dictate.

[19] Diderot in fact did prefer Italian opera, although he also praised Rousseau's comic opera, *Le Devin du village*, in a 'Querelle' pamphlet entitled *Les Trois Chapitres*. Diderot's other two 'Querelle' pamphlets—the *Arrêt rendu à l'amphithéâtre de l'Opéra* and *Au petit prophète de Boehmischbroda*—are also pro-Italian, but with a similarly conciliatory tone. It should also be noted that Rousseau made a preliminary contribution to the 'Querelle' with his *Lettre d'un symphoniste* in September 1753, in which he accused the musicians of the Opéra orchestra of deliberately playing poorly in order to cause the visiting Italian troupe to fail. For this he was burned in effigy and denied admittance to the Opéra, despite the fact that his own opera, *Le Devin du village*, was in the repertory. For a complete description of the chronology and literature of the 'Querelle', see Louisette Richebourg, *Contribution à l'histoire de la querelle des Bouffons* (Paris: Nizet & Bastard, 1937). See also the facsimile edn. of literature from the quarrel, Launay.

[20] Jean-Jacques Rousseau, *Lettre sur la musique française* (Paris: n.p., 1753), 1–2; Launay, i. 673–74. All references hereafter to Rousseau's *Lettre* give the original pagination, accompanied by the pagination from the Launay facsimile edn.

expression? Of a national music style? What is the relationship between music and language? Between melody and harmony? What is the role of the composer, the critic, the music theorist? What is the corresponding relationship between sensibility and reason? Finally, as an application of the answers to the above, how are we to judge a famous monologue recitative by Lully—reputed to be French recitative at its best—when it fails to conform to the principles of musical expression set forth by Rousseau?

All of this is to be settled through rational discourse. It is to be approached from the broad point of view of a philosopher, rather than the narrower view of a musician or poet. Rousseau emphasizes that the musician is guided by taste and genius; the philosopher alone can provide the underlying principles of art: 'It is up to the poet to make poetry, up to the musician to make music; but it belongs only to the philosopher to speak effectively about one or the other.'[21]

Rousseau acknowledges at the start that music consists of harmony, as well as melody and rhythm. However, for the question he has posed about French music, harmony is of little relevance. It has its principle in nature and 'is the same for all nations'.[22] The central argument in the *Lettre* is that melody and language determine the particular character of a national music style. And actually it is language which influences melody. Only a musical language can give rise to true melody and in turn to true music. This is also the case for instrumental music, which originated after vocal music and was influenced by it: 'I have said that all national music draws its principal character from its own language, and I should add that it is principally the prosody of a language that constitutes its character. As vocal music has preceded most instrumental music, the latter has always received its melodic contours and rhythm from vocal music . . .'[23]

---

[21] Jean-Jacques Rousseau, *Lettre sur la musique française* (Paris: n.p., 1753), 3; Launay, i. 675. As was mentioned earlier, Rousseau was not only a philosopher, but also a self-taught musician. His successful comic opera, *Le Devin du village*, paved the way for comic opera as an important genre in France. Yet, in the *Lettre*, Rousseau questions the existence of French music.

[22] Ibid. 4; Launay, i. 676. Later, in the *Essai sur l'origine des langues* and elsewhere, Rousseau strongly qualified his view of harmony as natural by making a distinction between harmony as raw material and harmony as it is used in music. In the latter case, it becomes a product of society—unnatural and varying from culture to culture. Indeed, as we shall discuss in the next chapter, Rousseau eventually viewed the very need for harmony as a sign of a decadent society, far removed from the ideal natural state when language and music were unified and when the sole need for language was for expression of the passions.

[23] *Lettre*, 9; Launay, i. 681. Rousseau's notion of the crucial relationship between language and music in the *Lettre* was not yet present in his music articles in the *Encyclopédie*, compiled in 1749. Nor had Rousseau taken such an extreme position in his criticisms of French opera in 1752 in his *Lettre à M. Grimm . . . sur Omphale*. It was only after he developed the notion of the centrality of language for musical expression that he criticized French opera in the sweeping general way that we see in the *Lettre* of 1753. For a description of the substantial changes in Rousseau's views between 1749 and 1753, see Wokler, 'Rousseau on Rameau and Revolution', 260.

Rousseau then goes on to describe the characteristics of a musical language that produces good melody, using Italian as his example. This is at the very heart of his argument, since it provides the criteria for determining the gloomy fate of French music. He begins with a general point about language—one which he would develop more fully in subsequent writings: that a musical language cannot be devoted to reason, since reason will only produce good grammar, rather than good music (as is the case with the French): 'If one asks which of all the languages has the best grammar, I would answer it is the one where the people reason the best; and if one asks which of all the people must have the best music, I would say it is the one where the language is most appropriate for it.'[24] Rousseau specifies the essential qualities that make Italian the most musical language in Europe. It is sonorous, gentle and harmonious, having more vowels than consonants, and vowel sounds that are clear and pure—all of which facilitate a melody with gentle expressive inflections. Its prosody is rhythmic and regular, with a clear and precise relationship between long and short syllables, further marked by regular rhythmic groupings or patterns of long and short syllables. This language rhythm in turn enhances musical rhythm, without which a melodic line would make little sense: 'Rhythm is to melody almost what syntax is to discourse.'[25] The overall effect of these combined qualities is that the Italian language above all is shaped by something that Rousseau refers to as 'accent'. This is a crucial concept that Rousseau would develop more fully in later works, although he puts it aside for the moment in a false gesture of modesty: 'This important point demands such a profound discussion, that it is best to reserve it for a better hand.'[26]

The French language, which lacks all these qualities, has proved itself incapable of producing good melody, with the result that the French have sought to compensate for this lack through a series of disastrous supplements—the most disastrous being harmony:

[24] *Lettre sur la musique française*, 16–17; Launay, i. 688–9. In the *Lettre*, the negative role of reason and the musical or unmusical nature of a language are merely presented as givens or a priori facts. As we shall see in Ch. 3, Rousseau subsequently develops a theory of language and melody, through an examination of their origins and history, to support these facts.

[25] Ibid. 8; Launay, i. 680.

[26] Ibid. 21; Launay, i. 693. As we shall see in Ch. 3, Rousseau presents the concept of 'accent' as a central part of his theory of the origins of language and melody. Essentially, he views 'accent' as a kind of natural inflection of the voice that was characteristic of man's first language. In this original state, language was used purely for the expression of feelings or passions—as opposed to thoughts or reasons. We have already seen in the *Lettre* that Rousseau equates reason with everything that is not musical, reinforcing this point in the following remark: 'In those countries where the sciences and all the arts have developed to a very high degree, music alone awaits to be born.' (*Lettre*, 22; Launay, i. 694.) The idea that the development of the sciences and the arts may not represent progress becomes a major theme in Rousseau's subsequent writings—to be discussed in the next chapter. It was already present in his *Discours sur les sciences et les arts*, published in 1750.

The impossibility of inventing agreeable melodies has obliged the composers to turn all their energies in the direction of harmony, and lacking real beauties, they have introduced beauties of convention ... instead of good music, they have created a learned music; to supplement melody, they have multiplied the accompaniments ... To avoid being insipid, they have augmented confusion; they think they are making music, but they only make noise.[27]

In a similar manner, the French make frequent use of ornamentation to compensate further for lack of melody.

Rousseau emphasizes once again that this process of compensation for having an unmusical language has a disastrous effect not only on the vocal part, but on the orchestral accompaniment as well: 'The symphony usually proceeds in measured rhythm ... and one often hears in the same piece the actors and the orchestra contradict one another and create obstacles for one another ... The symphonists are no longer able, even in performing good music, to endow it with force and energy.'[28] This reinforces his position that the influence of language on music is so pervasive that it affects a whole musical style.

Rousseau concedes that harmony itself is not disastrous, as long as it is used in conjunction with expressive melody, rather than as compensation for its absence. He in fact praises the Italians for their use of bold modulations, which are particularly well suited for pathetic or tragic expression—in which the Italians also excel:

Although one seldom studies the pathetic and tragic character [of Italian melody], one is soon surprised at the force that the art of the composer bestows upon it in these great works of music. It is with the aid of these skilful modulations, of this pure and simple harmony, these lively and brilliant accompaniments, that these divine melodies ... ravish the soul ...[29]

Rousseau further elaborates on the nature of appropriate accompaniment, and here he introduces a second major point—one that he claims he is the first to recognize, although the Italians do it in practice. It is the rule of 'unity of melody', which forbids the use of more than one melody at a time, since it is impossible for music to be expressive and pleasing unless all the parts work together to reinforce a single melody. Nothing should distract from the one melody, the ear cannot follow several at once, and they only cancel the effects of one another:

In order for music to become interesting, for it to carry the sentiments to the soul that one wishes to arouse there, all the parts must work together to reinforce the expression of a subject ... it is necessary ... that the whole ensemble carry only one melody at a time to the ear and only one idea to the spirit.[30]

[27] *Lettre*, 6–7; Launay, i. 678–9.   [28] Ibid. 14; Launay, i. 686.
[29] Ibid. 34; Launay, i. 706.
[30] Ibid. 35–6; Launay, i. 707–8.

Piling up melodies, harmonies, rhythms, notes, parts and instruments 'is only a bad supplement for lack of genius'.[31] The Italians not only avoid this error, but follow the unity rule by favouring unison accompaniments—a choice suitable for Italian melodies, but not for French: 'It is in this great rule that one must seek the cause of the frequent unison accompaniments that one observes in Italian music ...'[32] If harmonic chords or ornamental figuration are used in the accompaniment—for enhancing the expression of the melody—the composer must do so without violating the unity rule, 'observing with care that the orchestra is always dominated by the singing part'.[33] This rule also eliminates the use of fugues and other imitative forms: 'They are clearly the remains of barbaric and bad taste, which only exist, like the portals of our gothic churches, for the shame of those who had the patience to make them.'[34]

As a further attack on French accompaniment through the counter-example of the Italians, Rousseau emphasizes the positive effect of their use of incomplete harmonies: 'What! I said to myself, a complete harmony has less effect than a mutilated one, and our accompanists, in making all chords full, only make a confused noise, while the others, with less sounds, make more harmony, or, at least, make their accompaniment more expressive and agreeable.'[35] Not only does the Italian use of incomplete harmonies give the accompaniment a simpler and cleaner sound; it also allows individual harmonies to have a single unmixed expressive impact—the very same benefits provided by the unity principle.[36]

Finally, Rousseau turns to vocal music and also to the nature of the text—once again praising the Italians for the power of their expression in both recitatives and arias: 'These great works of Italian music which are ravishing; these masterpieces of genius which bring forth tears, which offer the most moving scenes, which paint the most vivid situations ... carry all the passions that they express to the soul ...'[37] Such texts, which

---

[31] Ibid. 35; Launay, i. 707. [32] Ibid. 36–7; Launay, i. 708–9.

[33] Ibid. 41; Launay, i. 713. Still another example of how care must be taken in observing the unity rule is duets. They pose a particular challenge, since it is not natural for two people to speak at the same time. Italians manage to observe the unity rule and to maintain a natural sense of expression by having the voices alternate with one another—as in a dialogue—or come together when appropriate for the text.

[34] Ibid. 44; Launay, i. 716. Rousseau admits that there was a time when Italian music was similarly barbaric, before the Italians came to their senses: 'In this time when music was hardly born, there was in Italy this ridiculous emphasis on harmonic science, these pedantic pretensions of doctrine that we have so dearly preserved.' (*Lettre*, 290.)

[35] Ibid. 52–3; Launay, i. 724–25.

[36] Interestingly enough, Rousseau recommends that the French return to the simplicity of Lully: 'Let us agree that the harmony of this celebrated musician is purer and less inverted, that his bass lines are more natural ... that his melody is clearer, that his accompaniments less overloaded ... and consequently much better than ours ... '(*Lettre*, 61; Launay, i. 733.)

[37] Ibid. 62; Launay, i. 734.

are perfectly matched to the dramatic situation, are in stark contrast to French texts, which are 'always detached from the subject, producing only a miserable jargon ... a collection made by chance of the very small number of sonorous words that our language can provide ... returning in every manner, except that which could give them any meaning'.[38]

Rousseau focuses for the remainder of the *Lettre* on recitative, where the influence of language is most direct: 'As each language has a declamation of its own, each language must also have its own recitative ... It is evident ... that the best recitative, in whatever language ... is that which is closest to speech ...'[39] He praises Italian recitative for the following strengths: 'That it can have a lively declamation and energetic harmony at the same time; that it can proceed as rapidly as speech, and also be as melodious as a true song; that it can be shaped by all the inflections with which the most vehement passions animate discourse ...'[40] It also uses sufficient modulations to reflect the powerful expressions in the texts, and, when appropriate, uses an orchestral accompaniment in a special kind of recitative, called *récitatif obligé* (another important concept that Rousseau postpones dealing with in great detail in the present work).

As for French recitative, he proposes to put it to a final test. He will examine a work considered to be a French masterpiece according to 'unanimous consent'. The expert Rameau himself has praised it for its expressive modulations. It is the famous monologue by Lully, 'Enfin, il est en ma puissance', from the opera *Armide*.[41]

Rousseau sets out to judge the recitative on its own terms—as a model of French recitative. This dooms it from the start. If it follows the declamation of the French language, then it must be totally lacking in melodic and rhythmic interest. On the other hand, if the music does not reflect the text, then it is only a false recitative. Applying these premises, he provides a line-by-line analysis of the recitative's failings— which we will consider in a moment. Line-by-line he carries his critique

---

[38] *Lettre sur la musique française*, 64; Launay, i. 736. Rousseau cites the French use of such stock imagery as 'flammes' and 'chaînes', which do in fact appear repeatedly in the libretti of Rameau's operas, as well as those of his predecessors.

[39] Ibid. 69–71; Launay, i. 741–3.   [40] Ibid. 75; Launay, i. 747.

[41] Rousseau's choice of the monologue 'Enfin, il est en ma puissance' was not his alone. It had been suggested by Diderot during the 'Querelle' in his pamphlet *Au petit prophète de Boemischbroda*, which was inspired by Baron Von Grimm's famous essay, *Le Petit Prophète*. In this pamphlet Diderot makes an appeal for rational discourse and recommends a comparison between analogous scenes from a French and an Italian opera, Lully's *Armide* and Terradella's *Nitocris*. Diderot rejects as invalid the numerous comparisons between Italian comic opera and French tragic opera. His own comparison comes out in favour of the Italian. Like Rousseau, he refers to Rameau's praise of the Lully monologue, which Rameau made in his treatise the *Nouveau système* in 1726, and would repeat in *Observations* in 1754.

to the inevitable conclusion, the notorious verdict, 'that the French don't have any music and can't have any; and if they ever did, it would be so much the worse for them'.[42]

Far from putting a rational end to the controversy, the *Lettre* provoked an even more heated campaign in defence of French music and in direct rebuttal of Rousseau.[43] It was against this background that Rameau presented a response to Rousseau in his short treatise entitled *Observations sur notre instinct pour la musique in 1754*. Instead of directly confronting Rousseau's charges against the French language, Rameau based his defence of French music on a point-by-point rebuttal of Rousseau's critique of the monologue.

Before we examine the critique and its rebuttal, let us first consider how Rameau prepares his defence. He places the defence of the monologue within the framework of the treatise as a whole, which is concerned with the aesthetic issue of how expression in music is achieved. The answer to this question furnishes Rameau with the guiding principle for judging the musical expression of the monologue and for refuting the charges made by Roussseau. The two writers agree that expressiveness is the sole criterion for judging the monologue. If they reach opposite conclusions, it is because they differ on the means of expression in music. This, then, becomes one of the most important themes in the dialogue, not only between Rameau and Rousseau, but among the other participants as well.

For Rameau it is harmony, rather than language or melody, that is the sole basis of music and expression. There can be no other, because harmony alone is given to us directly from nature and is known to us immediately through instinct as the source of expression in music (unless—like Rousseau—we block out that instinctive knowledge):

We have received a gift [from nature] which is called instinct. Let us consult it in our judgements ... A person whose mind is preoccupied while listening to music is never free enough to judge it. For example, if in his opinion he finds that the essential beauty of this art lies in the changes from low to high, from soft to loud, from fast to slow ... he will judge everything by these criteria without reflecting on their weakness or how little merit they have, and he will fail to notice that they are distinguished from harmony, which is the unique

---

[42] *Lettre*, 92; Launay, i. 764.

[43] The enormous political impact of the *Lettre* is discussed in Wokler, 'Rousseau on Rameau and Revolution', 251–6. It should be stressed that the anti-French position of the *philosophes* generally spared Rameau, who was considered something of an innovator—perhaps even a reformer—in comparison to composers, such as Destouches, who were considered the direct bearers of the archaic Lullian tradition.

basis of music and the principle of its greatest effects ... Melody alone derives its force from this source, from which it emanates directly ...[44]

More specifically, what is given to us in nature is the resonating body—Rameau calls it the *corps sonore*—which generates not only a principal or fundamental sound, but also a series of harmonically related overtones which are the consonant intervals of harmony: 'This principle is now known: it exists ... in the harmony which results from the resonance of all sounding bodies ...'[45] The fact that the intervals above the fundamental bass are generated by the bass means that melody has its source in harmony: 'Melody has no other principle than harmony as produced by the resonating body.'[46]

Equally important, it means that the emotional force of melody resides in harmony.[47] Rameau explains in further detail how harmony gives rise to expression in music through the *corps sonore*. Expression is determined by the relationship between the principal resonance, called the tonic, and the pitches that are a fifth above and below the tonic, called the dominant and sub-dominant respectively. He sees the effects of the latter two in terms of contrasting expressive families: 'These products can be divided into two genres based on the order in which their sounds are generated ... the dominant, which is a fifth above, and the sub-dominant, which is a fifth below [the principal sound] ...'[48] The family of the dominant is associated with a feeling of joy and strength, because the dominant is produced directly as an overtone which resonates along with the principal sound. (The dominant family includes the major mode, a rising melody, and all the keys with sharps in them.) The family of the sub-dominant produces a feeling of sadness or tension, because the sub-dominant is not generated directly as an overtone within the principal body or tonic—

---

[44] Rameau, *Observations* pp. iii–vi; *CTW* iii. 259–60. Rameau admits that melody and rhythm are an appropriate basis of expression in Italian comic opera, which essentially consists of physical actions. At the same time he makes it clear that the object of French opera is the expression of feeling, and harmony alone can accomplish this (vii–x). Rameau's distinction between French tragedy and Italian comedy does not resolve the quarrel, because the pro-Italian views of Rousseau—and also of Diderot and others—include Italian tragedy.

[45] Ibid. 2; *CTW*, iii. 267. Rameau's harmonic theory and his principle of the *corps sonore* will be taken up in greater detail in Ch. 4.

[46] Ibid. 10; *CTW*, iii. 271.

[47] This view of melody marks a shift in Rameau's thinking since the *Traité de l'harmonie* (Paris: Ballard, (1722) (*CTW*) i). It is a more extreme position on harmonic supremacy than Rameau holds in his earlier treatise. In the *Traité* he acknowledges the expressive power of melody despite its source in harmony. For example, in advising on how to set words to music he says that musical expression can be achieved 'as much by melody, harmony and rhythm' (*Traité*, 162; *CTW* i. 192). However, in *Observations* he seems to consider harmony and melody as so inseparable that he can no longer recognize any independent power of melody.

[48] *Observations*, p. xii; *CTW*, iii. 263.

according to Rameau, it vibrates in silence when set in motion by the principal sound.[49] (The sub-dominant family includes the minor mode, a descending melody, and all the keys with flats in them.) The expressive distinction between the two families is thus created by the way the sounds are generated and the directness or indirectness in relation to the principal resonating body or tonic.

An essential feature of these expressive contrasts is that we can experience them immediately and directly, through instinct. This faculty leads us to the harmonic relationships that can also be known through reason and mathematical calculations: 'We will show that the principle is verified by our instinct, and this instinct by the principle. In this fashion the cause is verified by the effect that we experience, and this effect by the cause.'[50] The two paths—instinct and reason—thus provide a mutual confirmation of the *corps sonore* as the basis of expression in music.[51] In this manner, Rameau establishes that all other criteria for judging musical expression—and especially melodic considerations—are irrelevant.

With these aesthetic principles established in favour of harmonic supremacy, Rameau proceeds to a detailed defence of the monologue, responding to Rousseau's critique point-by-point.[52] It is worth closely following this part of the exchange, which is perhaps less familiar, since it provides a vivid illustration of their conflicting views of musical expression, as they actually apply to music. (See Example 1.)

Rousseau's main criticism is that the dramatic situation calls for a profound change of expression that the music utterly fails to convey. The heroine Armide is tormented by conflicting passions—she is about to kill her prisoner and enemy Renaud, whom she really loves: 'As she sees him, she hesitates, becomes more tender, the knife falls from her

---

[49] The derivation of the sub-dominant always remained problematic for Rameau. In the *Démonstration*, he viewed it as a product of sympathetic vibrations, which was a revision of the derivation in the *Génération*, in which he believed they were generated as undertones. The one consistency in the various derivations is that the sub-dominant, in comparison to the dominant, was less directly related to the tonic. (*Démonstration du principe de l'harmonie, servant de base à tout l'art musical théorique et pratique* (Paris: Durand, Pissot, 1750) (*CTW* iii. 151–254); *Génération harmonique, on Traité de musique théorique et pratique* (Paris: Prault Fils, 1737) (*CTW* iii. 1–150).)

[50] *Observations*, p. vii; *CTW*, iii. 261.

[51] Rameau's emphasis on instinct in the *Observations* marks still another shift from Rameau's earliest treatises, where reason and abstract mathematical calculations have a more central role. As we shall see in the next chapter, the shift was part of a more general tendency occurring at the time, towards recognizing an important role for instinct or sensibility in the artistic experience.

[52] This choice of strategy was praised in a contemporary journal (*Annonces, affiches at avis divers* (12 June 1754) 2): 'Our music is at least vindicated, and the monologue of Armide, defended by this great master ... M. Rameau has seized an issue overlooked by all those who have written against M. Rousseau.' The account presented here of this part of the debate is based on my earlier discussion, in 'The Development of Rameau's Thoughts on Modulation and Chromatics', *JAMS* 26, no.1 (1973), 69–91.

Example 1. Recitative from Lully's *Armide* (after the score published by Ballard in Paris, 1686). Bracketed figures are the implied chromatics or dissonances in Rameau's interpretation.

hands; she forgets her deed of vengeance ...'[53] Rousseau claims that neither the melody, the declamation, nor the accompaniment reflect her emotional transition from murderous rage to adoration. Above all, his critique focuses on the failure of the harmony to reflect her prodigious emotional change (the very same harmony that Rameau has praised for its expressiveness): 'The musician finishes ... where he began, without having ever left the harmonies that are closest to the principal key ... without having given the least expression to the harmony ...'

Rameau is in complete disagreement. Not only is there some harmonic contrast, but the harmony is as varied as it could be—including the use of chromatic tones, which signify harmonic departures or modulations: 'So many new sharps or flats, which are essentially chromatic tones, [are] distributed as perfectly as possible ...'[54] If we do not readily perceive these contrasts, it is because of the skill of the composer in 'hiding art through art'. Rather than using abrupt and harsh modulations—which is the sign of a limited talent—Lully's harmonic departures are simple and gentle, with agreeable connection or liaison:

Let us not be mistaken, however: the required harmonic departures are to be found in this simplicity ... in these gentle departures, in which the liaison, although agreeable, unmistakably allows us to feel the different movements that they paint ... we will always experience this ... as long as we are guided by feeling alone, without any irrelevant preoccupation.[55]

The issue of how much harmonic contrast there is in the recitative differs in kind from the broader and more philosophical disagreement over the respective roles of harmony versus melody. It actually involves a different reading of the music. More precisely, it involves a different perception of the harmonies implied by the continuo bass line and the melody.[56]

Rameau's harmonic defence begins with the first three lines of text, where he responds to Rousseau's main charge that there is an absence of key change when needed. (We will skip over some of Rousseau's repeated charges—such as his objection to the overuse or misuse of French ornaments or trills.) Rameau claims that the harmonic changes

---

[53] *Lettre*, 80; Launay, i. 752. Rousseau's critique of the monologue continues from this point until the end of the *Lettre*, 80–92 (Launay, i. 752–64).

[54] *Observations*, 98; *CTW*, iii. 315.   [55] Ibid. 105–6; *CTW* iii. 319.

[56] In accordance with continuo bass practice the accompanist improvises in filling in the chords, since the only notes that are given in the musical score are those in the melody and the bass line. The accompanist receives some guidance through the use of numbers or figures to indicate which pitches should be played above the bass notes. However, as can be seen in the musical score in Example 1, many of the bass notes appear without numbers, and the harmonies must be inferred through just the melody and bass line.

are the most suitable that one could desire. There is a contrast between the 'softness' of minor and the 'vigour' of major which corresponds perfectly with the phrases of the text: 'There is everything that can be used to create the most perfect expression that one can desire.'[57]

Enfin, il est en ma puissance, [minor]
[Finally, he is in my power,]
Ce fatal Ennemi, [move to major]
[This fatal enemy,]
Ce superbe Vainqueur. [major]
[This superb conqueror.]

In the next line Rousseau complains that the harmony degenerates to word painting on the word 'sleep' (m. 5). It is given a gentle chord despite Armide's fury: 'He [Lully] has forgotten Armide's fury, in order to take a little nap ...'[58] Rameau counters that individual chords should not be considered in isolation. The harmony in question is part of an entire phrase which moves from the sub-dominant to the dominant and finally to the tonic (mm. 4–8). The expressive contrast between the weaker sub-dominant and the more forceful dominant has already been established earlier in the treatise. As used here, the progression closely reflects the growing strength of Armide's feelings:

Lully ... certainly was not asleep on these last lines: he begins in the key of the sub-dominant ... he passes to the dominant where the energy is redoubled ... he also has the voice start low, and then rise rapidly, making us feel all the fury which comes over Armide ... the dominant, chosen for the cadence which precedes the last verse, makes ... the following tonic cadence strongly desired.[59]

Rousseau sees the final tonic cadence as an individual progression, and claims it is 'ridiculous ... in the middle of a violent emotion'.[60]

Le charme du sommeil [sub-dominant]
[The charm of sleep]
le livre à ma vengeance, [dominant]
[delivers him to my vengeance]
Je vais percer son invincible cœur. [tonic]
[I shall pierce his invincible heart.]

The remainder of Rousseau's critique concerns the prolonged passage (mm. 9–22) in which Armide's resolve begins to weaken and her inner struggle gradually builds to an intense level. Once again, Rousseau objects to the use of the same chords and keys when the text demands a sharp contrast. For example, he cites the abrupt change in

[57] *Observations*, 76–7; *CTW*, iii. 304–5.   [58] *Lettre*, 82; Launay, i. 754.
[59] *Observations*, 78–9; *CTW*, iii. 306.
[60] *Lettre*, 83; Launay, i. 755.

the text in the following lines, and claims that the harmony is almost the same for both:

Qu'il éprouve toute ma rage. [tonic on D]
[He will feel all my rage.]
Quel trouble me saisit? [D becomes D7 as dominant of G]
[What is troubling me?]

Here they both agree that a tonic chord becomes a dominant (mm. 11–12). The issue is whether or not this change provides sufficient harmonic contrast. Rousseau finds it seriously lacking: 'Heavens! It is only a question of tonic and dominant at a moment where all harmonic ties should be broken.'[61] For Rameau, the conversion of a chord from tonic to dominant represents a contrast as dramatic as when 'day becomes night'.[62] The chord change actually establishes a move to the expressive key of the sub-dominant. He claims that a similar change occurs for the words 'What makes me hesitate?' (mm. 13–14). The move to the sub-dominant each time corresponds to Armide's increasing uncertainty.

Rameau also asserts that there are further expressive harmonic moves in the passage. For example, he extols the timing of the return to the principal tonic after the suspense created by the preceding key changes—just as the text reaches the dramatic words, 'I shall strike' (mm. 16–17): 'The key . . . which reigns in the whole monologue, which alone predominates, and which is desired more strongly than ever after all the different keys . . . returns and suddenly strikes on the tonic, exactly to express the decisive word . . .' Rousseau finds the setting of these words expressively neutral.

The point of furthest remove between the two harmonic interpretations is in their disagreement over the climactic passage which Rousseau aptly describes as 'the most violent moment in the whole scene' (mm. 18–22).[63] Her disconnected utterances contradict one another: 'I shall finish this . . . I tremble! I shall be avenged . . . I swoon!' Rousseau protests that the setting is completely unsuitable: 'Who would believe that the musician has left all this agitation in the same key, without the least intellectual transition, without the least harmonic departure, in such an insipid manner, with a melody that is so poorly characterized . . .'[64]

In Rameau's response to these accusations he presents his most striking harmonic interpretation: 'Not only is all this agitation not in the same key, but there are chromatic changes every half-measure.'[65] What this means, according to Rameau's analysis, is that there is a change of

---

[61] Ibid.85; Launay, i. 757. [62] *Observations*, 90; *CTW*, iii. 311.
[63] *Lettre*, 86; Launay, i. 758.
[64] Ibid. 86–7; Launay, i. 758–9.
[65] *Observations*, 96–7; *CTW*, iii. 314–15.

key within every measure, and each change implies a new chromatic tone—an additional sharp or flat which belongs to the new key. The chromatic tones need not be present in the music—indeed, there are few in this passage. They are automatically implied by the new key or tonic which requires new sharps or flats. Equally important, they have an expressive effect, primarily through the change of key:

This is not the only musical composition where the harmonic foundation implies chromatics, without their slightest appearance in any of the parts, and where the feeling that we experience from them is born directly from the basis of the harmony. It is necessary to have more than eyes . . . to judge an art where the cause resides as much in what is implied as in what is expressed . . .[66]

> Achevons [tonic on G becomes G7 as dominant of C]
> [I shall finish this]
> Je frémis! [tonic on C moves to A7 as dominant of D]
> [I tremble!]
> Vengeons-nous [tonic on D becomes to D7 as dominant of G]
> [I shall avenge myself]
> Je soupire! [tonic on G]
> [I swoon!]

Rameau's interpretation of this passage essentially completes his defence of the recitative. It helps to explain how Rameau and Rousseau could disagree so fully on the issue of harmonic contrast. On the one hand, Rameau invokes the concept of implied tones where Rousseau sees none at all. On the other hand, even when they agree that the tonic becomes a dominant, they disagree on whether or not this amounts to a harmonic contrast. A further distinction—related to both of these points—is that Rameau's analysis is concerned with the overall harmonic context and the syntactic relationship among chords within a phrase or larger unit, while Rousseau essentially views chords or cadences as individual entities. It is hardly surprising that the eminent theorist Rameau should present a more sophisticated harmonic analysis—one that takes into account overall key relationships.

For both writers more is at stake, however, than simply the issue of harmonic contrast. We have already seen that Rousseau's principal condemnation of the monologue—or any French recitative—is founded on the unmusical nature of the French language. If he is concerned with the harmony of the monologue, it is simply to show that 'even if this scene were as perfect as one pretends, we could only conclude . . . that it is French music well done; which would not preclude

---

[66] *Observations*, 107; *CTW*, iii. 320. Rameau's notion of implied tones—required in some way through the musical context—appears throughout his theoretical treatises. His use of it here creates a large gap between his harmonic interpretation and that of Rousseau. The concept of implied harmonies will be dealt with in chapter 4, in a discussion of Rameau's view of chordal syntax.

that since the genre has been demonstrated to be bad, that this is absolutely bad music . . .'.[67] Rameau's defence goes well beyond his proof of harmonic contrast, and takes into account this sweeping condemnation. Not only is harmony the source of expression in music, but even when the text or the melodic line appear to be the source, the true foundation can only be in the harmony: 'It is principally on the basis of harmony, from which the melody applied to words is derived, that the singer receives the feeling that he must paint: the words only serve . . . as an indication: we have just proven that . . .'[68]

A final point about Rameau's defence of the harmony in the monologue has to do with the intentions of Lully. Rameau recognizes that he has taken some liberties in his harmonic interpretations—that several of the key changes included in his analysis are not actually indicated in Lully's musical score. Rameau claims that Lully's genius and instinct allowed him to provide the appropriate harmonic foundations, even without his having a complete understanding of the musical choices that he made:

There is a use of chromatics which does not actually appear in the figured bass of Lully, but which appears as the foundation of the different expressions . . . Whatever the figures are, one can judge, through the different feelings that the actor and audience experience, that the composer could only have been guided by the harmonic foundations that I present.[69]

With this claim Rameau has come full circle, back to the notion of an immediate instinctive response with which he began the treatise. It is even more applicable to the composer than to the listener or critic. On this point, Rousseau makes a similar observation when describing how a musician or composer makes a choice: 'For this choice the musician is not obliged to present reasons, but simply to feel the results. It is up to him to have genius, taste, to find what is effective.'[70] Rousseau also adds that it is up to the theorist to explain why something is effective—a remark which is similar, once again, to Rameau's claim that reason and instinct provide mutual confirmation for one another. As we shall see in the next chapter, the belief in taste or instinct was an important idea at the time—accepted by both, although leading to very different conclusions.

[67] *Lettre*, 78–9; Launay, i. 750–1.   [68] *Observations*, 102; *CTW*, iii. 317.

[69] *Observations*, 104–5; *CTW* iii. 318–19. It is worth noting that Rameau's harmonic interpretation of the monologue in the *Observations* differs from his earlier analysis and praise of the same piece in the *Nouveau système* of 1726—with far fewer implied chromatic tones in the earlier work. (*Nouveau système de musique théorique . . . pour servir d'introduction au traité de l'harmonie* (Paris: Ballard, 1726) (*CTW* ii).) A major point in my article, 'The Development of Rameau's Thoughts on Modulation and Chromatics', is that the differences between the two analyses reflect significant changes in Rameau's views on modulation and chromatics.

[70] *Lettre*, 59–60; Launay, i. 731–2.

The foregoing account of the debate between Rameau and Rousseau in the two texts under consideration presents their views on expression in some detail. In order to grasp the tenor of their arguments, you should turn to the first two items of the appendix.

3

Music as Expressive Art:
Rameau versus Rousseau on Expressive Means and Content

WE have seen in the preceding chapter that one of the principal differences between Rameau and Rousseau is over the means of expression in music—with Rameau arguing for harmonic supremacy, and Rousseau for melodic. This in turn is related to more fundamental differences in their views of what is natural in music. Rameau's first principle, from which all else follows, is that harmony has its source in nature, in the generation of sound. The generative process determines expressive effects as well as principles of harmonic procedure. Most important of all, since the source of expression comes from nature the effects are universal, transcending time and place, and are accessible through instinct or reason. Rousseau, on the other hand, is more concerned with human nature, and especially with the role of language in musical expression. This leads to a focus on the vocal line and melody, and also to a concern with national or cultural differences, rather than universal qualities.

This contrast between Rameau and Rousseau is of particular significance because—as Rousseau scholars have observed—the two positions 'represent two completely different ways of understanding the world and exemplify a conflict that is found at this time in many other areas of thought'.[1] A main concern of this chapter is to clarify further the essential differences between Rameau and Rousseau by considering how their specific quarrel on the means of expression in music relates to the larger issue of expressive content, or what it is that music is supposed to express. This in turn will require examination of subsequent developments in Rousseau's thought.

For Rameau, expression is identified with text setting, with conveying its sentiments as precisely as possible. As we have seen in the preceding chapter, this is done primarily through a kind of harmonic punctuation, using different cadences and key changes or modulations to reflect expressive contrasts in the text from one phrase to another.

---

[1] Lionel Gossman, 'Time and History in Rousseau', *Studies on Voltaire*, 30 (1964), 319.

This view of expression was maintained by Rameau throughout his career—from his earliest treatises, through *Observations*, and beyond. Indeed, in the *Nouveau système*, published in 1726, he presents an illustration of the expressive powers of harmony, using the monologue by Lully which would appear in *Observations* in 1754. Already in the earlier treatise he describes musical expression in terms which emphasize an analogy with language: 'In setting a text to music, it is necessary to consider how the phrases of the text relate to one another in meaning, and to try to make the music conform to these relationships through its modulations.'[2]

In his emphasis on the importance of text, Rameau recognizes its role in aria as well as recitative—all must proceed in the spirit of recitative. He even extends this way of thinking to instrumental dances and symphonies which occur in opera. Although they have no text, he makes the following recommendation: 'He who does not take words for his guide always imagines a subject which holds him in the same subjection.'[3] It is worth noting that Rameau advanced this view of expression not only in his theoretical writings, but in his operas as well. His text settings, in arias and recitatives, closely follow the detailed nuances of the text, relying primarily on harmony to do so.

In contrast to Rameau's views on expressive content, Rousseau is not concerned with the meaning of words or ideas in a text, but with a more direct form of expression, conveyed by the intonations of the human voice itself, as it expresses the underlying feelings in a text. In subsequent writings Rousseau develops the idea more fully that true expression is immediate and direct, through a natural language of the passions, and—when translated into music—through melody. The degree of expressive content or feeling depends on the degree of closeness between the melodic line and the natural language of the passions.

There is a special irony in the contrast between Rameau and Rousseau on expressive means and content. Rameau focuses on harmony, which is a purely musical element, and yet he shows great concern for text and its content. Rousseau, on the other hand, stresses melody, which is closely related to language, but nevertheless de-emphasizes the importance of text—at least in its specific content.

[2] Rameau, *Nouveau système*, 41; *CTW* ii. 51. For a comparison between the analysis of the Lully monologue in *Nouveau système* with that in *Observations*, see my article, 'The Development of Rameau's Thoughts on Modulation and Chromatics', 80–2. Although there are differences between the two analyses, as well as a shift toward a stronger position on harmonic supremacy in *Observations*, Rameau's views on the expressive goals of music remained unchanged.

[3] Rameau, *Traité de l'harmonie*, 162–3; *CTW* i. 192–3. For an analysis of his opera *Hippolyte et Aricie* in terms of expressive treatment of recitatives, arias, and instrumental pieces, see my dissertation, 'A Hierarchic Interpretation of the Theories and Music of Jean-Philippe Rameau' (Ph.D. diss., University of Chicago, 1979).

The distance between Rousseau and Rameau on musical expression, already considerable in the positions presented in the *Lettre sur la musique française* and the *Observations*, respectively, grew even wider as Rousseau developed a theoretical foundation for his views in subsequent writings. As we shall see, a salient feature of these later writings was an increasingly radical rejection of the entire French musical tradition—Rousseau's position became the complete antithesis of Rameau's.[4] Before we consider these further developments, it is useful to reverse direction and to review the traditional views on expression that Rameau and Rousseau inherited and to some extent shared. Only by understanding their shared heritage and points of agreement can we understand more fully how they drew so completely apart.[5]

One of the most important ideas that they inherited was the neo-classical doctrine of art as imitation of nature, and especially the nature of the passions. The doctrine stemmed from Aristotle's *Poetics*, which was revived during the Italian Renaissance, became widespread during the seventeenth century, and remained at the centre of criticism well into the eighteenth century. This revival of the Greek *mimesis*, although subject to many different interpretations, placed an emphasis on the representational side of art—that it must say something, have meaning. Literary theory initially dominated all the arts, borrowing the techniques and goals of the ancient art of rhetoric. Imitation in music referred to music with text, principally opera.[6] In all the arts, imitating the passions was to be so powerful that it could move the passions or 'affections' of the audience, producing a purifying or cathartic effect.

In France, the concept of imitating the passions took on a special meaning under the prevailing influence of Cartesian rationalism during the second half of the seventeenth century. Descartes posited a rational mechanical universe, subject to universal laws that could be known

---

[4] Catherine Kintzler, like Gossman, recognizes this extreme antithesis. It is the principal theme of her book, *Jean-Philippe Rameau: Splendeur et naufrage de l'esthétique du plaisir à l'âge classique*, 2nd edn. (Paris: Minerve, 1988). Kintzler sees Rameau as representing French classical thought—which in turn was completely embedded in the rationalist philosophy of Descartes—and argues that Rousseau's aesthetic doctrine, promoting the centrality of pure feeling or sensibility, was constructed to contradict classical theory, forming a parallel with it in all of its component parts. She further argues that Rousseau's challenging doctrine eventually led to the downfall of French *tragédie lyrique* and French classicism in general.

[5] The present summary of this background is indebted to the philosophical study by Rosalie Sadowsky, 'Jean-Baptiste Abbé Dubos: The Influence of Cartesian and Neo-Aristotelian Ideas on Music Theory and Practice' (Ph.D. diss., Yale University, 1960). Another valuable source is Georgia Cowart, *The Origins of Modern Musical Criticism: French and Italian Music, 1600-1750* (Ann Arbor, Mich.: University Microfilms International, 1981).

[6] Music in fact was only included among the expressive arts during the 16th cent., when it shifted from its traditional position as part of the mathematical *quadrivium* in the medieval scholastic curriculum to join the linguistic disciplines of the *trivium*, leaving acoustics and theory among the sciences. The view of music as both art and science will be taken up in greater detail in the next two chapters.

solely through innate reason. According to this doctrine, knowledge through any authority other than reason was suspect, and truth was always an abstract formal principle, hidden beneath the appearance of sensible reality. Even the passions had their place within this realm, since they could transmit ideas and incite the mind to think and to act.

The close bond between the passions and reason was reflected in literature through a formal or intellectualized portrayal of the passions, using stereotyped images and figures of speech. With language serving as a model, musical imitation similarly involved the use of characteristic musical figures to which rhetorical meaning was ascribed.[7]

Still another part of the French tradition was the neo-classical literary doctrine of Nicolas Boileau-Despréaux. In his *L'Art poétique* (1674) he upheld the rules of Greek tragedy and the classical belief in the moral or educative function of art.[8] As a strict neo-classicist, he insisted that *tragédie lyrique* was subject to the same rules as spoken tragedy. He assailed musical librettos for their hedonism, their emphasis on amorous intrigue, and also for their frequent scene changes, in violation of the rules of unity.

In a series of subsequent debates there was an attempt to free music from these constraints. Led by Charles Perrault during the celebrated 'quarrel between the ancients and the moderns', the defence of *tragédie lyrique* rested on a more relativist position, viewing the departures from antiquity as signs of innovation and progress. The controversy thus revolved around the issue of the extent to which artistic principles were universal and could remain fixed throughout the ages. It also concerned the issue of recognizing *tragédie lyrique* as a separate genre in its own right.[9]

With the success of Lully's operas, the progressives prevailed. There was an acceptance of the view that librettos must serve the special needs

---

[7] The widespread use of musical figures as a rhetorical device eventually became known as the *Affektenlehre* or the 'Doctrine of the Affections', a term used by German musicologists since the 19th cent. However, as George Buelow observes, 'no one comprehensive, organized doctrine of how the Affections were to be achieved in music was ever established in Baroque theory'. (George Buelow, 'Rhetoric and Music', in *The New Grove Dictionary of Music and Musicians*, ed. Stanley Sadie (London: Macmillan Publications, 1980), xv. 800.) Terminology and definitions were inconsistent among the various writers during the 17th and 18th cents., although they did in fact attempt to categorize types of affections and their representation in music.

[8] Under the influence of Cartesianism, furthermore, the neo-classical rules became strict doctrine, confirmed or proven by reason, rather than mere suggestions for literary procedure as they had been in the early 17th cent.

[9] For the recognition of opera as a genre in its own right the relativists did not have to reject the influence of antiquity. Aristotle himself advocated that each art had its own proper ends and its own individual methods of imitation.

arising from the union of poetry and music, and that opera must be judged by separate standards from spoken tragedy.[10] At the same time, language and rhetoric still served as models for imitation or expression in music. Once again, music for most critics was identified with music with text, principally opera.

Such was the prevalent view of musical expression during the early eighteenth-century debate over French and Italian opera—the debate between Lecerf de la Viéville and Raguenet that foreshadowed the later 'Querelle'.[11] While the protagonists differed with one another on how a text should be set, there was little disagreement on the importance of text. Nevertheless, the pro-Italian arguments of Raguenet show some shift away from the importance of reason in musical expression, and point to an increasing role for the senses. He admires Italian opera, and especially the aria, because it is sensuous—although it appeals to reason as well. His recognition of the importance of the senses also leads to a more relativist position, aligning Raguenet with the 'moderns' in their call for independence from antiquity.[12] This same relativism allows him to recognize merits in French opera as well, and he praises it for its skilful treatment of recitative, the tender affections and the use of spectacle.

In Lecerf's pro-French response, he rejects a role for the senses, and invokes antiquity to support his position. His praise of French opera is based on its appeal to reason and its obedience to the classical rules of simplicity and moderation. Citing examples from operas by Lully, with special emphasis on recitative, he praises the degree of precision with which it can portray the passions or affections. Italian opera, on the other hand, relies on brilliant and dazzling effects, on appealing almost

[10] Not only did it emerge as a genre in its own right, but, according to Catherine Kintzler, it was a form of tragedy that produced a mirror-like inversion of the essential features of spoken tragedy. She emphasizes musical tragedy as a parallel to spoken tragedy, rather than a subsidiary form of tragedy. (Kintzler, *Rameau*.)

[11] This quarrel was related in part to the renewed enthusiasm and interest in Italian music after the death of Lully in 1687. Georgia Cowart observes that comparisons and rivalry between French and Italian music were a long-standing tradition in France (dating back to the early seventeenth century) as the French were exposed to Italian music, and especially to opera, through performances in France, or through travels to Italy. Lully himself was born in Italy, arriving in France at the age of 14 in 1646. For a discussion of the earlier comparisons, see Cowart, *Origins of Modern Musical Criticism*, Ch. 1.

[12] Georgia Cowart observes that the musical debate between Raguenet and Lecerf was strongly influenced by the literary quarrel between the 'ancients' and the 'moderns'. She notes that the title of Raguenet's work, *Parallèle des Italiens et des Français en ce qui regarde la musique et les opéras* (Paris, 1702), reflects its indebtedness to Charles Perrault's *Parallèle des anciens et des modernes en ce qui regarde les arts et les sciences* (Paris, 1688). Lecerf's response, which was presented in his *Comparaison de la musique italienne et de la musique française* (Paris, 1704), shows a similar absorption of literary issues. Cowart emphasizes, as one of her major points, that Lecerf's espousal of neoclassical literary doctrine—'his careful construction of a set of standards and his subsequent evaluation of different bodies of music acccording to those standards give his work a modern critical outlook'. (Cowart, *Origins of Modern Musical Criticism*, 71.)

exclusively to the senses and the pleasures of the ear. It will be noted that in this debate, which still retains some of the earlier themes of the 'ancients' versus the 'moderns', Lully is now assigned a place on the side of the 'ancients'—with the Italians taking his place to represent the 'moderns'.[13] The issue, this time, revolved to a great extent around the importance of reason versus the senses.

Shortly after the initiative by Raguenet, there was a more serious challenge to the absolute rule of reason. It came from the Abbé Dubos in his *Réflexions critiques sur la poésie et la peinture* in 1719. Under the influence of Hobbes, Locke, and the British sensationalist school, Dubos assigns a primary role to sensibility, rather than reason, in the imitation of the passions.[14] He also makes it clear that music not only has its place among the imitative arts, but is capable of the most powerful expression among the arts.

Still following the Cartesian assumption of a mechanical orderly universe, Dubos assumes the universality of the passions. Now, however, they are conveyed directly through sensible experience—on the part of both the artist and the audience. The idea of passion is no longer the model, but passion itself. Artistic sensibility allows the artist to choose a pathetic or moving subject, and the work of art intensifies the original passion.

The elimination of the intervention of reason in the artistic experience also eliminates the need for intellectualization or formalization of the passions by the artist. Language is no longer the model, and music acquires a new status as an art form.[15] The materials of music and painting, indeed, are seen as closer to the original passions, while poetic images are less direct. Opera, in turn, is viewed as potentially more intense in its expressive powers than is spoken tragedy, since it combines music and poetry: 'The natural signs of the passions that music evokes and which it artfully uses to increase the impact of the words to which it is set, must then make these words more able to touch us, for these natural signs have a marvellous power to move us.'[16]

---

[13] Shortly thereafter, Rameau would undergo a similar reversal, at first being identified with a more modern, and indeed Italian-influenced, style—in contrast to the old-fashioned style of Lully—in the quarrel between the Lullists and the Ramists; and then switching to become associated with traditional French style—in contrast to the more modern Italian *galant* style—in the 'Querelle des Bouffons'.

[14] Dubos met Locke and other English writers of the sensationalist school when he became *chargé d'affaires* to England in 1702.

[15] It should be noted that the sensationalist philosophy of Locke and his followers did not call for the complete elimination of a role for reason, but rather an elimination of the Cartesian notion of innate ideas. It was only in Dubos's application of sensationalism in the realm of art that reason was dispensable.

[16] From the translation in Peter le Huray and James Day (eds.), *Music and Aesthetics in the Eighteenth and Early-Nineteenth Centuries*, abridged edn. (Cambridge: Cambridge University Press, 1988), 19.

Dubos's emphasis on sensibility also has implications for the nature of text in opera. The text should be simple and free of elaborate imagery, sharing with music the goal of direct expression of the passions. Natural language, which is closest to the original passions, is viewed as a kind of instinctive vocalization or inarticulate language. This is what music should mirror, rather than the precise poetic images or ideas in a text. In so doing, music should rely primarily on melody, since its tones are most similar to natural vocal sounds and inarticulate language: 'Just as the painter imitates the forms and colours of nature so the musician imitates the tones of the voice—its accents, sighs and inflections. He imitates in short all the sounds that nature herself uses to express the feelings and passions.'[17] Once again, music's strength comes from its capacity for immediate and direct expression.

The new role for sensible experience also increases the importance of taste in determining artistic values. In this regard, however, Dubos still reflects neo-classical mentality, emphasizing the universality of taste rather than individual response, despite the primacy of sensual experience. Conformity is based on the mechanical world-view, and arises from the fact that all men have similar instincts, passions, and response mechanisms, which ultimately prevail over individual differences of temperament or disposition. Above all, a judgement based on sensibility is infallible. To have a pleasing or moving experience is proof that the art object is pleasing or moving. In so far as there is such a thing as an 'educated response' to art, it is only a product of cumulative sensible experience. It does not introduce a role for reason or the intellect.[18]

This challenge to the absolute rule of reason in the artistic experience found a receptive audience. There were four editions of the *Réflexions* during Dubos's lifetime, followed by three more shortly after his death in 1742.[19] The advancement of the sensibility position and the new emphasis on taste, however, did not result in the total displacement of reason or an abandonment of universal laws in explaining art or music. Rather, the two coexisted—at times competing, but more often combined to varying degrees within the works of individual writers.[20]

---

[17] Ibid. 18.

[18] With the elimination of the role of reason or the intellect in the artistic experience, the classical concern for the moral or educative function of art is also undermined. For example, Dubos's emphasis is on the ability of music to please or move the individual.

[19] The last was published in 1770. Translations were published in cities throughout Europe—in Amsterdam, Leipzig, Berlin, Copenhagen, London, and Breslau.

[20] René Wellek notes, for example, that while many critics espoused taste and sensibility, they were less radical than Dubos in their anti-intellectualism. 'They usually managed to reconcile taste

One of the strongest proponents of the Cartesian rationalist position was Rameau, who devoted his entire career to explaining music—in all its aspects—in terms of universal formal principles. Even in his aesthetic treatise, the *Observations sur notre instinct pour la musique*, where he reflects the growing interest in sensible experience, he presents this experience as an alternative path for reaching the conclusions that could also be reached through reason. As a further rationalist control, he places harmony—which is subject to scientific laws—in a primary role in the direct evocation of feelings or passions, and assigns melody a more secondary position.[21] This was a reversal of the more prevalent view—as represented by Dubos and others—which identified melody with immediacy of expression. It enabled Rameau to absorb the notion of instinct or sensibility without sacrificing his view of the precise expressive powers of music and the means of achieving it through universal harmonic principles. The mutual reinforcement between instinct and reason, moreover, was not confined merely to the listener's response; it was in fact essential to the compositional process as well: 'Perfect understanding helps to put genius and taste into action; without it, they would become useless.'[22]

At the other end of the spectrum we find Rousseau, for whom sensibility is the definitive quality of true artistic expression, and reason is its antithesis. Like Dubos, he espouses the idea of an inarticulate and chant-like natural language of the passions, from which he too arrives at a position of melodic supremacy. Rousseau, however, goes much further than Dubos in explaining his view of expression, formulating a theory of the origin of melody and language. It is a theory so radical and sweeping in scope that it calls for a redefinition of society, human nature, knowledge, and truth itself.[23]

Having traced the principal aesthetic and musical issues that formed the background for Rousseau and Rameau, we are now ready to follow

---

and judgement . . . They defended the view that taste was both acquired and spontaneous, innate and cultivated, "sentimental" and intellectual.' Wellek goes on to observe, however, that 'these reconciliations of opposites raised a problem which proved dangerous to the basic assumptions of neo-classicism, which demanded, after all, an objective standard of value and beauty'. (René Wellek, *A History of Modern Criticism: 1750–1950*, vol. i. *The Late Eighteenth Century* (New Haven; Conn.: Yale University Press, 1955), 24.) These inner tensions in the concept of imitation will be taken up in Chs. 5 and 6 below.

[21] As noted in the preceding footnote, Rameau's view of instinct or taste was close to that of many critics who saw taste as 'a quicker reason, a short cut to the results of reason' (Wellek, 24).

[22] *Traité*, Preface; *CTW* i. 5. The influence of Cartesian rationalism on Rameau's theories is analysed in detail in Kintzler, *Rameau*. Other intellectual and philosophical influences will be examined in Ch. 4 below.

[23] As we shall see, Rousseau links the natural language of the passions with a particular state of society, before historical development and societal changes. This differs from Dubos, who views the natural language as an instinctive and universal response.

the lines of disagreement that developed after their exchange in the *Lettre sur la musique française* and the *Observations*, and especially the development of Rousseau's theory of the origin of melody and language. It should be noted that the theory was not yet present in the *Lettre*. There he simply presented the importance of language for melody as a given or a priori principle, without further explanation. It was only after Rameau put forth his aesthetic and theoretical arguments in the *Observations*—by way of answer to Rousseau, and also as further explanation of harmonic supremacy—that Rousseau countered with his own theory for explaining the superior role of melody.

Before that, however, Rameau wrote one more reply to Rousseau's *Lettre*—this time making a direct attack on the *Lettre*'s important new principle, that of 'unity of melody', and once again proclaiming the supremacy of harmony. Rameau included this attack in his *Erreurs sur la musique dans l'Encyclopédie*, published in 1755. As was noted earlier, the title of this essay is somewhat misleading. Far from being restricted to the music articles of the *Encyclopédie*, the essay also deals with the broader issue of Rousseau's doctrine of melodic supremacy—as illustrated in the following attack on this doctrine:

As long as we only consider melody as the principal source of effects in music, we will not make much progress, since it [melody] has even less power than rhythm ... Expression is born from neither a high nor a low pitch, but solely from the relationship between keys, interlaced by a certain transition from one to the other ... It is thus only from harmony, mother of melody, that the different effects that we experience in music arise directly ...[24]

Since Rousseau's doctrine of melodic supremacy was not yet present in his music articles in the *Encyclopédie*—written in 1749—Rameau's *Erreurs* should be viewed not only as a critique of the *Encyclopédie* articles, but also as part of Rameau's response to the *Lettre*.[25] Rousseau's theoretical response to Rameau went through a number of

[24] *Erreurs sur la musique dans l'Encyclopédie* (Paris: Jorry, 1755), 44–6; *CTW* v. 219–20.
[25] It was in fact Rameau's most direct defence of his theory of harmony. We have already noted that in Rameau's earlier response to the *Lettre*, in his *Observations*, he took an indirect approach, defending French opera and also the expressive role of harmony by rebutting the *Lettre*'s criticisms of Lully's recitative. It is not clear why Rameau belatedly switched to a more direct confrontation with Rousseau or why he chose to identify the *Encyclopédie* articles as the primary area of confrontation. Perhaps the extremity of the *Lettre*'s attack on French opera initially diverted Rameau's attention from the strength of Rousseau's anti-harmony position. What is clear is that in the *Erreurs* Rameau was not so much initiating a quarrel (although his attacks on the *Encyclopédie* did inadvertently initiate a quarrel with the editors of the *Encyclopédie*), but rather continuing one that was launched by Rousseau's *Lettre* and its assaults on some of Rameau's most basic beliefs about harmony. Many scholars, however, tend to follow the position of Alfred Oliver, who views the *Erreurs* mainly as a gratuitous and even 'sulky' display of bad temper. (See Oliver, *Encyclopedists as Critics*, 102.)

stages. At the time of the *Erreurs* there was no immediate published response by Rousseau. D'Alembert came to his defence in the 'Avertissement' to Volume 6 of the *Encyclopédie* in 1756. In his praise of Rousseau—seasoned with an effective dig at Rameau—d'Alembert also suggested that a response by Rousseau was in preparation:

M. Rousseau, who not only has much knowledge and taste in music, but also the talent of thinking and expressing himself with clarity, which musicians do not always have, is too capable of defending himself for us to undertake his cause here. In the *Dictionnaire de musique* which he is preparing, he will be able to return the arrows shot at him, if he so decides ...[26]

Through manuscript studies by Rousseau scholars, we now know that Rousseau did indeed prepare a prompt response to Rameau in 1755. Entitled 'Du principe de la mélodie ou reponse aux erreurs sur la musique', it was eventually rejected in that form by Rousseau, who then distributed its contents in his *Essai sur l'origine des langues* in 1781 and also in a more direct response to Rameau, entitled *Examen de deux principes avancés par M. Rameau.* Neither of the latter two were published during his lifetime, but appeared in 1781, after his death. As it turns out, the only version of Rousseau's theory of melody that was published during his lifetime was in the *Dictionnaire de musique*, published in 1768—where the theory is to be found in a number of articles dealing with aesthetic issues, the most complete presentation being the article entitled 'Opéra'.[27]

Rousseau's theory of melody, as formulated in the manuscript and in the *Essai sur l'origine des langues*, entails a reconstruction of the parallel histories of language and melody. Starting from a hypothetical common origin in a pre-societal state of nature, Rousseau traces their subsequent historical development in order to explain not only their present condition, but their essential nature as well.[28] The crux of the

---

[26] Jean le Rond d'Alembert, 'Avertissement des editeurs', *Encyclopédie, ou dictionnaire raisonné*, vi (Paris: Briasson, David l'aîné, Le Breton, Durand, 1756), p. i; *CTW* v. 289.

[27] The MS studies of Rousseau's response were undertaken independently by two Rousseau scholars, and the results published in Robert Wokler, 'Rameau, Rousseau, and *Essai sur l'origine des langues*', *Studies on Voltaire and the Eighteenth Century*, 127 (1974), 179–238, and Marie-Elisabeth Duchez, '"Principe de la mélodie" et "Origine des langues": Un brouillon inedit de Jean-Jacques Rousseau sur l'origine de la melodie', *Revue de musicologie*, 60 (1974), 33–86. The present study is indebted to both of these scholars for tracing the development of Rousseau's theory and pointing to its direct connection with the musical quarrels between Rameau and Rousseau. Because of the complex nature of Rousseau's response—including a philosophical theory, as well as a more direct reply to Rameau—Rousseau seems to have wavered in choosing the most appropriate forum for his response. The MS draft of 1755 is published in full in both the articles cited here.

[28] A number of Rousseau scholars have pointed out that the notion of a common origin for language and music was a prevalent one at the time. Catherine Kintzler notes that even Rameau concurred in this view—she cites statements to that effect in the *Code de musique pratique ... avec de*

theory is that language originated purely for the purpose of expressing feelings or passions, rather than physical needs, as people initially assembled in an ideal state of nature. Expression was direct and spontaneous, through an inarticulate but highly inflected form of vocalization—in Rousseau's terms, a voice shaped by 'accent'—further enlivened through the use of rhythmic patterns or cadences, resulting in a vocal line that was essentially singing. The first language was actually a union of expressive languages: poetry rather than prose, singing rather than speech—a rhythmic and accented voice, conveying passions rather than reason. Music and language were one:

> The origin of languages is not at all due to man's first needs ... It is neither hunger nor thirst, but love, hate, pity, anger, that brought forth the first vocalizations ... to move a young heart, to repulse an unjust aggressor, nature dictates accents, cries, plaintive sounds: these are the most ancient words invented, these are why the first languages were singing and passionate before becoming simple and methodic.[29]

And on the basis of this origin, Rousseau gives the following definition of the essential or ideal nature of melody and its role in music: 'It imitates the accents of language ... not only does it imitate, it speaks, and its inarticulate but lively, ardent passionate language, has a hundred times more energy than speech itself.'[30] Historically, the Heroic Age of Greece epitomized the perfect union between language and music, having a language that was both musical and expressive, shaped by the natural intonations and accents of the passionate voice—in contrast to the precise articulations of the French language: 'A language which has only articulations ... has only half of its potential richness; it expresses ideas, it is true, but to express feelings, images, it is necessary to have rhythm and sounds—that is to say, melody: that's what the Greek language had, and what is lacking in ours.'[31] This expressive ideal reflected in turn a geographic ideal; the gentle meridional climate

---

nouvelles réflexions sur le principe sonore (Paris: L'Imprimerie Royale, 1761) (*CTW* iv. 1–264). Kintzler observes, however, that for Rameau the question of origins or historical development has nothing to do with the essential nature of music, which can only be determined by the natural phenomenon of the resonating string. (*Ecrits sur la musique par J.-J. Rousseau*, ed. Catherine Kintzler (Paris: Editions Stock, 1979), preface, pp. ix–liv.)

[29] *Essai sur l'origine des langues*, ed. Jean Starobinski, Folio/Essais Series 135 (Paris: Gallimard, 1990), 67 (from ch. 2, entitled 'That the first invention of speech came not from needs but from passions').
All subsequent references to the *Essai* are to the Starobinski edn.

[30] Ibid. 124 (from ch. 14, 'Concerning melody').

[31] Ibid. 115–16 (from ch. 12, 'Origin of music'). Rousseau repeated this tribute to the ideal language of the Greeks in numerous articles in the *Dictionnaire* (in 'Accent', or 'Récitatif', for example), and in the 'Lettre à Burney avec fragmens d'observations sur l'Alceste italien de M. Gluck' (1776).

of Greece, fertile and rich, required a language only for the expression of the passionate feelings of the heart.[32]

During the course of history a process of degeneration set in, initially in Greece, manifested by the emergence of philosophy and subsequently influenced by a loss of political freedom:

As language was perfected, melody, in being subject to new rules, lost imperceptibly its former energy, and the calculation of intervals was substituted for the finesse of inflections. ... The study of philosophy and the progress of reasoning, having perfected grammar, deprived language of its lively and passionate tone which initially made it so singing.[33]

The process of degeneration was dramatically accelerated by the catastrophe of the barbaric invasions from the North during the late Roman Empire. They brought with them a harsh language of need, which replaced the poetic language of feeling: 'These crude people who were products of the North accustomed everyone's ears to the roughness of their speech; their voice harsh and bare of accent was noisy without being sonorous.'[34] This in turn had a damaging effect on melody: 'Song soon became only a slow and boring succession of sounds that were forced and shouted, without gentleness, without rhythm and grace.'[35]

The most serious consequence of these developments was that they led to the use of several voices and to the birth of harmony. Far from being the natural source of melody or expression (as Rameau claimed), harmony was introduced into music as a supplement or form of compensation for the absence of natural feelings or passions or melody; it was a negative product of culture and society: 'Song thus stripped of all melody, and consisting uniquely of the force and duration of sounds, ultimately suggested a means of making it more sonorous with the aid of consonances. Several voices ... found by chance some chords ... and thus began the practice of discant and counterpoint.'[36]

Harmony is also un-natural because its procedures are governed by artificial conventions, by rational principles or laws; it is based on derivations that are formulated in terms of proportions or ratios that are the product of mathematical calculations, rather than the natural proportions of the resonating string—all of which has nothing to do with true expression: 'When one calculates for a thousand years the proportions between sounds and the laws of harmony, how will one ever make of

---

[32] The role of climate in the development of languages was an important theme for other Enlightenment figures. Condillac's *Essai sur l'origine des connaissances humaines* (Paris, 1746) was a direct source of inspiration for many of them.

[33] *Essai*, 138 (from ch. 19, 'How music has degenerated').   [34] Ibid. 139–40.

[35] Ibid. 140.

[36] Ibid. 140–1.

this art an art of imitation . . . ?'[37] Even further from nature are the minor mode and dissonant chords used in harmony, since they are not produced by the resonating string.

Harmony is thus disqualified as the natural source of expression on two grounds, the second perhaps more important than the first: (1) The harmonies used in music cannot be equated with the natural proportions of the resonating string; and (2) The pleasures that we derive from harmony alone operate purely in the realm of physical sensation, and this cannot be the source of expression in music. Rousseau repeatedly insists that the physical phenomena of nature are devoid of any moral effect or meaning, which can only come from expressive melody: 'Successions of sounds or chords may perhaps amuse me for a moment; but, in order to charm me and make me feel tender, these successions must offer something which is neither sound nor chord, and which moves me in spite of myself.'[38] Ironically, melody is the natural source of expression because, unlike purely physical sensations, it has meaning, and yet that meaning depends on culture and society: 'If the greatest power that our sensations have over us is not due to moral causes, why are we so sensitive to impressions which are meaningless for barbarians? Why is our most moving music only an empty noise to the ear of a Caribbean?'[39]

Melody, however, is also further corrupted under the influence of harmony. It is now shaped by fixed harmonic intervals, rather than the more continuous and accented vocalizations of true passionate expression. Above all, music and language have become separated:

The genres, modes, scales, all received new faces; it was harmonic succession that ruled the march of the voice parts. This march having usurped the name of melody, one cannot in fact recognize in this new melody the traits of its mother; and our musical system having become by degrees purely harmonic, it is not surprising that oral accent has suffered, and that music has lost almost all of its energy. That is how song became, by degrees, an art completely separated from speech, from which it drew its origin.[40]

---

[37] Ibid. 123 (from ch. 14, 'Concerning harmony').

[38] Ibid. 128 (from ch. 15, 'That our strongest sensations are often aroused by moral impressions').

[39] Ibid. 126–7.

[40] Ibid. 142 (from ch. 19). Jacques Derrida argues that Rousseau inadvertently introduced the seeds of corruption that caused the separation of music and language at the very moment of origin— the need for supplement or compensation is always already there: 'This fissure is not one among others. It is *the* fissure: the necessity of interval, the harsh law of spacing. It could not endanger song except by being inscribed in it from its birth and in its essence.' Derrida emphasizes that this inscription from birth is something Rousseau says 'without wishing to say it' (Derrida, *Of Grammatology*, 200). We have already noted that Derrida sees a logical inconsistency in Rousseau's view of imitation in art because of the problematic concept of supplementation: 'Rousseau must at once denounce *mimesis* and art as supplements . . . and recognize in them man's good fortune, the expression of passion, the emergence of the inanimate.' (Ibid. 203–4.)

The completeness of the victory of convention over spontaneous expression varied from culture to culture, depending on the degree of closeness to the conditions of the ideal state. Warm and fertile southern climes (as in Italy) produced a softer and more musical language, still geared to the expression of feelings. Harsh northern climates (as in France) produced a harsher and more gutteral language, which was best suited for arguments and philosophy.[41]

Beyond these general points about musical expression, Rousseau's theoretical reconstruction also has significant implications for his views on specific musical forms or genres. This can be seen in his *Dictionnaire de musique*, where the theory of melody is a dominating presence. While its impact can be felt in articles throughout the work, its influence is particularly strong in the numerous entries dealing with opera—in many cases radically altering the meaning of traditional concepts.

Rousseau wrote the *Dictionnaire* between 1755 and 1767, which was precisely the period when the musical quarrels deepened and the theory of melody took shape. Although the *Dictionnaire* was until recently believed to be simply a recasting of his original music articles in the *Encyclopédie*, it is more nearly an original work. It is twice as long as the earlier book, with more than half of it devoted to new articles that had not originally appeared.[42] Through this extensive expansion and revision, the *Dictionnaire* served as a major vehicle for Rousseau in promoting his theory and, not incidentally, in advancing his arguments in the prolonged debate about music.[43]

[41] Rousseau's theory of the origin of melody—although closely connected with the musical quarrels—was also an integral part of an overall social philosophy that he had started to develop well before his entry into the musical debate with Rameau. The theme, linking civilized society with decline, was already present in 1750, in Rousseau's *Discours sur les sciences et les arts*. It appeared again in 1754 in the *Discours sur l'inégalité*, which originally contained a rudimentary draft of the *Essai sur l'origine des langues* as well. (There has been considerable disagreement among scholars as to the date of composition of the *Essai* and its chronological relationship to the *Discours sur l'inégalité*, with many scholars arguing that the latter preceded the *Essai*, although without any definitive settlement to the dispute.) The *Essai* stands apart from the others in its focus on music and language. If the musical quarrels played a role in the *Essai*—and the manuscripts show that they did—then they provided a stimulus for the further development of ideas that were already important aspects of Rousseau's philosophy.

[42] There are 524 new articles out of a total of 904. Most of the important new ones deal with aesthetic issues, many of them specifically related to opera. Among those that carried over, most were revised, often substantially, leaving only 166 that are almost identical to the original. For a detailed comparison, see Thomas Webb Hunt, 'The *Dictionnaire de musique* of Jean-Jacques Rousseau' (Ph.D. diss., North Texas State University, 1967), appendix 6.

[43] That the *Dictionnaire* served as a vehicle for debate was recognized in Rousseau's own time, as can be seen in the remark cited above from d'Alembert's 'Avertissement' to vol. vi of the *Encyclopédie*, where he promised that Rousseau would respond shortly to Rameau in the forthcoming *Dictionnaire de musique*. Rousseau himself acknowledged a connection between the *Dictionnaire* and his response to Rameau in the 'Avertissement' to his *Examen de deux principes avancés par M. Rameau* (1781). Rousseau explained that he had not intended to publish the *Examen*, which he had already put on paper in 1755, in response to Rameau's *Erreurs*. However, he subsequently

The most important article in which the theory is presented is the lengthy and newly written one entitled 'Opéra'. It is of particular significance because, as noted above, it is the principal version of his theory that was published during Rousseau's lifetime. All the elements of the theory are there: an original ideal state, subsequent decline or decay, and a process of compensation or supplementation—with opera as the main focus, rather than music in general. Progressing through all these stages in the reconstruction of the history of opera, Rousseau reaches the same conclusions as in the *Lettre*: the Italian language is musical and the French is not, which in turn determines the respective states of opera in the two countries. The case is settled with even greater finality in this work, since it now has theoretical support.

It is important to note in the theory that the separation of music and language after the decline of the ideal unity of Greek tragedy is true of all countries, including Italy. As a result of this separation, even Italian opera initially resorted to futile remedies:

At the birth of opera, its inventors, wishing to avoid the un-naturalness of uniting music with discourse in the imitation of ordinary human life, thought it best to transport the scene to the heavens and the underworld, and not knowing how to make men speak, they prefered to make gods and devils sing, rather than heroes and shepherds.[44]

The result was dramatic action that was lacking in interest, which in turn led to further attempts at compensation through the use of lavish scenery, machinery, and spectacle.

The Italians, however, had the potential to find more meaningful solutions: they had the capacity to create both expressive music and expressive poetry, and, since their music and poetry were compatible with one another, they had the potential effectively to combine the two. The key to it all is having a musical language—all the more important after the separation of music and language:

When language has neither gentleness nor flexibility, the rigidity of its poetry prevents it from being adapted to melody; the gentleness of melody in turn prevents it from lending itself to good verse declamation, and one feels in the forced union of these two arts a perpetual constraint that shocks the ear and destroys the attraction of both the melody and the declamation. This weakness is without remedy, and anyone who wishes to force the application of music to a language which is not musical, will make it even harsher than it already was.[45]

reconsidered, saying that it would 'serve as clarification for certain articles in my *Dictionnaire*, where the form of the work did not permit me to enter into long discussions'. (The text of the *Examen* is reprinted in *Ecrits sur la musique par J.-J. Rousseau*, ed. Kintzler, 338.)

[44] Rousseau, *Dictionnaire de musique* (Paris: Duchesne, 1768, 342. All quotations from the *Dictionnaire* are from the facsimile of the 1768 edn. (Hildesheim: Olms, 1969; reprint, New York: Johnson Reprint Corp., 1969).

[45] Ibid. 347.

During the course of the eighteenth century, Italian opera did in fact find a solution through the creation of lyrical poetry that lent itself to musical settings and inspired talented composers. The texts of Zeno and Metastasio consisted of recitatives and arias that expressed the energy and violence of feelings and passions: 'These new poems that genius has created, and which it alone could sustain, drove away effortlessly the bad musicians who only knew the mechanics of their art … the Vincis, Leos, Pergolesis, disdained the servile imitation of their predecessors, and opening a new path … achieved their goal almost with their very first steps.'[46]

Rousseau warns, however, that maintaining a balanced and close relationship between music and text is a level of perfection that is not easy to sustain: 'The musician, if he is more artistic than the poet … makes us completely forget the play, and changes the spectacle into a veritable concert. If the advantage, on the other hand, is with the poet, the music, in its turn, will become almost neutral …'[47]

Italian opera, having found a balance between music and text (in large part through the musicality of the Italian language) could rid itself of the futile and destructive remedies that the French, with their unmusical language, were still forced to employ:

It is thus very natural that music, having become passionate and pathetic, has rid itself … of these bad supplements which it no longer needs. Opera, purged of all this *merveilleux* which was destroying it, became a spectacle that was equally touching and majestic, worthy of pleasing people of taste and of arousing sensitive hearts.[48]

The fact that under the proper conditions opera can achieve powerful expression and a balanced relationship between music and language is an important concession by Rousseau. It leaves an opening for his retention of traditional operatic conventions, although they must be properly understood within the framework of the theory of loss and compensation. Above all, he retains the traditional goal of imitation, which he includes in the article 'Opéra' almost side by side with his dark conclusions about the loss of the Greek ideal of unity: 'Considered as a component of nature, music limits its effects to sensations and physical pleasures resulting from melody, harmony, and rhythm … But as an essential part of opera, of which the principal goal is imitation, music

---

[46] Rousseau, *Dictionnaire de musique*, 345–6.   [47] Ibid. 346.

[48] Ibid. 347. Diderot took an almost identical position to Rousseau's on the importance of maintaining a balanced relationship between music and text in opera, and on the importance of having a musical text in order to achieve such a balance. Diderot presented this view in an essay entitled *Observations sur un ouvrage intitulé 'Traité du mélodrame'* (1771), in which he played a mediating role during a debate over the relative importance of music versus text. The history of opera can be viewed as a continuous search for a balanced relationship between the two.

becomes one of the fine arts, capable of painting scenes, arousing feelings . . ,'[49] Once again, this view is far from the total rejection of opera that the theory might imply: it in fact leaves an opening for the possibility of reform.[50]

Rousseau's concern with music as an imitative art also leads to further insights about the nature of imitation or expression in music. And here he makes a contribution to the traditional concept of imitation that surpasses most contemporary statements in clarifying music's expressive powers. He observes that these powers derive from music's greater freedom from pure representation, in comparison to the other arts. Instead of representing objects or painting images, music has the power to affect us directly, to excite feelings and movements within us, doing so through movement itself. Melody is a succession of inflections—the field of music is time—in contrast to painting:

> The imitation of painting is always cold, because it lacks that succession of ideas and impressions that warm the soul by degrees . . . the art of the musician consists in substituting for the insensible image of the object, the movements that its presence excites in the soul of the spectator: it does not represent things directly; but it awakens in our soul the same feeling that one experiences in seeing it.[51]

Because of this non-representational quality, music has the power to evoke impressions of which painting is incapable:

> It is one of the great advantages of the musician to be able to paint things that we cannot hear, while it is impossible for the painter to paint what we cannot see; and the greatest achievement of an art whose only activity is movement, is the power to form even the image of repose. Sleep, the calm of night, solitude and even silence enter into the numerous tableaux of music.[52]

He adds that these same suggestive or impressionistic capabilities make

---

[49] Rousseau, *Dictionnaire*, 339. Rousseau's emphasis on imitation is also close to that of d'Alembert, presented in the 'Discours préliminaire des éditeurs' to vol i of the *Encyclopédie* (1751), pp. xi–xii: 'All music that does not paint anything, is simply noise.'

[50] That Rousseau's concept of corruption still allows for the possibility of reform—that 'evil is not without remedy'—is a point stressed by Jean Starobinski as well as other Rousseau scholars. See Rousseau's *Essai sur l'origine*, ed. Starobinski, 51–3.

[51] Rousseau, *Dictionnaire*, 349–50. Rousseau here is making an important distinction between music and painting. In the *Essai sur l'origine des langues* he warns against false analogies. While the effect of colours comes from their permanence, the effect of sounds comes from their succession. Yet Rousseau himself makes a repeated analogy between music and painting, as in the following example from the *Essai*, also appearing in the *Dictionnaire*: 'Melody does precisely for music what design does in painting—it is melody that outlines the traits and the figures, of which chords and sounds are only the colours' (from ch. 13, 'Concerning melody', 118–19.)

[52] Rousseau, *Dictionnaire*, 349.

music ideally suited for the direct expression of feelings, which is the primary goal of art.[53]

In this manner, Rousseau adapts the traditional concept of imitation (a process already well launched by Dubos and other proponents of the sensibility position), making it more amenable to the particular expressive capabilities of music, and in fact recognizing expressive powers in music that surpass the other arts. An equally important modification—and this is entailed in the notion of direct expression—is the complete exemption of reason in the artistic experience. Not only does it lose its former centrality; it is seen as antithetical to expression. Rousseau thus goes considerably further in an anti-rationalist direction than any of his predecessors, presenting the most dramatic challenge to the neo-classical mentality and its insistence on universal laws. At the same time, he stops safely short of making the complete break with contemporary doctrine that his own radical theory might imply.

Because of this odd mixture of the traditional and the new, with serious consideration often given to the former, the *Dictionnaire* is filled with thoughtful critiques—at times, with suggestions for reform—as well as clarifications of the practice of his day. A striking example is in the article 'Récitatif', where he presents some important distinctions between the respective roles of aria and recitative. Starting with the Rousseauian premise that current opera can never recapture the ideal declamation of the Greeks and therefore must compensate through the artificial conventions of recitative and aria, he expresses concern for achieving a balanced relationship between music and text. This is a concern that applies not only to the French, but perhaps even more to the Italians: 'Music dominates too much in our arias, so that the poetry is almost forgotten. Our lyrical dramas are sung too much ... An opera that is only a succession of arias would be almost as boring as a single aria of comparable length.' And here he clarifies a major function of recitative: 'It is necessary to divide and separate arias by the use of text; but it is necessary that this text be given a musical setting as well ... recitative is the means of uniting music and words; it is also the means for setting the arias apart from one another ...'[54]

---

[53] The notion of the superiority of music because of its impressionistic or suggestive powers, rather than direct representation, was so prized by Rousseau that he repeated the idea verbatim in a number of places: in two articles in the *Dictionnaire*—'Imitation', as well as 'Opéra'; and in the *Essai sur l'origine des langues*. As we shall see, it was an important theme for Diderot as well.

[54] Rousseau, *Dictionnaire*, 400. Rousseau objects to the use of spoken dialogue (as opposed to recitative) since it is important to have consistency and to maintain the use of music throughout an opera. The alternation of speech and song, as is the practice in French comic opera, is too disparate—like changing languages in the middle of a work. It destroys all sense of reality and continuity. For similar reasons, Rousseau rejects the use of dance and pantomime in opera: 'How can we introduce in the same work two languages that are mutually exclusive, and join the art of pantomime with that of text which renders it superfluous?' (Ibid. 351).

Interestingly enough, after defining recitative as 'a declamation in music, in which the musician must imitate, as much as possible, the inflexions of the voice', he proposes that recitative should rely on harmonic key changes or modulations in order to reflect the changing emotions in the text: 'In recitative, where the expressions, feelings, ideas, vary at each instant, one must employ modulations equally varied that can represent ... the successions expressed by the discourse ...'[55]

Of even greater significance, he recommends an expanded role for the orchestral accompaniment in his discussion of *récitatif obligé*. For this special kind of recitative, he proposes the use of orchestral passages in symphonic style alternating with vocal recitative, and claims that the orchestra can be even more expressive than the voice:

These alternating passages of recitative and melody vested with the full splendour of the orchestra, are the most touching, ravishing, energetic elements in modern music. The actor ... transported by a passion which does not permit him to say everything, interrupts himself ... during which time the orchestra speaks for him; and these silences, filled in this way, affect the listener infinitely more than if the actor himself had said everything which the music is conveying.[56]

He also adds that this technique was unknown in France until his opera *Le Devin du village*.[57] Evidently, the close relationship between melody and language does not preclude an important role for harmony or for the orchestra, when determined by expressive needs and the nature of the genre.[58]

In similar fashion, the article 'Air' provides a clearer view of how the music in arias can achieve a true imitation of the passions. Once again, melody is assigned a crucial role—controlling the overall design—but harmony is not excluded from the process:

The arias of our operas are ... the canvas or foundation on which imitative musical scenes are painted. Melody is the design, harmony is the colour. All the picturesque objects of nature, all the deep feelings of the human heart, are the

[55] Ibid. 401.   [56] Ibid. 404–5.

[57] Ibid. 405. Many would dispute that Rousseau was the first to use the technique, in France or elsewhere, but he undoubtedly helped to make it more popular. Gluck's use of it in *Alceste* was later praised by Rousseau—in the 'Fragmens d'observations sur l'Alceste italien de M. le chevalier Gluck' (*Ecrits sur la musique*, ed. Kintzler, 395–7.)

[58] Rousseau's recognition of the expressive powers of the orchestra also implies a recognition of a more important status for instrumental music. This is a principal thesis in Snyders, *Le Goût musical*. Snyders sees an important role for both Rousseau and Diderot in recognizing the special expressive powers of instrumental music. He observes, however, that they did not completely abandon the more traditional view of music as opera (see in particular, pp. 89–90 and p. 134). For a discussion of the rapidly developing importance of sonatas and symphonies and the gap that existed between aesthetic doctrine and popular taste, see Weber, 'Musical Taste. He notes that the wealthy patrons who supported instrumental music were not the same people as those who established aesthetic doctrine. For a detailed analysis of the gradual process by which the traditional doctrine of musical imitation became undone, see John Neubauer, *The Emancipation of Music from Language* (New Haven, Conn.: Yale University Press, 1986).

models that the artist imitates. The goals of imitation are to capture our attention and interest, to charm our ear, and to move our heart.[59]

He also adds (and this closely reflects the traditional Baroque view of expressive content) that each phrase in the aria text should paint the same picture or feeling, that there should be only one subject in the text, and that the music should express this overall image or feeling: 'The different phrases of an aria are only a number of different ways of presenting the same image. That is why the subject must be one.'[60]

In each of the above examples, it is worth stressing that the strong presence of lingering traditional elements by no means cancels the radical nature of Rousseau's departures from the accepted views of his day or the seriousness of his rupture with Rameau. It simply confirms that there were significant areas of agreement between them as well, and that these must be recognized if we are to have an accurate measure of their disagreements.

We have noted at the start that Rousseau and all the Enlightenment *philosophes* were constantly engaged in musical dialogue, both spoken and written, making much of their thinking on music a communal activity. While Rousseau's tone, as well as his content, often convey a deep sense of isolation—even from his fellow *philosophes*—his profound understanding of ideas that presumably were unacceptable to him belies the totality of his isolation. We would argue that Rousseau was listening to others, and was indeed a very good listener. He was engaged in dialogue in the best sense of the word.

In the next two chapters we will see how other themes were introduced and how the other participants joined in.

The translations in the appendix for this chapter focus on the subsequent arguments by Rameau and Rousseau on the issue of harmonic versus melodic supremacy: Rameau's *Erreurs sur la musique dans l'Encyclopédie*, selected passages; and Rousseau's *Dictionnaire* article 'Opéra', in its entirety.

[59] Rousseau, *Dictionnaire*, 29. [60] Ibid. 30.

4

Music as Science:
The Contribution of d'Alembert

In the preceding chapter on music as expressive art we have traced a gradual shift in French neo-classicism, moving from Cartesian rationalism in its purest form toward a growing recognition of an important role for sensibility in the artistic experience. We have also observed that the change did not occur uniformly, that a broad range of views coexisted, and that Rameau remained close to the rationalist end of the spectrum, while Rousseau forged a path to the most extreme end of the sensibility range.

As we turn now to a consideration of music as science and the scope and method of music theory, we might expect that the alternatives to reason would have less of an impact in that realm. No one—not even Rousseau—would deny that there was a part of music that was subject to rational principles and systematic investigation. All in fact agreed that harmony was the appropriate sphere for systematic inquiry, and that Rameau had achieved a breakthrough in music theory precisely because of his application of scientific principles.

Despite this consensus, however, the realm of music as science underwent a series of conflicts or debates which, if not identical to those in the aesthetic realm, were closely analogous. This of course was more than coincidence. Whether the subject was art or science, the Cartesian concept of truth or knowledge, still widely accepted in France until well into the eighteenth century—was increasingly exposed to serious scrutiny or challenge. A principal concern of this chapter is the gradual breakdown of Cartesian rationalism within the scientific realm of music. It will be shown that Rameau himself contributed to that breakdown—that despite his Cartesian claims and rhetoric, it was musical practice that ultimately determined his rules and laws of harmony.[1]

---

[1] The discrepancy between Rameau's Cartesian claims and some of his actual explanations of music is also discussed in my review of Catherine Kintzler's *Jean-Philippe Rameau: Splendeur et naufrage de l'esthétique du plaisir à l'âge classique*, in *JAMS* 38, no. 1 (1985), 169–78. For further discussion of specific Cartesian elements in Rameau's theory, see Charles B. Paul, 'Jean-Philippe Rameau (1683–1764), the Musician as Philosophe', *Proceedings of the American Philosophical Society*, 114, no. 2 (1970), 140–54. Paul recognizes the importance of Descartes's influence on Rameau but finds a number of other intellectual traditions in evidence. He also emphasizes Rameau's concern for actual musical practice as a guiding factor in the development of his theory.

Still another reason for the close paralleling of issues in the respective realms of music as art and as science is that the boundaries between the two were by no means fixed. Discussions in music theory seldom proceeded without references to music as expressive art.[2]

The question of scientific boundaries or appropriate limits for music theory was another part of the musical dialogue in which Rameau, once again, found himself the subject of controversy, especially as his pronouncements became increasingly metaphysical. This time, it was d'Alembert who was the principal challenger—although Rousseau once again held the position that was furthest from that of Rameau. Since the opposition between Rameau and Rousseau was closely related to the issues of the preceding chapter, and especially their respective views on the means of expression in music, we shall deal with that before turning to d'Alembert.

For Rameau, with his basically rationalist position, music as science is almost all-encompassing. There is no separate domain for music that is untouched by rational objective principles. It will be recalled that in Rameau's view instinct or sensibility is an alternative path for reaching the principles that could be known through reason—a view heavily emphasized in the *Observations*.[3] If Rameau recognizes any gap or difference between music as art and as science, it is only for those instances where musical practice cannot be explained by rules or principles—even after adapting or bending the principles to fit practice.[4] In such cases, Rameau invokes the notion of genius, taste, instinct, or music as art, thus signifying that there is a part of music which transcends rules or principles. (In the *Traité*, for example, he allows an otherwise forbidden extended chain of dissonant seventh chords by

[2] Claude Palisca traces the changing relation between music as art and as science during the 17th cent., in 'Scientific Empiricism in Musical Thought', in Hedley Howell Rhys (ed.), *Seventeenth-Century Science and the Arts* (Princeton, NJ: Princeton University Press, 1961), 91–137. He reminds us that during the medieval period music was considered a branch of science rather than art, and held a place among the mathematical *quadrivium*. Palisca sees a synthesis occurring during the Renaissance between music as art and as science, but observes that it broke down by the end of the 16th cent. The 17th cent. is characterized as a period when music and science were separate, but when scientific discoveries and methods continued to have an influence on musical writings. There was, however, a tendency for a time-lag to occur between the scientific discoveries and their absorption into music theory.

[3] Rameau never clarified how instinct and reason reach the same conclusions, other than simply to assert that the resonating string had the power to attain this mutual confirmation. The French scholar Marie-Elisabeth Duchez argues that Rameau's view at this time represented a psychoacoustic reality that science seized upon over 200 years later—current acoustical science now takes into account the psychic phenomenon of human reception. Duchez concludes that Rameau's principle of the fundamental bass not only had a scientific *raison d'être*, but enlarged the scientific domain of music without knowing it. (Marie-Elisabeth Duchez, 'Valeur épistémologique de la théorie de la basse fondamentale de Jean-Philippe Rameau: connaissance scientifique et représentation de la musique', *Studies on Voltaire and the Eighteenth Century*, 245 (1986), 91–130.)

[4] As we shall see, Rameau made such efforts at adaptation (although never completely successful) in his derivation of the minor mode, the sub-dominant, and the dissonant seventh chord.

saying that 'good taste obliges us sometimes to break these rules'.[5]) These cases, however, are relatively insignificant for Rameau, and have little influence on his belief in a comprehensive theory of harmony.

For Rousseau, on the other hand, music as expressive art is almost all-encompassing. The physical or scientific part of music, once converted into a means of expression, is no longer a physical or scientific phenomenon. Harmony, as used in music, is man-made, a product of culture. Given its origin and role in music history, as a form of compensation for the loss of true expression in music, it can only transcend this negative role by lending support to melodic expression. But in this capacity it is barely recognized as a science at all by Rousseau.

Rousseau's interpretation of the consequences of converting a physical or natural phenomenon into art also contains another ironic contrast with Rameau. For the latter, the fact that the physical raw material of harmony is a natural phenomenon is proof that harmony is the basis not only of music theory, but of natural expression in music. For Rousseau, the same fact leads to the opposite conclusion: the closer harmony is to being a purely physical phenomenon, the further it is from true musical expression.[6]

The extremity of Rousseau's attack on music as science removed him from the heart of the scientific debate, leaving it instead to d'Alembert. He was one of the pre-eminent scientists of the Enlightenment, well recognized for his work in the field of rational mechanics, and was elected to the Académie Royale des Sciences at the age of 24, in 1741. He was also a cosmopolitan man of letters, and served with Diderot as co-editor of the *Encyclopédie*. Though he was initially responsible for writing and editing science articles, his work rapidly expanded to embrace a broad range of fields, including music. He was also the author of the widely admired 'Discours préliminaire' to the *Encyclopédie*.

His more direct contribution to music theory began with his authorship of the simplified version of Rameau's theory, the *Elémens de musique théorique et pratique*, published in Paris in 1752. During the subsequent scientific debates that erupted with Rameau, d'Alembert was the chief spokesman for the *philosophes*. He entered into the debates not only to defend Rousseau against Rameau's *Erreurs dans l'Encyclopédie*, but also to present his own growing criticisms of Rameau's scientific assumptions. Before considering the views of Rameau which

[5] Rameau, *Traité*, 311; *CTW* i. 341.

[6] As we have seen, in Rousseau's *Lettre sur la musique française* he dismisses harmony as a possible influence on a national music style because harmony comes from nature and is the same for all nations. Apparently he is referring to harmony as physical raw material—rather than harmony as used in music, where it becomes a product of culture. Whatever Rousseau's intention, there is of course self-contradiction in these two different views of harmony.

became the subject of debate, however, it is useful to retrace our steps once again, and to examine Rameau's ideas on music as science before dissension arose.

From the very beginning of Rameau's career he sought to make music theory a science. In 1722, in his first theoretical treatise, the *Traité de l'harmonie*, he defined the goals of music theory in rationalist terms that reflected the prevalence of Cartesian science at the time.[7] It involved a search for a unique and self-evident principle which could be stated in mathematical terms:

Music is a science which must have rules which are certain; these rules must be derived from a self-evident principle, and this principle cannot be known to us without the use of mathematics. I must confess that despite all the experience that I could acquire in music, having practiced it for such a long time, it is nevertheless only with the use of mathematics that my ideas have taken shape, and that light has followed darkness which I did not perceive in the past.[8]

Briefly stated, the self-evident principle for Rameau posits that the lowest sound or fundamental of a perfect chord is the source or generator of the consonant intervals of that chord. (Rameau's 'perfect chord' is commonly known as a 'major triad'.) More specifically, the fundamental bass is the source of the major third and the perfect fifth in the major triad. Equally important, through the application of the principle of the identity of octaves, it does not matter in which octave the fundamental bass actually appears in the chord; it always remains the fundamental bass. The far-reaching consequence of this principle is that the various positions of a chord—depending on whether the fundamental bass occurs in the lowest position, or whether it lies above the other members of the chord (in current terminology, referred to as 'root' position and 'inverted' position, respectively)—are interpreted as having the same fundamental bass. (Octave equivalence also allows the intervals of a chord to be reduced to their respective positions within the octave.) In this view of chordal structure, the root position and the inversions are not separate chords.

From the fundamental bass as first principle, Rameau attempts to derive all the harmonies and rules of harmonic procedure used in eighteenth-century tonal practice, applying deductive Cartesian logic. While he essentially fulfils this goal, he does so through a pliant use of the principle, or through the constant interplay between musical instinct and logic, starting with the formulation of the principle of the fundamental bass itself. Rameau arrived at his concept of the

---

[7] Catherine Kintzler observes that the influence of the Cartesian doctrine was so pervasive in France that it was like a 'virus' or fever that raged, taking hold of Rameau as well as many others. (Kintzler, *Rameau*, 35).

[8] *Traité*, Preface; *CTW* i. 3.

fundamental bass as generator before his awareness of the actual generation of the consonant intervals as overtones. In the *Traité*, he still used
the traditional derivation of consonances, relying on the divisions of a
monochord by small integers, and defining the consonant intervals of
harmony purely in terms of the mathematical ratios resulting from the
comparison of string lengths.[9] At this stage, and indeed in subsequent
stages, an instinctive awareness of the functional relationship between
the fundamental bass and chordal inversions must have played a role in
his notion of the lowest sound as generator, since the divisions of the
monochord did not actually generate the physical sounds of intervals.
Similarly, it must have been instinct rather than pure logic that made
Rameau insist on the identity of octaves. In mathematical terms, the
unison and the octave are not identical—the octave ratio $2:1$ could not
represent an equality with the principal sound.[10] Nevertheless,
Rameau's assumption of octave identity is at the very heart of his
theory.

In Rameau's comprehensive system, the principle must yield not
only the major third and perfect fifth, but, as noted, all harmonies used
in eighteenth-century tonal practice: the minor mode, the sub-dominant, and the various dissonant chords then in use. These harmonies,
however, could not be extracted from the fundamental bass with the
kind of simple and direct derivation that produced the major triad
(neither the monochord, nor the subsequent discovery of the overtones
could produce these additional harmonies as directly), and Rameau
was forced (not only in the *Traité*, but throughout his career) to construct them through a series of ingenious manipulations and flexible
applications of the principle of the fundamental bass.

While Rameau scholars have duly noted the inconsistencies and
errors in his repeated efforts to derive the varied harmonies from a
single generative source, few would deny that there is a remarkable
logic to Rameau's incorporation of these harmonies within his system.
The principle that determines the structure of chords also determines
their succession: the intervals of the fifth and the third, which comprise

---

[9] This traditional method, dating back to Pythagoras and still used by Zarlino in the sixteenth
century, also featured prominently in Descartes's *Compendium musicae*, written in 1618. It was
translated into French in 1668 as the *Abrégé de la musique*, a work cited by Rameau in the *Traité*.
Rameau's derivations and their background are examined in Jacques Chailley, 'Rameau et la
théorie musicale', *La Revue musicale*, 260 (1964), 65–95. A more focused study of the discovery of
overtones and its implications for Rameau is presented in Thomas Christensen, 'Eighteenth-
Century Science and the *Corps Sonore*: The Scientific Background to Rameau's Principle of
Harmony', *Journal of Music Theory*, 31 (1987), 23–50.

[10] Rameau's insistence on this identity, which is essential to his entire theory, led to intense
disputes with the physicist Leonard Euler, who placed greater emphasis on the significance of
ratios. Rameau criticized Euler in a pamphlet of 1753, *Extrait d'une réponse de M. Rameau à M.
Euler sur l'identité des octaves* (*CTW* v. 167–88), and argued for the identity of octaves on the
grounds that we experience them as replicas of the principal sound.

the perfect chord, are also the most perfect intervals for the progression of the fundamental bass.

As it turns out, these few basic principles yield a comprehensive system that shows a profound understanding of the logic of tonal music and its chordal syntax. (The strength of Rameau's influence to the present day has far less to do with his view of harmonic generation than with his deep understanding of tonal syntax.) It is worth pausing briefly to examine this syntax, and especially the role of dissonance in defining the tonic. It illustrates not only the strength of his logic, but also the constant interplay between logic and musical instinct. If science or acoustics could provide only some of the guiding principles for Rameau—and it certainly did that—then his perception of an inherent logic within tonal music itself must have provided the rest.[11]

In his system of chordal syntax, the most far-reaching syntactic principle is that each chord within a key has a unique function. The three essential chords of a key (the tonic, dominant, and sub-dominant) are totally distinct and have non-overlapping functions, as long as the key is maintained. From these three chords the functions of the remaining chords are derived.[12]

The tonic is the most important chord in defining a key. Above all, it is the only chord without dissonance, the only triad or perfect chord—and the tonic may be major or minor. All other chords within a key must be dissonant, even if the dissonance is merely implied rather than expressed. Dissonance normally is formed by adding a seventh to a perfect chord. Rameau attests to the importance of dissonance in the following remark:

[11] A more detailed examination of Rameau's views of chordal structure and syntax is provided in my 'Rameau's Views on Modulation and their Background in French Theory', *JAMS* 31, no. 3 (1978), 467–79. Still another discussion, focusing on later developments in Rameau's views of chordal syntax and his concept of the tonic, is in my 'The Development of Rameau's Thoughts on Modulation and Chromatics', 69–91. For a detailed account of Rameau's theory in general, although dealing primarily with its significance for d'Alembert, see Thomas Christensen, 'Science and Music Theory in the Enlightenment: D'Alembert's Critique of Rameau' (Ph.D. diss., Yale University, 1985). Christensen's forthcoming book on Rameau is entitled *Jean-Philippe Rameau: The Science of Music Theory in the Enlightenment* (Cambridge University Press). Other studies, dealing with more specific aspects of his theory, appear in Jerome de La Gorce (ed.), *Jean-Philippe Rameau: Colloque international organisé par la Société Rameau, Dijon, 21–24 septembre 1983* (Paris, Geneva: Champion-Slatkine, 1987). Among older studies, the most thorough is by Matthew Shirlau, *The Theory of Harmony* (London: Novello, 1917). There is also a summary of his various treatises by Joan Ferris, 'The Evolution of Rameau's Harmonic Theories', *Journal of Music Theory*, 3, no. 1 (1959), 231–55.

[12] Rameau introduces the term 'sub-dominant' in his second treatise, the *Nouveau système*, which was written shortly after the *Traité* in 1726, and intended as a further elaboration of ideas presented in the *Traité*. The present discussion of Rameau's view of chordal syntax focuses on his original formulation in these two earliest treatises. The concept, however, remains essentially unchanged throughout his career (with only minor adjustments as his view of the generative process changed).

The necessity of dissonance is found first in the three fundamental tones which constitute a key [the tonic, dominant and sub-dominant]. Since each of them in turn can give the impression of being the key … [the musician] with the help of dissonance attached to the harmony of a fundamental chord which is not the principal tone, has the means of making it clear which key he intends to present.[13]

But the absence of dissonance in a perfect chord does not suffice to indicate the tonic. It is a necessary but not a sufficient condition. Rameau also distinguishes the tonic as the chord that follows the dominant seventh chord. The tonic is the only chord which can do so, and conversely, the dominant seventh is the only seventh chord which can precede a tonic (Rameau calls this dominant the 'dominant-tonic'). The resulting progression down a fifth from dominant to tonic is called a 'perfect cadence'.

An alternative cadence for establishing the tonic is the progression up a fifth from the sub-dominant to the tonic, called by Rameau an 'irregular cadence' (he also calls it an 'imperfect cadence', and in current terminology it is called a 'plagal cadence'). It involves the exceptional formation of dissonance, by adding a major sixth rather than a seventh to the perfect chord on the sub-dominant, producing the chord of the 'added sixth'. Once again, the cadential progression determines the unique function of the dissonant chord as well as the tonic. The only fundamental chord which can carry this dissonance and which can progress in this way is the sub-dominant.[14]

The role of the remaining chords, which are all dissonant seventh chords is modelled after the perfect cadence. Each seventh chord is considered the unique dominant of the chord a fifth below (Rameau calls them simply 'dominants'). The most important distinction between the function of the simple dominants or seventh chords and the dominant seventh is that the former cannot go to a perfect chord or tonic: they must go to another simple dominant and another—until the dominant seventh is reached, which can then proceed to the tonic. If the dissonance is absent in a chord which follows a simple dominant (and Rameau makes its actual presence optional) then it is automatically implied.[15]

[13] *Nouveau système*, 56; *CTW* ii. 66.

[14] Any question of ambiguity between the sub-dominant chord of the added major sixth and the seventh chord on the second degree of the scale—both having identical notes, is answered by the way in which the chord progresses. If it resolves to the tonic, then it must be a sub-dominant chord. In a later treatise, the *Génération*, Rameau exploits the potential ambiguity between the two chords through the notion of 'double emploi' (Rameau, *Génération harmonique*, 107–19; *CTW* iii. 68–74).

[15] Rameau also imposes a number of other restrictions on the use of simple seventh chords. Normally he forbids a seventh chord on the tone a half-step below the tonic (the leading tone), which in turn eliminates a seventh chord a fifth above or below. This leaves only three highly recommended sevenths—on the notes of *La*, *Re*, and *Sol*.

In addition to the perfect and irregular cadences and the progression of seventh chords by fifth, Rameau introduces a number of alternative chords and cadential progressions. They are viewed, however, merely as substitutions or variants of the original chords and progressions, a means of varying the harmony, but without affecting the basic premises of chordal syntax.[16]

Having applied a logical and scientific method to explain the structure and behaviour of a multitude of chords and chord progressions used in eighteenth-century tonal practice, Rameau could claim that the 'perfection' of the music of his day was now matched by a similar progress in music theory, which he had found lagging until then. What were once a large number of chords and chord progressions were reduced to a few essential ones, governed by a few underlying principles.

In Rameau's second treatise, the *Nouveau système* of 1726 (which was presented as a companion to the *Traité*), he recognized the experimental findings of Sauveur of the overtones produced by a resonating body.[17] The discovery of this phenomenon led Rameau to a reformulation of the principle of the fundamental bass, which he presented in two subsequent treatises, the *Génération harmonique* of 1737 and the *Démonstration du principe de l'harmonie* of 1749. In these works Rameau eliminated the more speculative and outmoded mathematical derivation of harmonic intervals based on the divisions of a monochord, and replaced it with his newly formulated principle of the *corps sonore*. According to this principle, a resonating body will generate not only its fundamental or lowest sound, but also a series of harmonically related overtones through the successive divisions of the resonating body, producing the octave, the perfect twelfth, and the major seventeenth—or, when reduced within the octave, the intervals of the perfect fifth and major third. This marked a change to a more physical or experimental basis for his theory of harmony, since the overtones were actual sounds, generated simultaneously with the principal sound.[18] In the *Génération*,

---

[16] A further means of varying the harmony is to leave the original key, but even then the basic premises of chordal syntax remain unchanged.

[17] Thomas Christensen notes that Rameau's use of the title *Nouveau système* was taken from the title of the report on Sauveur's findings that was drafted for the Académie in 1701 by Bernard de Fontenelle, entitled 'Sur un nouveau système de musique'. (Christensen, 'Eighteenth-century Science and the *Corps Sonore*', 26.)

[18] Even Rameau's use of physical or experimental evidence involved some rationalization, since he was selective and recognized only consonant intervals in the overtone series—despite the growing body of acoustical knowledge developed by Daniel Bernoulli and others, showing that in many instruments these were not the only sounds and that inharmonic partials were produced as well. It was on these grounds that Bernoulli, Euler, and other physicists attacked Rameau's principle of the *corps sonore* as the foundation of music theory, although, as Thomas Christensen observes, there is the irony that Bernoulli's experiments did in fact show that the harmonically related overtones in a vibrating string were more powerful and sustained than the inharmonic

Rameau repeatedly emphasized the new physical or experimental component to his theory, as in the following remark: 'Music is a physico-mathematical science; sound is its physical object, and the ratios found between the different sounds are the mathematical component.'[19] At the same time, he retained the Cartesian rationalist framework of his original formulation, and essentially used the new findings to confirm what he had already said in the *Traité*.[20] He claimed that everything still proceeded from a unique and self-evident principle that could be formulated in mathematical terms.[21]

The significance of the change to physical proof was nevertheless considerable for Rameau. Consistent with his goal of treating music as a science, it brought him closer to an important development occurring in France at the time—the rise of Newtonian experimental science, and a corresponding challenge to Cartesian metaphysics.

Voltaire was one of the earliest disciples of Newton in France, and helped to disseminate his ideas with his publication of the *Elémens de la philosophie de Neuton* in 1738. The transition, however, did not occur without resistance, or without lingering traces of Cartesian thought long after Newtonian science had been generally accepted. D'Alembert eventually became the leading spokesman for Newtonian science, expounding the new method in the 'Discours préliminaire' to the first

modes of vibration. (Ibid., 38.) Rameau also erred in the *Génération* by adopting the dubious physical explanation of overtones proposed by the Académician Mairan—that they were mechanically transmitted through the motion of atomistic particles in the air (a mistaken hypothesis abandoned by Rameau in the *Démonstration*). Despite these drawbacks, however, there is a consensus among Rameau scholars that his principle was based on well-confirmed properties of a vibrating string (rather than of all vibrating bodies), and thus incorporated important results from the scientific acoustical research of his day.

[19] Rameau, *Génération harmonique* 30; *CTW*, iii. 29.

[20] Rameau's retention of a Cartesian framework, recognized by many Rameau scholars, is given particular emphasis by Catherine Kintzler in her analysis of the eventual breakdown of French classicism (see Kintzler, *Jean Philippe Rameau*, 36–8, 186–7).

[21] We have already noted that the new derivation of harmony through the principle of the *corps sonore* did not solve Rameau's problem that only the major triad could be generated directly through the fundamental bass. If anything, the principle of the *corps sonore* made his attempt to derive all harmonies from a single generating principle even more difficult. He could not produce empirical evidence for the direct generation of the minor triad, the various seventh chords, nor of the sub-dominant. As many critics have observed, Rameau's attempt to solve these problems resulted in new inconsistencies and erroneous calculations and experiments that were as pseudo-scientific as the outmoded mathematical derivations of the *Traité*. In the *Génération*, for example, his derivation of the minor mode relied on an erroneous assumption of lower harmonics or vibrating undertones, agitated by the vibrations of the principal sound. He admitted that they vibrated so weakly that they couldn't be heard—that the minor was a product of both art and nature—but nevertheless claimed that his principle was upheld. In the *Démonstration*, he rejected the notion of undertones, substituting an equally problematic reliance on sympathetic vibrations. In that treatise, he also introduced an alternative derivation of the minor mode, relying on a second vibrating body a minor third below the principal one. Despite all these efforts, he never reached a satisfactory solution for the generation of the minor mode, the sub-dominant, or the varied seventh chords.

volume of the *Encyclopédie* in 1751. By the mid-1750s Newtonian science had made its conquest.[22]

Rameau submitted the two new treatises, the *Génération* and the *Démonstration*, to the Académie des Sciences in 1737 and 1749 respectively, seeking official scientific sanction for his theory. A report signed by Académie members Mairan, Nicole and d'Alembert praised the *Démonstration* for its scientific approach to music theory: 'Harmony, previously guided by arbitrary laws, has become through the efforts of M. Rameau a more geometric science, and one to which the principles of mathematics can be applied with a usefulness more real and sensible than had been until now.'[23]

Recognition for Rameau reached a high point in 1751, with the appearance of the first volume of the *Encyclopédie*. D'Alembert singled him out for praise in the 'Discours préliminaire'; and Rousseau, who was principal author of the articles on music, paid a form of tribute by incorporating much of Rameau's theory into his articles—although even then he expressed reservations about Rameau's heavy reliance on rational principles and mathematical calculations.[24] D'Alembert's admiration was expressed without reservation, praising Rameau as both composer and theorist:

[22] Henry Guerlac characterizes the period of the late 1730s and 1740s as one in which the 'French scientific community was deeply divided by the contest that raged between the partisans of Descartes and Malebranche and the young defenders of Newton's System of the World' (Henry Guerlac, 'Where the Statue Stood: Divergent Loyalties to Newton in the Eighteenth Century', in Earl R. Wasserman (ed.), *Aspects of the Eighteenth Century* (Baltimore: Johns Hopkins University Press, 1965, 318). While Guerlac emphasizes the profound change in scientific concept from Descartes to Newton, he also points to lingering Cartesianism and to the diversity of the scientific effort of the 18th cent. He concludes by suggesting that Newton himself retained a belief ('not wholly unlike those he attacked') that there was a mechanism in the universe that could be explained in terms of rational principles or general laws.

[23] Quoted and translated in Christensen, 'Science and Music Theory', 21–2. Christensen notes that d'Alembert was the principal signer of the Académie report and probably the author. This was d'Alembert's first careful reading of Rameau. Endorsement by the Académie and by the scientific community in general was something sought by Rameau for his theories throughout his career. D'Alembert later qualified his strong praise of the treatise, challenging in particular Rameau's change of title from the original 'Mémoire' to 'Démonstration'. As we shall see, d'Alembert objected to Rameau's implication that he had furnished complete scientific demonstration or proof for his theory.

[24] A letter from Rousseau to d'Alembert of 26 June 1751 indicates that the latter prevailed upon Rousseau to remove angry or wounding remarks against Rameau that the articles evidently had contained (Cited in Christensen, 'Science and Music Theory', 30). Christensen emphasizes d'Alembert's active role in correcting Rousseau's music articles in the *Encyclopédie* and his concern for presenting Rameau's theories as fully and accurately as possible, in all likelihood working in close consultation with Rameau. Christensen notes that in a number of cases d'Alembert added entries of his own to Rousseau's articles, as well as corrections. D'Alembert's efforts on behalf of fidelity to Rameau add considerable weight to Rameau's recollection (in his letter of 1757 entitled 'Réponse de M. Rameau à MM. les éditeurs de l'*Encyclopédie* sur leur dernier Avertissement') that he had been asked to write the music articles for the *Encyclopédie*, but had declined. (See *CTW* v. 360.)

The French finally seem to be persuaded that Lully left much to be done [in music]. M. Rameau, in carrying the practice of his art to such a high degree of perfection, has become both the model and the object of jealousy of a great number of artists ... But what distinguishes him most particularly, is to have reflected with much success on the theory of this same art; to have found in the fundamental bass the principle of harmony and melody; to have reduced by this means to more certain and simpler laws, a science formerly devoted to arbitrary rules or dictated by blind experience.[25]

D'Alembert's inclusion of this tribute to Rameau in the 'Discours préliminaire' has particular significance, since (as has been mentioned) he also used this introductory essay as a vehicle for promoting New-tonian science and for denouncing Cartesian metaphysics. Throughout the essay, in a new spirit of scientific positivism, d'Alembert conveys a mistrust of building a 'system' of knowledge based on a priori or 'innate ideas'. He insists instead on the Newtonian method of careful observa-tion and experimental rigour, applied in the discovery of facts or simple laws of physical relationships—as opposed to underlying causes.[26] D'Alembert's scepticism about metaphysical systems is summed up in the following statement: 'The universe is only a vast ocean, on whose surface we perceive a few more or less large islands, whose connection with the continent is hidden from us.'[27] It should be noted in this statement that d'Alembert still assumes a hidden unity or con-nectedness in the universe, which was a prevalent belief at the time, shared by many of the *philosophes*. What is new is his emphasis on how little of the whole man can know.[28]

In the following year, d'Alembert reinforced his tribute to Rameau by bringing out the simplified version of his theory, the *Elémens de musique théorique et pratique* (1752). This more readable account (which was reprinted several times in France, and published in translation in Germany and England, and known in translation in Italy as well) was

[25] d'Alembert, 'Discours préliminaire des éditeurs', *Encyclopédie* vol. i. p. xxxii. Warm recep-tion for d'Alembert's preface made him a leading spokesman for the *philosophes*.

[26] Closely allied to his emphasis on experimental science is his espousal of the sensationalist philosophy of Locke, to whom he also pays homage in the same essay. In noting the tributes to past thinkers, Enlightenment scholar Giorgio Tonelli stresses that French Enlightenment philosophers (as well as British) believed that 'the great revolution in philosophy had been accomplished by ... thinkers of what they considered the preceding century'. More specifically, they paid tribute to the 'famous triumvirate' of Bacon, Newton, and Locke, considering them as the founders of the new science. (Giorgio Tonelli, 'The "Weakness" of Reason', *Diderot Studies*, 14 (1971), 221.)

[27] D'Alembert, 'Discours préliminaire', *Encyclopédie*, vol i, p. xxvi.

[28] Tonelli sums up this sense of the limitations of knowledge in the following manner: 'The Enlightenment was indeed the Age of Reason, but one of the main tasks assigned to reason in that age was to set its own boundaries, carefully establishing the field of possible human knowledge versus things considered above the limits of human understanding.' Tonelli distinguishes this from 'scepticism', which 'questions the possibility that human reason could reach any absolute truth with demonstrative certainty'. It is the former which he considers as a general and typical 18th-cent. attitude. (Tonelli, 218–19.)

largely responsible for the dissemination and warm reception of Rameau's theory.[29] The immense success of this popularization, combined with recognition for Rameau from within the scientific community, seemed to assure his position as leading theorist as well as composer.[30]

The principle of the *corps sonore*, however, was destined to have a contrary impact. So confident had Rameau become, as a result of having this physical proof from nature, that he proceeded to extend his theory beyond the realm of music, first making it the basis of all the arts and sciences, and eventually extending it to religion and the universe as a whole. With every step that Rameau took towards converting his original theory into a complete metaphysical system, he was moving further apart from d'Alembert and the *philosophes*. The latter in turn were taking steps of their own. Most of them continued to believe that there was unity and order in the universe, but they became increasingly aware of the limitations of man's ability to know it in a systematic or comprehensive way.[31]

The first sign of Rameau's extension of the principle appeared in 1750, as he presented the *Démonstration* to some of the leading mathematicians of his day. In a letter to Johann Bernoulli (27 Apr. 1750), and one to Leonard Euler (30 Apr. 1752), and again in the *Nouvelles réflexions de M. Rameau sur sa Démonstration du principe de l'harmonie* (published in 1752), he claimed that 'the principle of all the arts resides in music with the greatest certainty and perceptibility'.[32]

[29] A detailed study of d'Alembert's treatment of Rameau's theory is made in Christensen, 'Science and Music Theory'. Christensen notes that the *Elémens*, which draws on a number of Rameau's treatises, relies most heavily on the *Démonstration* for its discussion of harmonic theory (d'Alembert had reviewed this treatise for the Académie in 1749). Another important source is the *Génération*, ch. 18, which forms the basis of the discussion on composition in the *Elémens*. There are also some scattered references to the *Traité* and *Nouveau système*. In addition to d'Alembert's extensive use of Rameau's written material, he also seems to have been in direct contact with Rameau during this period—a time when he was both writing the *Elémens* and editing Rousseau's music articles for the *Encyclopédie*. Rameau expressed his admiration for the *Elémens* in an open letter to the *Mercure* in May 1752.

[30] For an interpretation of d'Alembert's motivations in writing the *Elémens*, see Thomas Christensen, 'Music Theory as Scientific Propaganda: The Case of d'Alembert's *Elémens de Musique*', *Journal of the History of Ideas*, 50 (1989), 409–27. Christensen argues that d'Alembert wanted to promote Rameau's theory because he saw in it a paradigm of rational systematization which corresponded to his own work in rational mechanics—i.e. d'Alembert saw the *Elémens* as a means to promote his own concept of scientific method.

[31] As we shall see in the next chapter, Diderot eventually grew totally sceptical about the usefulness of mathematical proportions. This was a change that separated him not only from Rameau and other Cartesians, but from d'Alembert as well.

[32] Rameau, Preface to the *Nouvelles réflexions ... sur sa démonstration* (Paris: Durand, Pissot, 1752) (*CTW*. 96; Rameau's letter to Bernoulli is in *CTW* vi. 195–6, the letter to Euler in *CTW* v. 146). Catherine Kintzler notes that the idea of extension appeared abruptly around 1750, with the success of the *Démonstration*, and that it had not existed in Rameau's writings before that time. She sees this metaphysical Cartesianism as a kind of folly or even malady that was prevalent at the time. Rameau 'becomes too rational to be reasonable'; he becomes 'possessed by the demon of theoretical imperialism'. (Kintzler, *Rameau*, 36, 39 respectively).

It did not stop with the arts. In his next treatise, the *Observations*, published in 1754, he made it clear that the principle was the basis of all the arts and sciences:

The principle in question is not only that of all the arts of taste ... but of all the sciences subject to calculations. This cannot be denied without denying that the sciences are founded on proportions and progressions, of which nature has informed us through the phenomenon of the resonating string, in such a pronounced way, that it is impossible to reject the evidence. It is impossible to deny it! No proportions, no geometry.[33]

The respective roles of music and mathematics had now been reversed: where music was once based on a mathematical model, mathematics was now based on a musical model. Rameau repeated this position shortly thereafter, in the *Erreurs*, in 1756.[34]

With the appearance of the latter, d'Alembert was provoked to a response, which he included in his *Encyclopédie* articles 'Gamme' and 'Fondamental', published in Volume vii in 1757. Not only did he question the validity of applying the principle and its proportions to other fields, he also challenged the usefulness of proportions within music itself.[35]

No argument, however, could dissuade Rameau from the irreversible journey on which he was launched. In an increasingly bitter series of exchanges with d'Alembert, he repeatedly confirmed and even strengthened his position. When his next treatise appeared (the *Code de musique pratique* in 1761) it was published with a new set of essays in response to d'Alembert, and each of these focused on the comprehensiveness of the principle of the *corps sonore*.[36] Rameau completed the journey from theory to theology in his 'Lettre de M. Rameau aux philosophes' of 1762, which contains the following statement:

[33] *Observations*, pp. xv–xvi; *CTW*, iii. 265.   [34] *Erreurs*, 115–18; *CTW* v. 256–8.

[35] As we shall see, he takes up this point in the 'Discours préliminaire' to the 2nd edn. of the *Elémens*. The response to the *Erreurs* in these articles was in addition to the 'Avertissement' to vol. vi of the *Encyclopédie*, already cited.

[36] Rameau, *Code de musique pratique CTW* iv. 1–264. The essays in the 1761 edn. of the *Code* also included the 'Lettre à M. d'Alembert sur ses opinions en musique, inserées dans les articles 'Fondamental' et 'Gamme' de l'Encyclopédie'. In a subsequent printing of the *Code*, in 1762, the 'Origine des sciences, suivie d'une controverse sur le même sujet' was also attached, containing still further arguments by Rameau in defence of his position. (Along with the *Code*, they appear in *CTW* iv. The facsimiles for this vol. were based on the originals, which were in the editor's possession. It is an authentic arrangement, with all the works bound together, as requested by Rameau.) Still one more essay by Rameau should be recognized as part of this series of exchanges, the 'Conclusion sur l'origine des sciences', which was published in 1762 in the *Journal Encyclopédique*. It has been called to our attention by Philippe Lescat, in 'Conclusion sur l'origine des sciences', in de La Gorce (ed.), *Jean-Philippe Rameau Colloque International*, 409–24. Lescat observes that Rameau's defence of his position in this late work shows a new emphasis on the sense of hearing as superior to the other senses, thereby showing geometry's further dependence on music.

If the Creator, without wishing to reveal himself other than through his great works, has granted some secondary causes which contribute to our existence, shouldn't we believe that, to contribute similarly to the progress of our intelligence, he would have created a principle which he would make palpable to our senses, for the sake of engageing us in making comparisons?[37]

The principle of the *corps sonore* had become a substitute or symbol for divine revelation.[38]

D'Alembert correctly perceived that his disagreement with Rameau went beyond specific issues concerning the *corps sonore*. What was at stake was the very nature of music theory, or music as science. Interestingly enough, he addressed this larger issue as he brought out a second edition of the *Elémens de musique théorique et pratique*, based on Rameau's theory. In the new edition, published in Lyon in 1762, he added a 'Discours préliminaire' which was devoted in large part to a discussion of how to perfect music theory.[39] It is worth stressing that as openly critical as d'Alembert was in this new edition of the *Elémens*, he nevertheless saw sufficient merit to Rameau's theory to bring out a second edition. This act itself must be considered as an aspect of the dialogue.

Drawing upon his previously developed position on scientific method, and especially his espousal of Newtonian science, d'Alembert's proposals for perfecting music theory focus on the fact that music

---

[37] Rameau, 'Lettre de M. Rameau aux philosophes' (Paris: *Journal de Trévoux*, August 1762); *CTW* vi. 514. As has been noted, Rameau's impulse to create a complete metaphysical system based on mathematical proportions was still a prevalent one at the time, with a number of influential writers articulating their own particular form of metaphysics. Charles B. Paul cites Bernard de Fontenelle as one of the most eloquent proponents of the contemporary *esprit géométrique* (Paul, 'Rameau, the Musician as Philosophe'). Fontenelle espoused the use of mathematical proportions to achieve a mathematical synthesis within the various arts and sciences, and also between them. Paul also mentions the influence of the architect Charles-Etienne Briseux, who was cited by Rameau for his belief that architecture and all the arts are based on musical proportions. Finally, Paul adds Nicolas Malebranche's philosophical doctrine of Occasionalism, which was widely influential in the 18th cent. It attempted to reconcile Cartesian science with religion by explaining the mechanical laws of the universe in terms of God as first and only cause. Paul notes that Rameau's final conversion of the resonating string to a symbol of revelation was an example of Occasionalism.

[38] Rameau reiterates this position in one final treatise (the complete version of which was recently discovered in Stockholm by Herbert Schneider) entitled 'Vérités également ignorées et intéressantes, tiré du sein de la nature.' It has been published with an introduction and critical notes in Herbert Schneider, *Jean-Philippe Rameaus letzter Musiktraktat* (Stuttgart: Franz Steiner Verlag, 1986).

[39] Jean le Rond d'Alembert, *Elémens de musique théorique et pratique, suivant les principes de M. Rameau. Revue, corrigée, & considérablement augmentée* (Lyon: Bruyset, 1762); facsimile edn. of 'Discours préliminaire' in *CTW* vi. 457–77. D'Alembert had also written a letter responding to Rameau which appeared in *Le Mercure de France* in Apr. 1761, shortly followed by two more by Rameau. The 'Discours préliminaire' to the 1762 edn. of the *Elémens* contained d'Alembert's culminating arguments in the series of exchanges with Rameau. It was also the last time that he responded to Rameau, although Rameau kept the increasingly bitter debate alive until his death in 1764.

is a physical phenomenon, and therefore must follow many of the guiding principles used in the physical sciences. D'Alembert's recommendations include both a positive programme and a series of negative warnings.

The positive programme is Newtonian. He exhorts the music theorist to follow a method of relying on experience. This means observing facts, relating them to one another, and making them depend on a single fact, if possible—or at least on a small number of facts. The foundation, then, must be empirical evidence rather than abstract a priori principles.

On the negative side, he warns that the music theorist—or any experimental scientist—cannot expect conclusive evidence, or what is called 'demonstration', which is appropriate solely for geometry or abstract mathematics. While the principle of the resonating string has helped to reduce the rules and elements of music to a coherent system (which in itself is an achievement) the theorist cannot assume that it has been demonstrated as the unique principle of harmony.[40] On the contrary, the theorist must recognize that there are gradations of certainty, rather than absolute truths; that the principle explains some things better than others, and some things not at all. The nature of evidence in the physical sciences is conjectural; a new discovery can be made which will supersede the old. There is, moreover, no necessity that one principle must explain everything.[41] In the preface, in fact, he recommends the work of the Italian theorist Tartini, bringing to our attention his experimental findings on combination tones.

D'Alembert makes a number of additional points, which are closely related to methodology. He claims that his new edition not only clarifies

[40] 'Discours', p. xiii; *CTW* vi. 466. The inappropriate use of the term 'demonstration' is serious enough for d'Alembert, that—as noted above (see n. 23)—he admonished Rameau for having used it in the title of his treatise, the *Démonstration*. Rameau had originally submitted it to the Académie under the title 'Mémoire'.

[41] Ibid., p. xvii; *CTW* vi. 468. D'Alembert's argument, that a single principle need not explain everything, is emphasized by Jonathan Bernard as the underlying source of many of d'Alembert's more specific and technical disagreements with Rameau. Bernard also sees d'Alembert's position as leading to a more logical and coherent formulation of Rameau's theory. For a detailed analysis of their disagreements see Jonathan Bernard, 'The Principle and the Elements: Rameau's Controversy with d'Alembert', *Journal of Music Theory*, 24 (1980), 37–62. A similar analysis of their disagreements is to be found in Françoise Escal, 'Musique et Science', *International Review of the Aesthetics and Sociology of Music*, 14 (1983), 167–90. Escal observes that while the disagreements grew more severe with Rameau's increasingly metaphysical pronouncements, d'Alembert was more concerned with practical rules and empirical considerations than Rameau even in the 1st edn. of the *Elémens*; he also finds that d'Alembert viewed melody as more autonomous in relation to harmony. With the 2nd edn. of the *Elémens*, these differences grew stronger, with d'Alembert placing even greater emphasis on the limitations of music theory, arguing against the use of abstract calculations and rationalist extensions of the harmonic principle, and denouncing claims by Rameau that the principles of harmony were capable of absolute certainty or demonstrated proof. Not only was Rameau's principle a matter of hypothesis, but music itself—and especially judgements about its pleasing quality—was purely a matter of relative taste.

Rameau's theory, but also further simplifies it. His new derivations in this edition now rely on just a principal resonating body, as opposed to Rameau's use of auxiliary vibrating bodies in his derivations of the sub-dominant and minor mode. D'Alembert also gives a greater nod to the importance of melody. He tells us that physical derivations are distinct from historical ones, and that historically melody preceded harmony.[42]

Still further warnings are in order. D'Alembert finds the inclusion of mathematical calculations useless and even illusory in explaining music, since the proportions are only approximations of the intervals used in actual practice.[43] Finally, there is a warning of some of the worst abuses in music theory. One is indulging in scientific speculation concerning the causes of the pleasures derived from harmony. Music as art or pleasure does not lend itself to the kinds of explanation appropriate for music as science—and once again, even the latter are of a conjectural nature. Worse than that (and here he refers to Rameau indirectly) is the error of going beyond music, of trying to find non-existent relationships between music and other sciences.

All this adds up to a sizeable area of disagreement with Rameau, much of it of a serious nature. We may speculate about why d'Alembert brought out a second edition of the *Elémens*, and why he continued to devote himself to perfecting the flaws of the theory. D'Alembert provides at least a partial answer in the 'Discours préliminaire' to the *Elémens*, where once again he praises Rameau's theory for achieving a reduction in the number of seemingly arbitrary rules and for showing their connectedness through the principle of the *corps sonore*. He cites a fairly long list of musical phenomena whose explanation has been

---

[42] 'Discours', p. iv; *CTW* vi. 461. D'Alembert thus aligns himself with the more prevalent view of the origin of melody (presented as a full-blown theory by Rousseau) while still accepting Rameau's derivation of melody from harmony.

[43] Ibid. pp. xxx–xxxi; *CTW* vi. 474–5. Despite d'Alembert's reservations about defining musical intervals in terms of mathematical proportions, he retained much of the *esprit géometrique* in his approach to science in general. Scientific certainty meant knowledge that could be expressed in mathematical terms. An analysis of d'Alembert's scientific method and its relation to his intellectual role in the French Enlightenment is made in Thomas Hankins, *Jean d'Alembert: Science and the Enlightenment* (Oxford: Clarendon Press, 1970). One of the main points in the study is that d'Alembert was more Newtonian in his far-reaching statements about scientific method than he was in his own scientific research. There, Hankins shows, he was more rationalist and mathematical than he was experimental. Hankins thus confirms Guerlac's view that during the 18th cent. there was diversity of scientific method, including residual signs of Cartesian rationalism—even after the so-called conquest of Newtonian science (Guerlac, 'Where the Statue Stood'). Thomas Christensen's study of d'Alembert concurs that he was a rationalist. Indeed, a major point in Christensen's 'Science and Music Theory in the Enlightenment' is that it was d'Alembert's rationalism, rather than Rameau's, that was the principal source of disagreement between the two. Christensen further argues that d'Alembert's concern for methodological rigour and deductive logic was largely at the expense of musical common sense, and that Rameau's explanations (often bending the principle to reflect practice) were invariably more musically insightful.

clarified and simplified through this process: the structure of chords, harmonic progressions, the derivation of the major and minor scales, the use of dissonance, the enharmonic and chromatic and diatonic genres, and—finally—the principles and laws of temperament and tuning. Rameau's theory thus survived d'Alembert's growing disenchantment because it provided effective explanations for some of the most crucial features of tonal practice.

This answer invites still further speculation about Rameau as theorist. Given his preoccupation with abstract formulations and metaphysical principles, how did he achieve such effective results in explaining tonal practice—going in fact well beyond d'Alembert's sizeable list? The solution to this puzzle lies with Rameau himself. His powers of observation—undoubtedly strengthened by his own direct experience as a composer of tonal music, were too keen to allow him to be totally committed to abstract thinking or deductive logic. Indeed, we have argued all along that it must have been his powers of observation, and especially his insights into musical relationships, that allowed him to determine what it was that music theory was supposed to explain through a unifying principle.[44] Nor did he ever become so rigid in his commitment to the principle that he would sacrifice practice for the sake of the system. Each time there was a conflict between the two, it was practice that prevailed. We have already cited his most well-known departures from the single principle of the *corps sonore*, in his derivations of the dissonant seventh, the minor mode, and the sub-dominant, where he had recourse to a number of different generating principles. Rameau himself acknowledged that they arose less directly from nature and that they were a product of art as well as science. This recognition, to be sure, had little effect on his belief in the comprehensiveness of the principle. Nevertheless, it showed him to be less rigid and readier to adapt theory to fit practice than his rhetoric would imply.[45]

[44] As we shall see in Ch. 6, Diderot's experience as a practising artist had a similar influence on his way of viewing art.

[45] Despite the importance of musical instinct or observation in Rameau's formulation of his theory, it is difficult to assign it a place in his formal methodology. This problem is underlined by the French scholar Marie-Elisabeth Duchez, who argues that neither 'the scientists of the eighteenth-century, nor Rameau himself, understood the real basis of his deductions'. Duchez explains that basis in terms of a subconscious inductive process: 'The coherent system of hypotheses which form the basis of Rameau's deductions results from an almost subconscious inductive synthesis comprising not only the results of the experience of harmonic resonance emitted by the corps sonore, but also the hypotheses with which his previous knowledge furnished him ... placed in connection with his empirical musical experience.' (Marie-Elisabeth Duchez, 'D'Alembert diffuseur de la théorie harmonique de Rameau: déduction scientifique et simplification musical', in Monique Emery and Pierre Monzani (ed.), *Jean d'Alembert, savant et phillosophe: portrait à plusieurs voix, Actes du Colloque organisé par le Centre International de Synthèse-Fondation pour la Science, Paris, 15–18 juin 1983* (Paris: Archives contemporaines, 1989), 486.) Duchez finds that the source of disagreement between Rameau and d'Alembert was one of epistemology: d'Alembert was 'the scientist who studied music', and Rameau was 'the musician who, also and

Interestingly enough, Rameau's empirical observations seemed to sharpen even while his abstract metaphysical tendencies grew stronger—a phenomenon that perhaps has been insufficiently recognized by Rameau scholars. One of the most striking examples is to be found in *Observations*, which was a fairly late treatise, published in 1754. Side by side with Rameau's metaphysical claims for the all-embracing nature of the *corps sonore* are new and important harmonic interpretations based purely on musical context. More specifically, Rameau presents new distinctions in the various uses of the perfect chord or tonic, above all observing the difference between the perfect chord that functions as the tonic of a piece as a whole, and the perfect chord that may serve temporarily as a tonic. In each case, the physico-mathematical properties of the perfect chord remain unchanged and the context determines the distinction.[46] This precedence of practice over principle is all the more noteworthy, precisely because it occurred (as noted above) at a time when Rameau was attaching so much importance to metaphysical considerations concerning the *corps sonore*.[47] In assessing Rameau's Cartesianism and metaphysical tendencies, undeniably strong as they were, it is important to recognize the discrepancy between his Cartesian claims and some of his actual explanations of music.

D'Alembert perhaps never quite reached this recognition, but in bringing out a second edition of the *Elémens* with its new 'Discours préliminaire' he gave testimony both to what he valued in Rameau, and to what he thought should be rejected. It should be added that d'Alembert was similarly even-handed in the realm of music as art. His famous essay, 'De la liberté de la musique', which addresses the issues of the

above all, lived it' (p. 483). The serious consequence of this epistemological difference is that d'Alembert's version of Rameau's theory, which is so widely read, is a distorted over-simplification of Rameau's rich and complex musical thought. Above all, d'Alembert was unable to seize the compositional or operational possibilities in Rameau's theory, which represent its greatest value, and emphasized almost exclusively its role as scientific paradigm, which was perhaps its weakest part.

[46] Rameau's observations actually yield three different kinds of tonic: one is the 'reigning tonic', which refers to the key of a piece as a whole, or the principal harmony; another is the tonic which arises as the piece moves or modulates from one key to another; and finally, there is the tonic that is so temporary and is cancelled so quickly that it is only 'sensed' as a tonic—as opposed to the two types of actual tonic. The date when Rameau first made tonic distinctions has been placed considerably earlier by Thomas Christensen, who has discovered among d'Alembert's papers a previously unknown manuscript by Rameau, entitled 'L'Art de la basse fondamentale'. For a discussion of this work, which focuses on musical practice, see Thomas Christensen, 'Rameau's "L'Art de la basse fondamentale"', *Music Theory Spectrum*, 9 (1987), 18–41.

[47] For a discussion of the expressive implications of the harmonic distinctions, see my 'Development of Rameau's Thoughts on Modulation and Chromatics'. The practice of having a temporary tonic preceded by its dominant is currently referred to as the use of a secondary dominant. Rameau's terminology focuses on the temporary tonic itself, referring to it as a 'sensed' tonic.

'Querelle des Bouffons', was written in 1759, well after the departure of the Italian players and after the heat of the quarrels had subsided. It emphasizes that taste and judgement are relative matters, and proposes a new kind of French opera that combines what is best in French and Italian style. (Among other things, the new operas should retain the symphonies, ballets, and overture from French opera, and the aria style of Pergolesi from Italian opera.)[48] Above all, the essay calls for the freedom to choose what is best.[49]

With d'Alembert's position in mind, it is useful now to turn back to Rousseau for a consideration of some of his more specific views on music as science. Far less moderate than d'Alembert, Rousseau made sweeping statements or claims, in large part as a response to Rameau. An important point, however, is that in similar fashion to Rameau Rousseau took positions that were more extreme than his actual explanations of music as science.

We have already seen in the preceding chapter that many of Rousseau's articles dealing with opera and aesthetics in the *Dictionnaire* retained a fairly traditional concept of imitation, while presenting a radical theory of corruption and decay that would seem to imply the impossibility of natural expression or true imitation. The articles on music theory or music as science in the *Dictionnaire* show a similar incorporation of the accepted harmonic theories of his day (including Rameau's) despite Rousseau's radical belief that harmony is an artificial construct and a symptom of decay. In articles throughout the *Dictionnaire*, Rousseau engages in a search for viable harmonic theory, and in fact offers insightful comments and criteria for what that should be.

In some ways Rousseau even surpasses d'Alembert in his concern for recognizing the scientific limitations of theory and for establishing the

[48] D'Alembert, 'De la liberté de la musique', *Mélanges de littérature, d'histoire, et de philosophie*, iv. 377–454. By the time this essay was written, the French were writing comic operas with music in Italian style. As we shall see in Ch. 6, the operas of Duni—strongly admired by Diderot—were an extremely popular example of this development. His opera *Le Peintre amoureux de son modèle* had its première in 1757.

[49] Scholars agree that while d'Alembert's tastes may indeed have inclined him toward Italian music, there were political pressures as well that drew him to the pro-Italian side of the *philosophes*, especially as the *Encyclopédie* came increasingly under siege by the authorities. Many of d'Alembert's pro-Italian arguments closely echo the arguments of Rousseau, although with the important difference that d'Alembert is far more conciliatory toward the French. Despite d'Alembert's more moderate positions in 'De la liberté', however, Rameau viewed it as still another attack by his former supporter and admirer. For an examination of d'Alembert's views on music and the influence of political pressures, see two articles by John Pappas: 'Diderot, d'Alembert, et l'Encyclopédie', *Diderot Studies*, v (1963): 191–208; and 'D'Alembert et la querelle des Bouffons d'après des documents inédits', *Revue d'Histoire Littéraire de la France*, 65 (1965), 479–84. In the latter article, Pappas places particular emphasis on political pressures in explaining d'Alembert's pro-Italian views. He argues, on the basis of unpublished documents, that d'Alembert was actually not pro-Italian, contrary to the belief of most d'Alembert scholars.

boundaries between what is pure conjecture and what is demonstrated truth. But even for Rousseau the boundaries prove elusive. His treatment of theory in the *Dictionnaire* reveals a constant tension between the desire for universal or scientific laws on the one hand, and his belief that they cannot exist on the other. This shows up particularly in his discussions of the *corps sonore* and its role in harmonic theory. A number of examples will be cited which illustrate this tension. Once again, as in the articles on aesthetics, the selected examples also reveal Rousseau's extraordinary insights into the strengths and weaknesses of the music theory of his day.

One of the most telling examples is the article 'Harmonie'. In the following comment, Rousseau pays tribute to the principle of the *corps sonore* for providing a more scientific basis for harmonic theory:

For a long period, harmony had no principles, just rules which were almost arbitrary or based solely on the judgements of the ear, which in turn determined the quality of consonant progressions, which were also formulated in mathematical terms. But then, M. Mersenne and M. Sauveur made the discovery that every sound, no matter how simple in appearance, is always accompanied by other less audible sounds, which formed the perfect major chord. M. Rameau subsequently used this for his point of departure, and made it the basis of his harmonic system . . .

But before Rousseau goes too far in recognizing the scientific validity of Rameau's theory of harmony, he pulls back to his notion of theory as pure conjecture, offering the following somewhat contradictory observation: 'I must declare, however, that this system, no matter how ingenious it is, is not at all based on nature . . . that it was only established on some analogies or convergences that can be overturned tomorrow by an inventive man who finds more natural ones . . .'[50]

Rousseau does not wait for its overturn. He himself provides one of the most compelling critiques of the principle, showing its limitations on the following knowledgeable grounds: 'The resonating body does not give rise exclusively, to the sounds of the perfect chord . . . but to an infinity of other sounds, formed by all the partials of the resonating body, which are not at all included in the perfect chord. Why are the first ones consonant and the others not, since they are all equally derived from nature?'[51] Rousseau correctly observes that Rameau's harmonic theory entails a selective use of 'nature' rather than nature itself. Taking still another tack, he objects to the use of the principle as the basis for harmony by pointing out that under normal circumstances we do not hear the harmonics or overtones, but only a simple sound. While this observation itself is straightforward, the conclusion that he reaches is less so: 'The only good harmony is unison, and that as soon as we can make out the consonant overtones ... harmony has lost its purity.'[52]

The tension between what is conjecture and what is fact is even more pronounced in the article 'Consonance', where Rousseau attaches considerable weight to the *corps sonore* as the source of consonance: 'In regard to the pleasure that consonances give to the ear, unlike any other interval, we can see the source [of this pleasure] clearly in their generation. The consonances arise from the perfect chord, product of a single sound, and reciprocally the perfect chord is formed by the assemblage of its consonances.' However, once again Rousseau pulls back and indeed reverses direction, by expressing the following reservations about a natural or scientific basis for consonance:

But if one presses the question, and if one demands still further what is the source of the pleasure that the perfect chord gives the ear, while the ear is shocked by the combination of all other sounds, what would we be able to answer to that, except to ask in turn why green rather than grey delights our sight, and why the perfume of the rose enchants while the odour of the poppy displeases. It isn't that the scientists haven't explained all that; and what don't they explain? But that all these explanations are conjectural, and that one finds little solidity upon close examination![53]

Despite this scepticism towards rational or scientific explanations in music theory, Rousseau pays considerable tribute in the *Dictionnaire* to eighteenth-century theorists—singling out Tartini as well as Rameau in his article 'Système', and giving extensive and thoughtful coverage to their most important ideas.[54] His praise of Tartini is of particular interest, since it makes explicit his criteria for a good theory: 'Even if it [the theory] does not come from nature, it is at least, of all those published until now, the one which has the simplest principle, and in which all the laws of harmony seem to arise the least arbitrarily.'[55] In this comment, Rousseau reflects the widely accepted view of scientific method as a search for a few underlying principles that could explain a multitude of phenomena. If we must have harmony, he seems to be saying, then we must have harmonic theory. And in that case, the theory should conform to the above principles. It may never be more than conjecture or hypothesis, but if all goes well, the theory will be able to show how everything is linked, and how 'the true system of nature leads to the

---

[52] Ibid. 240.　　　[53] Ibid. 115–16.

[54] It should be noted that in Rousseau's article 'Système', which is largely devoted to the theory of Tartini, he justifies this choice on the grounds that the theory of Tartini is written in Italian, and is therefore less accessible to the public. It also happens to be his preferred theory—one which gives melody a more prominent role—but Rameau is still recognized as being the first to present underlying principles for what were once a series of arbitrary rules.

[55] Rousseau, *Dictionnaire*, 475.

most hidden detours of art'.[56] In this last remark, he seems to be saying that harmony indeed comes from nature.

These examples show clearly that Rousseau was far less extreme in his rejection of harmonic theory than his historical reconstruction would imply. At the same time, it would be misleading to deny the strength of his anti-harmonic convictions or his disdain for viewing harmonic theory as a series of laws stemming from nature. Ultimately, we must recognize and deal with the presence of two contradictory tendencies within Rousseau's musical thought: one, a radical rejection of the accepted views of his day; and the other, a serious consideration of those views, including adaptation to make them more viable. Given the dialogue context in which these opposing tendencies emerged, as well as the insightful nature of his treatment of the more traditional elements, we would emphasize once again that Rousseau attained these insights by listening carefully to the views of others—even to his strongest opponents in the debate.

The appendix translation for this chapter is d'Alembert's 'Discours préliminaire' to the second edition of the *Elémens de musique théorique et pratique*.

---

[56] Rousseau, *Dictionnaire*, 496.

5

Music as Art and Science
Synthesis by Diderot, 1748–1760

IN the preceding chapters we have traced some of the salient and con-flicting positions in the prolonged dialogue on music as art and as science. We have also seen that Rameau increasingly became a subject of controversy—for his views on expression in music, as well as music theory. The dialogue in both these areas continued to be marked by the characteristic Enlightenment search for underlying principles that could explain a multitude of phenomena.

The search, however, was accompanied by a gradual weakening of neo-classical theory in art, and an increasing awareness of the limita-tions of a priori or abstract principles in science. Much of the change was influenced by a new and greater importance attached to the respec-tive roles of sensibility in artistic expression, and of experience or em-piricism in scientific investigation. Although Rameau made an effort to adapt to these changes, his essentially rationalist outlook and his in-creasing immersion in metaphysical speculation left him in an isolated position *vis à vis* the *philosophes* at the time of his death in 1764.

D'Alembert, in his conciliatory fashion, attempted to preserve what was best in Rameau's theory by making a clearer separation between his metaphysical speculations and his more solid contributions in the de-velopment of harmonic theory. He also tried to improve the theory by simplifying Rameau's formulations and making them more intelligible. Rousseau was far more radical in his attacks, aiming not only at Rameau's metaphysics, but at reason itself. He proposed a view of music—and of art, language, and society—in which pure feeling was the sole component that was true to its nature.

Interestingly enough, the Enlightenment's challenge to neo-classicism in the realm of music as art, while moving away from abso-lute laws or rational systems, stopped considerably short of a concept of art as a totally subjective experience—either for artist or audience. Ernst Cassirer describes the situation in the following terms: 'The new approach ... considerably limits or gives up entirely the claim to rational justification of aesthetic judgement; but it does not relinquish its claim to universality. The question now is merely that of a more exact determination of the nature of this universality and of the manner in which it can be asserted.' He also observes that the question was not approached at the time with a 'really consistent line of reasoning' or a 'conscious orientation'.[1]

It is fitting in this penultimate chapter to turn to the contributions of Diderot, not so much because he built a systematic aesthetic theory, but because he was more directly concerned with the tensions inherent in neo-classicism, and attempted to achieve some reconciliation between the subjective and the objective in the artistic experience. We have already noted Diderot's penchant for dialectics. Each time that he adopted a position, he was simultaneously aware of the complexities and inherent tensions in that position, pulling him onward to a new formulation. His views on music consequently underwent almost constant change, with the important result that he carried many ideas further and achieved a greater level of synthesis among opposing ideas than had been attained before.[2] For this reason, he holds a special place in the present study.

It is also fitting to turn to Diderot for a kind of summation because of his sustained role as chief editor of the *Encyclopédie*—itself a kind of summation of Enlightenment thought. Diderot served in that capacity from the origin of the *Encyclopédie* in 1747, until its completion in 1769. Strongly influenced by his direction, the *Encyclopédie* was characterized by a pervasive and profound respect for science and a 'far-reaching scepticism about what conventionally passed for truth'.[3]

The consistency of point of view was no small feat, given the comprehensive scope of the *Encyclopédie*, the length of time it took to complete, and above all the co-operative nature of the enterprise. D'Alembert served as co-editor with Diderot from the original signing of the contract until his resignation in 1758.[4] In addition to the two editors, who

[1] Ernst Cassirer, *The Philosophy of the Enlightenment*, trans. Fritz C. A. Koelln and James Pettegrove (Boston: Beacon Press, 1955), 299.

[2] This synthesizing tendency has been observed by a number of Diderot scholars—as, for example, in the following remark by Otis Fellows: 'Diderot, like many of his fellow *philosophes*, had a genius for synthesis—assimilating the ideas of thinkers both ancient and modern, giving a new slant to these ideas, and finally, fusing them into novel and challenging form.' (Otis Fellows, *Diderot* (Boston: Twayne Publishers, 1977), 93.)

[3] Wilson, *Diderot* 140. Wilson's very complete biography of Diderot includes an illuminating discussion of the nature of Diderot's contributions to the *Encyclopédie*. In addition, there is a detailed account in Jacques Proust, *Diderot et l'Encyclopédie* (Paris: Armand Colin, 1962).

[4] Their contract, as originally agreed upon, was for a translation into French of Ephraim Chambers's highly successful *Cyclopaedia*, which had been published in England in 1728. By the time the prospectus for the French *Encyclopédie* appeared in 1750 the project had greatly expanded, acquiring the all-encompassing and ambitious scope that is implied in the title, *Encyclopédie, ou Dictionnaire raisonné des sciences, des arts et des métiers* (Encyclopedia, or Analytical Dictionary of the Sciences, Arts and Crafts). Although d'Alembert's activities gradually expanded, from his early responsibility for the mathematical articles to his involvement in a wide range of subjects, Diderot had primary responsibility on a more sustained and daily basis in his capacity as chief editor.

wrote hundreds of articles between them, the contributors included a long line of distinguished *philosophes*: Montesquieu, Voltaire, Rousseau, Holbach, Grimm, the Chevalier de Jaucourt, among others.[5]

Nor was the task made any easier by the repeated intervention of the authorities, who came to view the *Encyclopédie* as a kind of political tract.[6] As its subscribers grew in number, so too did its enemies. During the late 1740s and throughout the 1750s Diderot persevered in the face of unrelenting censorship, threats, and even imprisonment.[7] In 1759 the *Encyclopédie* was condemned by the *parlement* of Paris and by a royal decree of the King's Council, forcing the tenacious Diderot to go 'underground' for the writing and production of the final ten volumes.[8]

Diderot's editorial role also had an impact on the evolution of his own thought, since it constantly exposed him to new ideas. Rather than merely absorbing what he learned, he was engaged in a creative process, transforming ideas into new and innovative formulations.

Through the process of constant change, it is perhaps no exaggeration to say that at one time or another Diderot drew close to each of the positions on music as art and as science that have been presented in the preceding chapters—including some of the most divergent views. We would also add that some of the most dramatic changes took place in his

[5] They were identified by a scheme of initials given in the preface to the *Encyclopédie*. For a list of contributors of articles on music, see Oliver, *encyclopédistes as Critics of Music*, appendix A, 171–88.

[6] Indeed, the term *philosophe* acquired a broader meaning, referring not only to philosophers in the usual sense, but to members of a political party. It should be noted that the members of the party, in trying to circumvent the censors' slashes, took to conveying their message in an oblique or indirect manner in many articles in the *Encyclopédie*. Reading 'between the lines' was often more important than reading what was stated in the text.

[7] Principal opposition came from the Jesuits who succeeded in having vols i and ii suppressed in 1752. The licence for the whole was not revoked, however, and publication was allowed to resume shortly thereafter—probably in deference to the more than 2,000 people who had already subscribed. Continuation received only 'tacit permission', without the public and explicit approval *du Roi* that had been granted to the first two vols. when they originally appeared. The *Encyclopédie* went forward under these conditions, with new vols. appearing at the rate of one per year until 1757, when d'Alembert's article on Geneva precipitated a new censorship crisis, and led to his resignation as editor of the *Encyclopédie*. The controversial article proposed among other things that the austere Calvinist city-state of Geneva should put an end to its ban on legitimate theatre. This provoked violent reaction not only from the Genevans, but also from the long-standing enemies of the *Encyclopédie*, who became more convinced than ever that the enterprise was damaging to religion and morality. D'Alembert scholars have also noted that at the time of his resignation there were not only growing external pressures from the enemies of the *Encyclopédie*, but also internal differences over philosophical issues between d'Alembert and Diderot (discussed below). The consistency of editorial policy in the *Encyclopédie* thus had largely to do with Diderot's point of view and his sustained commitment to the enterprise for over 20 years, even as other prominent members defected.

[8] They were finally published in one release in 1765, with no official approval, but without opposition. For a complete account of the practice of clandestine printing see Robert Darnton, *The Literary Underground of the Old Regime* (Cambridge, Mass.: Harvard University Press, 1982).

attitudes toward Rameau. Diderot was one of the first among the *philosophes* to admire Rameau's theory. In his *Mémoires sur différens sujets de mathématiques*, published in 1748, he presented a concept of music that focused on harmony, and that was indebted to Rameau's principle of the *corps sonore*.[9] However, a little over a decade later, in *Le Neveu de Rameau* (1761), Diderot attacked Rameau as theorist as well as opera composer. Furthermore, in that same work Diderot aligned himself closely with Rameau's arch-enemy Rousseau, presenting a concept of music with melody as the principal vehicle for expression. The comprehensiveness of this attack on Rameau did not prevent Diderot from taking up the assault once more in the treatise entitled *Leçons de clavecin et principes d'harmonie, par M. Bemetzrieder*, published in 1771. In this work he not only assailed Rameau's theory, but proposed an alternative one that was free of the defects of Rameau's.

In explaining the changes in Diderot's musical thought, and especially his eventual rejection of Rameau, we would acknowledge at the outset that provocations by Rameau cannot be ignored. We have already seen how the once admired composer-theorist managed to arouse the animosity of all the *philosophes* through his attacks on Rousseau and the *Encyclopédie*, and through his increasing turn towards metaphysics. However, as important as these external factors are, they should not deter us from examining Diderot's thought more directly for further clues. In the present discussion we will argue that a significant shift in his epistemology played a major role in the changes in his views about music. More specifically, we will trace Diderot's growing scepticism about the relevance of general laws and abstractions and his espousal of the increasingly compelling concepts in the biological sciences as an alternative model to physics and mathematics. Not only did these changes affect his views on music as science, they also had an impact on his musical aesthetics.[10]

---

[9] Denis Diderot, *Mémoires sur différens sujets de mathématiques* (1748); ed. Jean Mayer, Hermann, ii. (1975). As we have noted elsewhere, Diderot's support for Rameau may have led him to provide editorial assistance to Rameau on his treatise, the *Démonstration du principe de l'harmonie*, which was published in 1750. Thomas Christensen's study of the original drafts of the *Démonstration*, and especially the Preface, leads him to believe that Diderot's role was confined to the Preface, which is an essay on method and the *corps sonore*. Christensen notes that the Preface has a more overt sensationalist interpretation of theory than in any of Rameau's previous works, and considers this a sign of Diderot's influence. (These arguments will appear in Christensen, *Rameau: Science of Music Theory*).

[10] Historian Peter Gay describes Diderot's changes in the realm of art as a departure from an early neo-classical outlook: 'Diderot long was unadventurous, content to leave most of the neo-classical structure untouched ... He drew on classical doctrines for his early ideals of art as imitation and art as moral ... It was not until the 1760s—always remaining himself, or, rather, becoming himself more and more—that he discarded inherited ideas and began to grope for a modern aesthetic.' (Peter Gay, *The Enlightenment: An Interpretation*, vol. ii, *The Science of Freedom* (New York: Alfred A. Knopf, 1969), 251.)

Let us begin with the early work in which he draws close to Rameau, his *Mémoires sur différens sujets de mathématiques*, published in 1748. The first *Mémoire*, 'Principes généraux d'acoustique', in addition to summarizing the major acoustical findings of Mersenne, Taylor, Sauveur, Euler, and others, adopts without reservation Rameau's principle of the *corps sonore* as the basis of music theory.[11] Like Rameau, Diderot emphasizes that music has universal principles, that compositional choices are not arbitrary or subjective. In support of this view, he notes that there is a consensus on the consonant intervals of harmony—the octave, fifth, and third—despite observed differences in musical taste from one historical period to another, and from one culture or nation to another. The consonant intervals are a universal source of pleasure because they have their foundation in nature, in the overtones, which provide us with the perfect chord. From this it follows, for Diderot, as well as Rameau, that harmonic progressions also have their foundation in nature: 'If this unanimous consensus has a real foundation in nature; if indeed all sounds are not equally suitable to form agreeable consonances, can one regard the succession of sounds and consonances as arbitrary? ... That is not plausible.'[12]

Like Rameau, Diderot attributes the universal principles of pleasure not only to the physical properties of consonance, but also to proportional relationships. And here he is referring to the simple ratios that exist between the frequency of the vibrating string as a whole and the respective frequencies of each of the consonant harmonics: 'We will demonstrate presently that musical pleasure consists in the perception of the relationships among sounds.'[13]

Music's embodiment of proportions as well as physical properties has methodological implications for music theory. Citing contrasting theoretical approaches from antiquity—Pythagoras versus Aristoxenes—Diderot finds each only partially successful. While praising Pythagoras for recognizing that the perception of proportional relationships is the source of musical pleasure, Diderot criticizes him

[11] Of the five *Mémoires* in this work, the first and the fourth deal with music. The fourth, entitled 'Projet d'un nouvel orgue', presents Diderot's proposal for a mechanical organ. It reflects both his strong practical interest in the technology of the mechanical arts and crafts, including considerable knowledge of musical instruments, and another more fanciful and inventive side. Little is known of his early musical training.

[12] Diderot, *Mémoires sur différens sujets de mathématiques*; Hermann, ii. 235–6. Diderot's support of Rameau's theory appears to coincide with close contact with Rameau. The abbé Raynal comments on their relationship in the *Correspondance littéraire*—also suggesting a forthcoming collaboration between the two: 'Diderot was intimate friends with M. Rameau, whose discoveries he will publish shortly. The sublime and profound musician has presented other works in the past where he has not shown sufficient clarity and elegance. M. Diderot will rework these ideas and he is very capable of bringing them to light.' (Quoted in *Denis Diderot: Écrits sur la musique*, ed. Béatrice Durand-Sendrail (Paris: Editions Lattès, 1987), 27.)

[13] *Mémoires*; Hermann, ii. 236.

for relying too heavily on proportions and overlooking the role of the ear. Aristoxenes, on the other hand, erred by banishing numbers and calculations and by relying solely on the ear in the choice of intervallic successions. Diderot is very close to Rameau in insisting that theory must be based on both proportions and experience.

Diderot is also close to Rameau, and to the general geometrical spirit of the time, in asserting the applicability of proportional relationships to all the arts and sciences: 'This principle [of proportional relationships] applies to poetry, painting, architecture, morals, all the arts and all the sciences ... Things which seemed the most arbitrary were suggested by relationships ...'[14] Both would agree, furthermore, that the beauty of consonance does not rule out the need for dissonance in music as a means of enhancing its pleasure. There is also a striking similarity between Diderot and Rameau in the view that intellect and feeling are alternative paths to musical pleasures: 'These relationships can affect our soul in two fashions, by feeling or by perception, with most men affected by the former.'[15]

As important as these agreements are, some differences between Diderot and Rameau appear even at this early stage. One of the most crucial is Diderot's emphasis on the listener's perception of relationships, rather than on the relationships themselves. And since the senses are involved in this perception, there are individual differences in response, despite the foundation of harmonic relationships in nature. For Rameau, the fact that harmonic proportions come from nature assures universal response. The gap between the two is somewhat narrowed by Diderot's recognition that not all listeners are equally skilled. He recommends as guide someone who is well instructed in these matters, and 'who has a pure organ, enjoys a healthy intellect, and for whom images are not distorted by the senses'.[16] This belief that there is a 'correct' way of experiencing harmonic intervals and their proportions—despite the role of the senses—also reflects Diderot's closeness to neo-classical doctrine at this stage of his career.

Diderot also goes further than Rameau in addressing the nature of the musical composition itself. Not only do listeners differ from one another, but musical compositions differ in the complexity of the proportional relationships that they contain. The greater the complexity, the greater the need for talent and concentration in order to enjoy them.

---

[14] *Mémoires*; Hermann, ii. 256.

[15] Ibid. 237. In the same year as the *Mémoires*, Diderot also expressed appreciation for Rameau as opera composer in his satirical and somewhat risqué novel, *Les Bijoux indiscrèts*. Ch. 13 of this novel presents a comparison of two opera composers 'Utmiutsol' and 'Uremifasolasiututut' (representing Lully and Rameau, respectively) and effectively captures the particular strengths of Rameau.

[16] Ibid. 236.

This also helps to explain different cultural responses: 'The melody of primitives will be too simple for us, and our music too complex for them.'[17]

Before leaving this early and fairly traditional work of Diderot's, it is worth noting one more important difference with Rameau. For the latter, the foundation of harmonic proportions in nature also means that harmony is the sole source of expression and meaning in music. Diderot never comes to this conclusion. Even at this early stage, there is an awareness of the complexity of the artistic experience, and especially the inherent tension between general laws and individual response, an awareness that only awaits further development.

A few years after the *Mémoires*, in the *Lettre sur les sourds et muets*, published in 1751, Diderot resumes his attempt to explain the sources of pleasure in music—this time focusing less on harmony and the resonating string, and turning instead to the expressive powers of music as conceptualized in the neo-classical doctrine of art as an imitation of nature and the passions. He does so as part of a larger inquiry about the nature of language and art. Diderot confirms his belief in music's imitative powers by answering a correspondent who has expressed scepticism about imitation in music. He cites her argument that '"there are some musical compositions to which no images are attached ... and which nevertheless give everyone great pleasure"'.[18] In his response, he defines the nature of artistic pleasure and distinguishes it from other forms of pleasure, making the concept of imitation a vital key to the difference between the two:

These musical compositions which affect you agreeably without evoking either picture, or distinct perception of relationships, only flatter your ear like a rainbow pleases our eyes, with a pleasure of pure and simple sensation; and yet they are considerably lacking the perfection that you require and that they could have if the truth of imitation were joined to the charms of harmony.

He goes on to say that the pleasure derived from artistic imitation is even greater than the pleasure obtained from nature itself: 'If only the stars could retain their original brightness when painted on canvas, you would find them more beautiful than they are in the firmament, because of the reflective pleasure that derives from

---

[17] Ibid. 237.
[18] Diderot, *Lettre sur les sourds et muets* (1751); ed. Jacques Chouillet, Hermann, iv (1978), 205. Diderot's answer to the correspondent was added to the original *Lettre sur les sourds*, and printed in May 1751—three months after the original appeared. The correspondent was a learned woman, Mlle de la Chaux, who clearly had the ability to ask perceptive questions.

imitation combined with the direct and natural pleasure of the sensation of the object.'[19]

As compelling as Diderot's arguments are in favour of musical imitation, he concedes that music is less precise than the other art-forms
and that perceptions depend to a greater extent on the individual:

Music has a greater need than painting or poetry to reach within us to those
favourably disposed organs. Its imagery is so faint and fleeting, that it is easy to
lose or misinterpret ... Painting shows the object itself, poetry describes it,
music barely arouses an idea. It has only intervals and the duration of sound as
resources; and what analogy is there between this type of colouring and actual
springtime, storms, solitude, etc. and most objects?[20]

He thus poses a challenge to the concept of musical imitation that is
more serious than the argument of his correspondent.

Diderot uses this challenge, however, not to undermine the expressive power of music, but to probe more deeply into its nature. In the
following speculation he comes to terms with the imprecision of music
and views it as a source of potential strength:

How is it that of the three arts that imitate nature, the one that has the most
arbitrary and imprecise expression speaks most strongly to the soul? Could it
be that by showing less of the object, it leaves more to our imagination, or that
since we need agitation in order to be moved, music is more appropriate than
painting and poetry for producing turbulence within us?[21]

Throughout this discussion, Diderot stresses the differences among the
arts.

Elsewhere in the work, he offers an illustration of music's expressive
power by examining a musical setting of a poem on a dying woman (a
setting that scholars, thus far, have been unable to identify). He emphasizes here as well that music cannot show the thing itself—in contrast to painting—but presents a kind of poetic image or symbol
instead. In the musical setting, Diderot assigns an important role to the
harmony and accompaniment in conveying the poetic image. They are
in fact capable of expressing some things that the vocal line cannot:

---

[19] Diderot, *Lettre sur les sourds et muets* (1751), 205–6. This passage is also discussed by Walter
Rex, who emphasizes the complexity of Diderot's views of imitation. See Walter Rex, 'A Propos of
the Figure of Music in the Frontispiece of the Encyclopédie: Theories of Musical Imitation in
d'Alembert, Rousseau, and Diderot', *International Musicology Society Report of the Twelfth Contress,
Berkeley, 1977* (Kassel: Barenreiter, 1981), 214–25.

[20] *Lettre sur les sourds*, Hermann, iv. 207. Diderot's emphasis in *Les Sourds* on the differences
among the arts is also presented as a response to the position of the abbé Batteux who argued that
all of the arts are subject to the same principle of imitation—the imitation of a universal ideal
nature, or *belle nature*. Batteux also observed that music was less capable of precise representations
and that it was better suited to imitating the simple affections. Batteux's position was presented in
Les Beaux-arts réduits à un même principe (1743).

[21] *Lettrre sur les sourds*: Hermann, iv. 207.

'When the musician knows his art, the accompanying parts will reinforce one another, either to strengthen the expression of the vocal part, or to add new ideas that the subject demands, but the vocal part could not convey.'[22] As for the appropriate harmony for the image of a dying woman, Diderot recommends the use of chromatic and dissonant chords that are normally forbidden. Without these transgressions—referred to with the term *licence*, which was also used by Rameau—musical language would be impoverished and lacking in energy.[23]

Diderot's recognition of a special kind of expressive quality in music, one that is less precise and at the same time more powerful, ties in with a larger theme in the *Lettre sur les sourds and muets*, that languages, as well as the arts, differ from one another in terms of their potential to express feelings. It is worth digressing for a moment to note his views on these differences, since they have important musical ramifications for both Diderot and Rousseau. Diderot views linguistic differences as a reflection of different stages in the development of language. The ancient languages are closer to feeling and are more capable of poetic expression; the more evolved or 'perfected' languages have the precision and clarity necessary for thought. He cites Latin as an example of the former, and French as an example of the latter. It should be noted, however, that Diderot does not exclude French from the realm of poetry and feeling; he simply points to a difference in aptitude. It is only when, shortly thereafter, Rousseau develops his version of the historical reconstruction of language, that French becomes incapable of expressing feeling.[24]

---

[22] Ibid. 185. We have already noted that Rousseau similarly acknowledges that the accompaniment can be more expressive than the vocal part (see above, Rousseau's concept of *récitatif obligé* in the *Dictionnaire*). Diderot presents this idea in a number of other works, including his *Lettre sur les aveugles* (1749), where a blind young woman makes the following strong statement: 'I can do without the interpretation of the singing parts as long as the symphonist is a man of genius and knows how to give character to his melody.' (Hermann, iv. 100.)

[23] The concept of *licence*, or the violation of rules, had a theoretical justification that in part stemmed from Longinus' classical treatise, *On the Sublime* (3rd cent. AD). Peter Gay notes that Longinus' notion of the sublime was generally very popular during the late 17th and early 18th cents. (It was disseminated in France through Nicholas Boileau's *Réflexions sur Longin* (1694).) Peter Gay emphasizes the appeal of the notion of sublimity and its link to *licence* in the following observation: 'It gave good reasons for unreasonable preferences, objective sanctions to subjective sentiments, legitimate justification for breaking the law' (Gay, *The Enlightenment*, ii. 304).

[24] Paul Hugo Meyer, in his commentary to his edition of the *Lettre sur les sourds*, points to the closeness between Diderot's views on the nature of language and those expressed by Condillac in his *Essai sur l'origine des connaissances humaines*, published in 1746 ('Diderot: *Lettre sur les sourds et muets*, edition commentée et présentée par Paul Hugo Meyer', *Diderot Studies*, 7 (1965): 15–18). Despite the earlier date of Condillac's *Essai*, Meyer raises some uncertainty about who was the original source of inspiration for these ideas, since there was considerable interaction between the two during this period. Meyer also observes Rousseau's indebtedness to both Diderot and Condillac for the development of his own views on language—although he notes that Rousseau transformed the reconstruction to fit his particular ideology.

Closely related to the dichotomy between feeling and thought is an important contrast that Diderot makes between poetic expression and discourse. In the latter case, he emphasizes that rational ideas are expressed successively, although reason makes comparisons among perceptions that occur simultaneously. Poetic expression, on the other hand, mirrors the indivisible state of the soul. Using poetic images or 'hieroglyphs', rather than thoughts, it conveys meaning and feeling at the same time. This applies to each of the arts, but, (once again) with different kinds of imagery and resources in each case.

Diderot also includes one of the strongest and most original arguments for the expressive powers of music in his observations on how a deaf mute from birth would conceive of music. The experience of the deaf mute holds a central position in the *Lettre*, since the mute relies on the language of gesture, which Diderot identifies with an early stage of language that is close to feeling.[25] Diderot's compelling hypothesis is that if a deaf mute were to form his concept of music by watching the facial expressions and gestures of those listening to music or playing an instrument, he would assume that musical sounds have as much meaning as words in discourse have: 'The signs of joy or sadness that are painted on our faces and in our gestures, when we are struck by a beautiful harmony ... might be compared to the effects produced by discourse ...'[26] The hypothetical situation demonstrates the primary role of the senses in the formation of ideas. Even more important, the impaired sense faculty of the mute and the resulting distortion in his concept of music symbolizes man's limitations in general in dealing with the totality of experience:

Isn't that ... a faithful image of our thoughts, of our reasoning, of our systems, in a word, of those concepts which have made a reputation for so many philosophers? Each time that they have judged things which seem to demand a faculty that we lack for attaining a full understanding, which is often the case, they have shown less wisdom and are often further from the truth than the deaf mute who I have been discussing.[27]

---

[25] Although Diderot and Rousseau both agree that the language of gesture is an early stage of language, Rousseau identifies it to a greater extent with the expression of physical needs rather than feelings: 'Visible signs make imitation more exact, but interest is more fully aroused by sounds. That makes me think that if we ever have physical needs, we would be able to do very well without speaking at all and would understand one another perfectly by the language of gesture alone.' (Rousseau, *Essai sur l'origine des langues*, ed. Starobinski, 63; ch. 1, 'Concerning different means of communicating our thoughts'.)

[26] *Lettre sur les sourds*; Hermann, iv. 147. Diderot's view of the extraordinary expressive powers of music also inspires his repeated use of a musical metaphor associating the tensions of the vibrating string with man's energies and passions—man is an instrument and his passions are the strings. For a discussion of this metaphor, see Jacques Chouillet, *Diderot poète de l'énergie* (Paris: Presses Universitaires de France, 1984), 249–79.

[27] *Lettre sur les sourds*; Hermann, iv. 147.

With this, Diderot seems to reconsider whether the deaf mute is so wrong about music after all: 'Even if we don't speak as distinctly with instruments as with our mouth, nor paint ideas as clearly with sounds as we do with discourse, nevertheless we do say something.'[28]

Diderot presents one final example of music's expressive power in his discussion of music as a communal experience. He observes that there is an incremental effect when an impassioned experience is shared: 'It is the nature of all enthusiasm that it communicates itself and increases according to the number of enthusiasts. Men have a reciprocal effect on one another, through the energetic and lively image that they convey when transported by passion ...'[29] The potential for this powerful communal experience is an important theme for Diderot throughout his career, reflecting his view of both an ideal music and an ideal society. Music had such powers in ancient Greece, for example, where youths received around a dozen years of training.[30]

Given Diderot's emphasis on the poetic mysteries of music, as well as its extraordinary expressive powers, it is surprising to find him re-affirming in the same work the more traditional rationalist position of the *Mémoires*. He not only reaffirms the view that the perception of proportional relationships is the source of beauty in all the arts, but restates it a few months later in the *Encyclopédie* article 'Beau'. His definition of beauty illustrates how closely he holds to the original formulation of the *Mémoires*, continuing to emphasize the objective nature of beauty, even while linking it to the perception of the in-dividual: 'I ... call *beautiful* outside of myself, whatever contains in itself that which can awaken the idea of proportional relationships in my understanding; and *beautiful* in relation to me, whatever does awaken that idea.'[31] In similar fashion, he links imitation with proportional relationships, defining the 'beauty of imitation' as the use of propor-tions 'in representations of works of art or of nature'.[32]

[28] Ibid. Diderot's quasi-experimental use of a hypothetical figure with one of his senses im-paired had already occurred in his *Lettre sur les aveugles* (1749). This emphasis on the senses was part of a widespread acceptance among the *philosophes* of the sensationalist philosophy of Locke, with Condillac in a leading role in its dissemination and further development. The experimental device of a type with a hearing impairment appeared in Condillac's *Essai sur l'origine des connaissances humaines*. It was an attempt to understand the normal through the abnormal.

[29] *Lettre sur les sourds*; Hermann, iv. 207–8.

[30] Diderot and Rousseau had similar views on the ideal nature of Greek music and Greek society. Rousseau, however, (as already noted) carried this notion to much more pessimistic conclusions about French music and society.

[31] Denis Diderot, 'Beau' in the *Encyclopédie*, ed. John Lough and Jacques Proust, Hermann, vi. (1976), 156. In *Lettre sur les sourds*, the importance of proportions appears in his response to Mlle de la Chaux, Hermann, iv. 202.

[32] 'Beau'; Hermann, vi. 158–9. What this involves is three different contexts for proportional relationships: those within nature; those within our understanding, which were awakened by the relationships in nature; and those within the work of art, which represent the relationships found in nature.

Diderot takes a decisive step away from this rationalist emphasis on proportional relationships not in his next aesthetic work, but in his scientific essay, *Pensées sur l'interprétation de la nature*, published in 1754.[33] This work has a strong bearing on his views on music, as well as the other arts, in that it presents a view of scientific method that rejects the use of mathematics, and attempts to close the gap between abstraction and concrete reality. The essay marks a shift toward the biological sciences which was symptomatic of scientific developments at the time. Putting aside the prevalent mechanical world-view, Diderot focuses on nature as a dynamic organic process in a perpetual state of flux: 'If beings are undergoing successive alterations, changing by the most imperceptible nuances; time, which never stops, must create the most enormous differences between forms that existed in very ancient times, those that exist today, and those that will exist in the future . . .'[34] The shift in Diderot's thinking draws him apart not only from Rameau, who was already becoming increasingly metaphysical, but also from d'Alembert, who maintained a commitment to Newtonian science and to the search, through experimentation, for universal laws that could be formulated in mathematical terms.[35]

Diderot's scientific stance in the *Interprétation* is distinguished by an overriding sense of the unintelligibility of the universe and the limitations of science and philosophy. In this he draws closer to Rousseau, who viewed science and reason as artificial conventions of society. The absence of permanence and stability, coupled with the impossibility of reflecting reality through mathematical principles, leads Diderot to call for a more purely experimental science. Description and interpretation

[33] Diderot, *Pensées sur l'interprétation de la nature* (1754); ed. Jean Varloot, with commentary by Herbert Dieckmann and Jean Varloot, Hermann, ix. (1981). It first appeared in 1753 under the shorter title, *De l'interprétation de la nature*; only some minor revisions and the altered title distinguish the 1754 edition.

[34] Ibid. 91–2. Although the *Interprétation* presents Diderot's strongest advocacy of the biological sciences, he had already taken an important step in that direction in the *Lettre sur les aveugles*, published in 1749. Indeed, his arrest and imprisonment for anti-religious beliefs stemmed from his strong espousal of biological materialism in this earlier work.

[35] According to d'Alembert scholars, this philosophical difference was a contributing factor to d'Alembert's departure from the *Encyclopédie*, where he was co-editor from 1750 until his resignation in 1758. Thomas Hankins, for example, notes that there was 'a widening gap between their views on the philosophical foundations of science . . . a gap that grew until eventually it broke the bond of friendship and common purpose, and probably contributed to d'Alembert's decision to leave the *Encyclopédie*'. (Hankins, *d'Alembert*, 66). Hankins notes that while Diderot's views changed considerably throughout his career, d'Alembert's position changed very little after his writing of the 'Discours préliminaire' for the *Encyclopédie*. Hankins explains the disagreement that developed between them in more precise terms: 'It was this problem of abstraction that first divided d'Alembert and Diderot. Abstraction, for d'Alembert, was the way to make physical problems amenable to geometrical analysis and therefore formed an essential part of his scientific method. But Diderot described abstraction as a common source of error' (p. 75). Diderot was most explicit about his intellectual differences with d'Alembert in *Le Rêve de d'Alembert*, written in 1769.

are to be its principal tools: 'Phenomena are infinite; causes hidden; forms perhaps transitory. Against so many obstacles that we find within ourselves, and that nature imposes from without, all we can do is slow experimentation and limited reflection.'[36] Interestingly enough, the impossibility of knowing anything more than an 'incomplete moment' in the history of nature does not preclude a unified view of evolution by Diderot in which all phenomena are linked to one another. He thus retained the widely accepted assumption of a unified universe, regarding it as essential for the existence of any science or philosophy.

The implications of this dynamic view of nature for art have to do with man's place in the evolutionary process. Diderot emphasizes man's uniqueness as a self-conscious being, having evolved to the highest level of existence through an 'infinity' of increasingly complex organizing stages. At the same time, he reminds us that this thinking and feeling creature is still part of nature, part of an irrational process that includes both structure and de-structure: 'He may be departing, or will depart from his [current] state through a never-ending decline, during which his faculties will leave him in the same way that they came . . .'[37]

The paradox in this view of the human condition is observed by Diderot scholar Lester Crocker: 'A process without meaning has produced a being who creates meaning and lives by meaning.'[38] In Diderot's universe, the demand for meaning is a 'hopeless quest'. There is one chance for order, however, and that is in the realm of art: 'Art alone, by creating its own peculiarly human reality, enables man to triumph over disorder, to satisfy the deep emotional and intellectual need for order.'[39] In doing so, however, art must deal with disorder. Crocker characterizes Diderot's fiction as 'deeply concerned with the problem of finding new and better aesthetic processes to express the experience of human and cosmic disorder'. He adds: 'He breaks out of

---

[36] *Interprétation*; Hermann, ix. 43. The scientific background for Diderot's shift toward the life sciences is discussed by Enlightenment scholar Colm Kiernan. He observes that 'there was in eighteenth-century France a cleavage within science itself'—referring to the diametrical opposites of the Newtonian sciences of physics and astronomy on the one hand, and the life sciences on the other. (Colm Kiernan, 'Diderot and Science', *Diderot Studies*, 14 (1971): 115.) Arthur Wilson points to the influence of Bacon's *Novum Organum* on Diderot's biological concept of scientific method. (Wilson, *Diderot*, 188).

[37] *Interprétation*; Hermann, ix. 94–5.

[38] Lester Crocker, 'The Idea of a "Neutral" Universe', *Diderot Studies*, 21 (1983), 75. Crocker also points out that this view of nature is very different from the picture of the Enlightenment presented in Carl Becker's *The Heavenly City of the Eighteenth-Century Philosophers*, which posits that Enlightenment thinkers believed that the universe is 'a beautifully articulated machine designed by the Supreme Being according to a rational plan . . .' (Crocker, 45). Crocker also emphasizes that there was no single Enlightenment mentality.

[39] Lester Crocker, *Diderot's Chaotic Order: Approach to Synthesis* (Princeton, NJ: Princeton University Press, 1974), 74.

the classical aesthetic imitation ... into forms that themselves have some kinship with anarchy ...'[40]

Diderot's search for new art-forms that could reflect the dynamic nature of reality focuses primarily on drama, where he deals with this issue both as theorist and as playwright. His first two plays are accompanied by theoretical discussions: *Le Fils naturel*, published with the *Entretiens sur 'le Fils naturel*' in 1757 (under the overall title *Dorval et moi*); and *Le Père de famille*, published with the *Discours sur la poésie dramatique* in 1758.[41] His views apply to opera as well as spoken drama, and they also have some bearing on music theory.

Diderot's theory of drama closely parallels the scientific approach presented in *Pensées sur l'interprétation de la nature*. Whereas in science he rejects the abstractions of mathematics as artificial constructs incapable of reflecting concrete reality, in drama he rejects the rigid genres of neo-classical theory and the artificial staging conventions of classic French theatre as unsuitable for the portrayal of real passions. In his emphasis on realism he calls for the creation of a new genre, the *drame bourgeois*, which is in between classical tragedy and comedy. While the comic genre deals with types, and the tragic deals with individuals, the new genre is distinguished from them by dealing with 'conditions', and especially the realistic social conditions of a new middle class.[42]

His reforms in favour of realism apply to lyrical tragedy as well as spoken drama. Diderot makes a special target of *le merveilleux*, which featured so prominently in French opera. He rules out magical scenes of enchantment, since there are no existing models in nature. Opera must deal with truth just as philosophy does; it must imitate nature and especially the strongest nature: 'Geniuses have brought the philosophy of our time from the abstract realm to the real. Can't we find someone who will perform the same service for lyrical poetry and bring it down from enchanted regions to the earth that we inhabit?'[43] It is interesting to note that although fantasy is a fault of French opera and not of

[40] Lester Crocker, *Diderot's Chaotic Order*, 160.

[41] Wilson notes that Diderot's impulse to write plays came 'suddenly', when he was in his early forties (Wilson, *Diderot*, 260). *Le Fils* was the greater success of the two, although neither were performed immediately at the Comédie-Française. The two plays were widely read and had many editions throughout Europe, as did their accompanying essays. It is worth stressing the dual perspective of Diderot as playwright and as dramatic theorist, since it is an important common bond with Rameau, who was both composer and music theorist.

[42] Diderot also places the action of the drama in the present and in realistic settings, with realistic staging. He also writes naturalistic rather than elevated dialogues. Literary scholar René Wellek observes that while the reforms of the *drame bourgeois* were innovations in France, there were models in England that were known and admired by Diderot (Wellek, *History of Modern Criticism*, i. 47.)

[43] Denis Diderot, *Entretiens sur Le Fils naturel* (published with the play under the overall title *Dorval et moi*), ed. Jacques Chouillet and Anne-Marie Chouillet, Hermann, x. (1980), 'Troisième Entretien', 150–1.

Italian, his praise of the latter is somewhat muted: 'The lyrical genre of a neighbouring people undoubtedly has its faults, but much less than it is thought.'[44] Like Rousseau, Diderot reserves his strongest admiration for the Greeks, and even proposes that opera should be based on ancient tragedy rather than bourgeois tragedy. This is particularly recommended since the opera libretto should be 'measured', and bourgeois tragedy 'seems to preclude versification'.[45]

Meaningful content in theatre also depends on powerful expression. And here Diderot's emphasis on the emotive reaches a new peak. He leaves little or no room for reflection in his concept of the artist and the creative process. Only the passionate artist can achieve greatness in art. He must be so aroused by emotions during the creative process that he is in a kind of feverish transport, a state beyond consciousness: 'It is a strong and permanent heat that embraces him, that makes him short of breath, that consumes him, kills him; but which gives life and soul to everything he touches.'[46] Furthermore, it is not just the artist who must have these powerful feelings, but the actor or singer, and eventually the audience as well. The theatre is an experience of emotional intensity: 'Oh dramatic poets, the true applause that you seek, is not the clapping of hands ... but that deep sigh which comes from the soul after the constraint of a long silence, which then brings relief.'[47]

These powerful effects, however, are not to be sought for their own sake. A major point of his dramatic theory is that virtue is the ultimate goal of theatre: 'The parterre of the *Comédie* is the sole place where the tears of virtuous and wicked men are mixed ... the wicked will leave the theatre less disposed to do evil ...'[48] In this view of art as a path to virtue Diderot is still close to the neo-classical tradition. His liberation from the rigid rules of antiquity does not mean a complete break with that tradition.[49]

Diderot's concern with powerful expression in the theatre also calls for an expanded role for the actor and a new emphasis on pantomime

[44] Ibid. 151. We have already noted that in the 'Querelle des Bouffons' Diderot joined Rousseau and the other *philosophes* on the Italian side, but took a more moderate and conciliatory tone.

[45] Ibid. 156.

[46] *Entretiens*; Hermann, 'Second Entretien', x. 99. Crocker warns us against confusing the emotive creative process with the finished work of art, and reminds us that out of disorder comes order: 'The genius, working in the way that is his, creates a new order ... As in nature, order arises out of a disorderly, energetic process.' (Crocker, *Diderot's Chaotic Order*, 55.)

[47] Diderot, *De la Poésie dramatique* (1758); ed. Jacques Chouillet and Anne-Marie Chouller, Hermann, x. (1980), 339.

[48] Ibid. 338.

[49] Peter Gay observes that moralizing in art, even at the expense of aesthetic values, was the most difficult aspect of neo-classicism for Diderot to relinquish. Gay explains that the *philosophes* felt that 'there was simply too much work to be done—too many injustices to be righted, superstitions to be exposed ... to permit the *philosophes* to abandon their poses as modern Socrateses, or modern Catos ...' (Gay, *The Enlightenment*, ii. 258).

and improvisation, in the ancient manner of the Greeks. This is a return to an important idea of the *Lettre sur les sourds*, that gestures are closer to feelings: 'We speak too much in our dramas; and consequently, our actors do not play enough. We have lost an art, which the ancients utilized so effectively.'[50]

Closely related to pantomime, opera has the important non-verbal resource of dance as well. Diderot emphasizes that dance is one of the imitative arts—it is pantomime in poetic form—and should not be treated as pure dance: 'I would like someone to tell me what is the meaning of all these dances, such as the minuet, the passe-pied, the rigaudon ... what does it imitate?'[51] Dance, like pantomime, should be closely linked to the drama. It should have its own means of representation, its own subject, with a similar role in scenes or acts to that of recitative or aria. Such use of dance also requires an imitative or expressive role for the orchestra: 'It is the orchestra that speaks; it renders the discourse, imitates the actions. The poet has dictated what the orchestra should say; the musician has written it ...'[52]

Opera of course consists largely of vocal settings with text, and here too Diderot emphasizes the importance of strong emotions, passions that are so powerful that they transcend the meaning of individual words. A text with such emotions is best set as accompanied recitative (*le style simple*), allowing the vocal line to follow the accents of the 'violent and inarticulate' cries of nature. With this concern for the violent and the inarticulate, Diderot points once more to an important role for the orchestra. He proposes the use of ritornellos in between the phrases of text as a means of reinforcing such emotions as fear, horror, fury, pain, or pity.[53] There are other types of text, however, which are more pictorial and which portray external objects rather than internal feelings. These texts do not lend themselves to recitative, and would best be set as melodic arias (*le style figuré*), with more ornate figuration in both voice and orchestra. Far from viewing the pictorial and expressive styles as equal, Diderot warns that pictorial imagery can undermine the expression of the natural cries of nature: 'Everything that he [the artist] devotes to the pictorial scene will deflect from pathetic expression. It will have a greater effect on the ears, less on the soul.'[54]

[50] *Entretiens*: Hermann, 'Second Entretien', x. 101.

[51] Ibid., 'Troisième Entretien', x. 152. Paul Henry Lang observes that Diderot's proposals for dance were actually carried out in France, resulting in an important contribution by Diderot to the new genre of the *ballet-pantomime* (Lang, 'Diderot as Musician', *Diderot Studies*, 10 (1968), 96).

[52] *Entretiens*; 'Troisième Entretien', x. 153.

[53] Diderot thus has the same position as Rousseau on the use of *récitatif obligé* as a powerful means of expression. Diderot cites Clytemnestre's expression of grief over the sacrifice of her daughter from Racine's *Iphigénie* as an example of a powerful text that would lend itself to such a setting (ibid., 'Troisième Entretien', x. 157).

[54] Ibid. 158.

Finally, Diderot's theorizing about drama shows a strong concern for the role of genius and imagination. Reflecting once again the views in the scientific essay, *Pensées sur l'interprétation de la nature*, Diderot presents a concept of imagination that rejects abstraction. Imagination begins when a person is forced 'to move from abstract and general sounds, until he arrives at a sensible representation, the last boundary and resting point of reason'. And although the use of imagination makes one a painter or a poet, its importance is not confined to the artist alone: Without imagination, 'one is neither a poet, nor a philosopher, nor a man of intelligence, nor a reasonable being, nor a man'.[55]

In the ebb and flow in Diderot's aesthetics between the reflective and the emotive, his theory of drama in this period clearly marks a shift away from his earlier concerns with abstractions and proportions, as seen in the *Mémoires*, the article 'Beau', and to some extent in *Lettre sur les sourds*. Diderot's rejection of abstraction in the scientific realm thus has a profound impact on his views of drama and music. Indeed, it carries over into the realm of imagination, which governs not only art, but all intellectual activity.

This period of intense emotionalism is also one in which Diderot's views draw closest to those of Rousseau. Both are wedded to sensibility, to inarticulate and direct expression of the passions, and to the belief that conditions were more suitable for these ideals in an earlier more primitive society. They also share a certain scepticism about universal laws and abstract principles. Many of these shared views stem from their customary practice of exchanging ideas and trying out new ones with one another, showing how deeply ingrained was the habit of dialogue.

Serious disagreements, however, arose between them toward the end of the 1750s, one of which concerned the theatre and morality. We have already seen that for Diderot virtue was the ultimate goal of theatre—a view that was generally shared by the *philosophes*. Ironically, it was Rousseau's strong moral position that turned him against the theatre, especially as he viewed it in the overall context of his social ideology. In his *Lettre à d'Alembert sur les spectacles*, published in 1758, he condemned the theatre as an institution, because it reflected an immoral society. Rousseau argued that religion must precede virtue.[56]

[55] *De la Poésie*; Hermann, x. 359.

[56] Rousseau's *Lettre à d'Alembert* was written primarily as an attack on d'Alembert's proposal that the Calvinist city-state of Geneva should allow legitimate theatre—a proposal made by d'Alembert in his ill-fated *Encyclopédie* article 'Genève' (see n. 7 above). However, the *Lettre à d'Alembert* was also an attack on Diderot, both in the Preface, where Rousseau openly announced a break between the two, and in the letter itself, where his anti-theatre position amounted to an indirect assault on Diderot the playwright. Peter Gay explains that the quarrels that divided Rousseau from his fellow *philosophes* were partly the fault of his style: 'As his former associates were to complain: Rousseau was a playwright who inveighed against the theatre, a moralist who aban-

Diderot's views on theatre, including lyrical theatre and music, continued to evolve after his first plays and essays. At the same time, his aesthetic activities expanded to the world of painting, where, at the request of the Baron von Grimm, he became art critic for Grimm's *Correspondance littéraire*. He wrote reviews of the official biennial Salon art exhibitions (called 'Salons') of the Accadémie de peinture et de sulpture from 1759 until 1781. The resulting series of Salons closely paralleled Diderot's continued aesthetic exploration in the realms of theatre and music, which we will consider in the final chapter of this study.[57]

The appendix translations for this chapter are from the *Entretiens sur 'Le Fils naturel'*.

doned his children, a religious philosopher who changed his confession twice for dubious reasons, a libertarian who could not get compulsion out of his mind, a deist who accused his fellow deists of irreligion, a professional celebrant of friendship who broke with everyone.' (Gay, *The Enlightenment*, ii. 530.) Arthur Wilson observes that Rousseau's attacks on his fellow *philosophes* must have greatly comforted the enemies of the *Encyclopédie*, showing them that the united front was broken. Wilson attributes the break in the close friendship between Diderot and Rousseau to a series of misunderstandings which started around 1757. He also explains that Rousseau had 'an extremely sensitive and imaginative nature, which impelled him to be suspicious of the motives of his friends and created an appalling conviction of ever-threatening menace and ever-darkling doom' (Wilson, *Diderot*, 291).

[57] Grimm's *Correspondance littéraire* was an exclusive hand-copied newsletter whose subscribers were a small and highly select group of enlightened foreign princes. It was intended to keep them abreast of the literary and artistic scene in Paris, and presented reviews and summary reports of events. Since the readers lived abroad and did not see the art works of the Salons, Diderot was challenged to capture the pictures for the imagination, thereby greatly sharpening his powers of observation and skills as a critic. He wrote nine reviews entitled 'Salons' after the title of the official exhibitions, which were at the Louvre.

6

Music as Art and Science
Synthesis by Diderot, 1761–1771, and Conclusion

A major part of Diderot's subsequent aesthetic exploration and further development of ideas involved a reassessment of emotionalism, in which he examined its negative as well as its positive traits. Ultimately, Diderot ended by reasserting the values of reason and reflection. One of the most significant products of this exploratory process was the dramatic dialogue, *Le Neveu de Rameau*, written in 1761.[1]

Scholars tend to agree that the period in which Diderot wrote *Le Neveu* witnessed some critical changes in his life and his philosophical outlook—changes which pulled his aesthetics in the direction of greater reflection and emotional restraint. Arthur Wilson observes that *Le Neveu* 'constitutes a discernible stage in Diderot's progress from *sensibilité* to self-conscious artistic control'.[2] Wilson attributes this change to a maturation process, 'which was essential for the production of those later works which have become the subjects of such ... wide admiration in the twentieth century'.[3] This maturation was induced by a series of crises in Diderot's life around 1759: the increasingly virulent attacks against the *Encyclopédie* (including the accusations of treason and personal danger for Diderot), defection of colleagues and collaborators from the project, sadness and foreboding owing to his father's death, and loneliness. Perhaps most significant of all, Diderot showed a growing uncertainty about his own talents as a writer. So great were his doubts—or perhaps, 'soul-weariness'—that Diderot published almost none of his writings after 1759: he 'laid all his bets on posterity'.[4]

For the present study, *Le Neveu* is of particular significance because Diderot's reassessment of the role of emotions in the creative process

---

[1] *Le Neveu de Rameau* (1761); ed. Henri Coulet, Hermann, xii. (1989), 69–196. Diderot made revisions in *Le Neveu* in 1762, 1766, 1767, and 1775. Diderot scholars nevertheless consider it a unified product of 1761, and, according to Otis Fellows, 'this despite interpolations and minor revisions extending to 1775' (Otis Fellows, 'The Theme of Genius in Diderot's Neveu de Rameau', *Diderot Studies*, 2 (1952), 174). The present discussion is indebted to Fellows's insightful analysis of Diderot's treatment of the theme of artistic creativity and genius.

[2] Wilson, *Diderot*, 423.   [3] Ibid. 345.

[4] Ibid. 345. The *Encyclopédie*, which Diderot continued to write clandestinely, was published in one release and with no opposition in 1765.

uses music as its prime example among the arts. The nephew of the title is Jean-François Rameau, closely modelled after the real-life figure of that name who was a failed composer, and whose uncle was the famous Jean-Philippe Rameau. Not only does the celebrated Rameau feature in the play as part of its musical background, but so too does the 'Querelle des Bouffons', with all its accompanying musical and aesthetic issues. Before we turn to the play's specific points about music, we must first examine the more general issue of Diderot's reassessment of emotionalism in artistic creation, since that too has an important bearing on music.

The play is essentially a dialogue between the self-questioning and philosophic figure, designated in the text as Moi, and the brilliant but erratic nephew, Lui. They are old but casual acquaintances who meet by chance at the Café de la Régence. It must be stressed at the outset that despite the extreme realism of the play—the authenticity of the Café de la Régence with its chess players, references to authentic details in Diderot's life for the portrayal of Moi, and to realistic aspects of Jean-François' real-life situation for Lui—it is nevertheless a work of fiction. As we shall see, the scholarly search for Diderot's meaning in the play has appropriately focused on the play as a whole, with considerable speculation as to how much either of the two characters represents the views of Diderot himself.

At the time of their meeting in the play, which is narrated by Moi, the nephew is facing a crisis in his life. He has recently been ejected from his parasitic existence as a kind of 'court jester' in the salon of the wealthy Bertin and his mistress, the actress Mlle Hus. Through much of the dialogue Lui takes inventory of his life, dealing with the question of why success has eluded him, and yet remaining unrepentant about his parasitic and hedonistic lifestyle.[5]

Diderot's portrait of the nephew holds an important key to his reassessment of intense emotionalism in the creative process. The nephew is not only emotional and erratic, he is extremely so. Constantly vacillating, the nephew himself is uncertain as to who or what he is.[6] And it is

[5] The encounter itself presumably was authentic, and must have occurred in 1760. As noted above, the plight of the nephew in the play closely mirrored the real-life situation of Jean-François Rameau. He actually was an eccentric character who made a precarious living as a teacher of singing and keyboard playing, and also was a hanger-on in grand houses. Many of the play's references to Diderot's life are accurate as well. Otis Fellows points to the play's inclusion of other authentic contemporary issues, observing that Diderot also wrote the play as a virulent satire aimed at 'the society of such men of wealth as Bertin, who not only gave wholehearted support to the adversaries of the *Encyclopédie*, but ... utilized his fabulous riches to support men of letters, actresses, and playwrights who were usually devoid not only of genius but of talent' (Fellows, *Diderot*, 89).

[6] Fellows points to the importance of instability or change as a theme in the play, noting that the introduction presents the Horatian epigraph 'Born under the malignant influence of change' (Fellows, 'Theme of Genius', 186). We have also seen in the preceding chapter that the idea of

precisely this erratic quality that helps to explain his failure as an artist. His uncontrolled impulses and lack of self-discipline have led to mediocrity.

Diderot provides a concrete illustration of the nephew in the throws of creative excitation and unbridled enthusiasm in the prolonged pantomime scene which occurs at the climactic moment of the play. Inspired by their discussion of music, the nephew plunges into an impersonation of an opera performance, miming the dancers, singers, and instrumentalists. As he does so, he enters into a sublime state of passion, completely losing himself in the performance—'with an enthusiasm so close to "la folie" that it is uncertain that he will ever pull out of it'.[7] While the nephew has extraordinary powers of expression and can captivate an audience, he falls far short of his goal of true artistic expression. The performance is jumbled, overloaded, disorganized, and finally ludicrous. Moi as narrator conveys both the power of the performance and its grotesqueness:

He piled up and mixed together thirty tunes, Italian, French, tragic, comic, of all sorts of characters; sometimes with a voice of a double bass he descended into the infernal regions; sometimes straining himself and mimicking a falsetto, he split the higher regions asunder ... But you would have gone off into bursts of laughter at the way he mimicked the different instruments ... he whistled the recorders, let the sounds of the transverse flutes flow, shouting, singing and throwing himself about like a mad man; performing by himself the male dancers, the female dancers, the male singers, the female singers, a whole orchestra, a complete opera-house ... running, stopping, with the air of one possessed, with gleaming eyes, foaming mouth. The weather was stifling, and the sweat which ran down the furrows of his brow and the length of his cheeks mingled with the powder from his hair ...[8]

Ultimately, the nephew's lack of restraint and discipline, his total abandon, make of his creativity 'a hideous mockery of genius'.[9]

This vivid portrayal of the grotesque side of uncontrolled emotionalism marks a decided shift from Diderot's earlier picture in

change or flux is very much a part of Diderot's view of nature, including human nature. In the play, the important idea of change is brought to life through the character of the nephew.

[7] Diderot, *Le Neveu*; Hermann, xii. 165.   [8] Ibid. 165–6.

[9] Fellows, 'Theme of Genius', 195. It should be noted that the emotive Lui not only performs two pantomimes, but engages in gestures throughout the play—making it far more than just a dialogue in spoken words. These are the expressive languages to which Diderot attaches great importance in many of his writings, as we have already seen. Diderot's imaginative use of non-verbal language in *Le Neveu* has been viewed by scholars as a far-reaching step in the history of literary genres. Walter Rex, for example, observes that in *Le Neveu* Diderot 'actually puts the theory of imitation to work, exploiting it as a literary device ...'. Rex further notes that in the prolonged pantomime scene there are perhaps four or five layers of imitation—it is an imitation of opera, which in turn involves a combination of several of the imitative arts. (Rex, 'A Propos of the Figure of Music', 220.)

the *Entretiens sur 'Le Fils naturel'*, where the sublime experience of the artist is made the *sine qua non* of true art. Now the artistic impulse must also reside in someone with the discipline and restraint of Moi.[10]

Diderot, however, avoids presenting a simple answer to the problem of the respective roles of reflection and emotion in artistic creativity. Throughout the play, the confrontation between the opposites of Lui and Moi serves to sustain a sense of the complexity and richness not only of the nature of art, but of morality, and of human nature itself.[11]

The interaction between Lui and Moi epitomizes this complexity. What is striking almost immediately is that despite Lui's parasitic life-style and his unrepentant attitude, he is not completely repellent to the highly moral Moi. A number of Diderot scholars have observed Moi's empathy or close feelings toward Lui. Sharon L. Kabelac, for example, notes that 'We see *Lui* as an "open-ended" character about whom Diderot can make no definitive judgement ...'.[12] The empathy, furthermore, is more than simply the attraction between opposites. Otis Fellows observes that Lui and Moi show an essential agreement on the crucial theme of talent or genius, which holds an important position in the play—with significant implications, once again, for music as well. And the very fact of agreement, despite their basic differences, adds greater weight to the content of their discussions on this subject. It is well worth citing the specific agreements that Fellows discerningly draws from their naturalistic and often rambling conversation:[13] (a) most significantly, they agree that genius is inborn and that there is a primordial role for nature in fashioning a man of genius; (b) a close

---

[10] Fellows notes that the idea of Moi as dispassionate observer, while already an important idea in *Le Neveu*, has artistic consequences that are more clearly spelled out in later works by Diderot—in the *Essai sur la peinture* of 1765, and above all in the *Paradoxe sur le comédien* of 1769 (Fellows, 'The Theme of Genius', 178). Gay concurs, but makes the additional point that 'he retreated neither from his affection for spontaneity and imagination nor from his admiration for the genius who is sublimely indifferent to rules, but came to see that feelings must be subjected to the control of reason and acquired new respect for the technical mastery of the craftsman' (Gay, *The Enlightenment*, ii. 282).

[11] Fellows notes that the dialogue was a preferred literary form in many of Diderot's major works because it provided him with the opportunity to present two sides of a problem—to hold it 'in the light and turn it around slowly before concluding with a conception which is not simple, which he does not wish to be homogeneous, and the synthesis of which he often leaves to the reader' (Fellows, 'Theme of Genius', 185–6.)

[12] Sharon L. Kabelac, 'Irony as a Metaphysics in *Le Neveu de Rameau*', *Diderot Studies*, 14 (1971), 99. Kabelac explains that Moi is empathetic and tolerant because he is attracted to Lui's originality and willingness to disregard conventions. In Moi, however, 'the excesses which Lui succumbs to are contained without being submerged'. Kabelac adds that Moi's situation or condition is also incongruous: 'He is a man of regular habits, but his ideas are promiscuous. One area of stability permits variety in another ...' (ibid. 100).

[13] The summary is based on Fellows, 'Theme of Genius', 188–92. Fellows observes that the theme of talent and genius as presented in *Le Neveu* has received scant attention from scholars, even among those concerned with the theme of genius in other of Diderot's works, or among those focusing on the many themes in *Le Neveu* (ibid. 171–2).

corollary is that the nephew's failure is due to neuro-biological factors—his extreme emotional mobility, for example; (c) they agree that genius—although a product of nature—is a rare product, 'a monstrous form of human species, differing in kind from the normal, and thus an anomaly and a deviant in time'; (d) genius, although inborn, exists within society and is affected by that society. The nephew, for example, has fallen victim to a corrupting Parisian social milieu. A true genius, perhaps, would not have succumbed to 'society's conspiracy against the truly great man', but nevertheless he is a concrete person, subject to everyday needs and circumstances that are not always within his control.[14]

Because of these crucial agreements, Fellows rejects the view of many scholars who see in their opposition a series of insoluble dilemmas, possibly representing two irreconcilable aspects of Diderot himself. Fellows emphasizes instead the close relationship between the seeming opposites of the emotive and the reflective: 'In Diderot's personality there are in evidence two elements, one of which derives from the other, and which, in some measure, explain the seeming contradictions ...' More specifically, he sees Diderot's 'excessive sensibility' as the source of his intellectual 'insatiable curiousity ... which drives him to ponder on Nature ...'[15]

In Diderot's treatment of the theme of talent and genius in *Le Neveu*, as well as in other works, he provides a whole new concept of genius that differs from the prevailing view of his time. Herbert Dieckmann explains the change and emphasizes Diderot's unique contribution: 'The transition from the conception of genius as mere talent to the conception of *the* genius as an individual was accomplished through a specific act of thought. ... Diderot accomplished this act of thought and thereby became conscious of the problem of "the genius" as a type of person.'[16] Dieckmann sees this change against a larger philosophical background of transition that we have already traced in Chapter 2—the

---

[14] Elsewhere, Fellows also notes that Diderot's treatment of the theme of talent or genius allows us to 'see and to some extent to understand why the nephew, though gifted with unusual power of expression, is unable to embody his musical talents in a form that has either permanence or validity' (Fellows, *Diderot*, 90).

[15] Fellows, 'Theme of Genius', 169. Kabelac also concludes that their differences do not end in a stalemate. She finds that Lui and Moi agree on the cause of Lui's failure—once again, it is because he lacks the stability that Moi has. While this comes close to a judgement against Lui, Kabelac softens this conclusion, emphasizing that man and nature are in a constant state of flux: '*Lui* is his demonstration that we can not discern the reality of a man (and thereby judge him); but *Moi* is his pragmatic acknowledgment that we do and we must ...' (Kabelac, 'Irony as a Metaphysics', 108–9).

[16] Herbert Dieckmann, 'Diderot's Conception of Genius', *Journal of the History of Ideas*, 2, no.2 (1941), 152. Wilson takes a similar view and describes the older concept of genius 'as simply talent carried to a higher exponential power', while for Diderot genius is 'a gift of nature different from talent not in degree but in kind' (Wilson, *Diderot*, 420).

transition from the absolute rule of reason, or Cartesianism, to the growing recognition of emotion and sensibility. With this expansion, the operations of genius acquired greater breadth. Dieckmann explains that Diderot's new concept of genius 'presupposes that the influence of the emotional faculties upon the mind is not only admitted or acknowledged, but recognized as leading to a higher level of cognition'.[17]

Turning now to the more specifically musical ideas in *Le Neveu*, we find that the play's reassertion of reflective values does not mean a rejection of powerful expression in music. Nor does it mean a return to Diderot's earlier support for the rationalist theory of Rameau. In the play's first reference to the uncle Rameau, Moi attacks him both as theorist and as opera composer. Rameau is described as

that famous musician ... who has written so many unintelligible and apocalyptic truths on the theory of music, which neither he nor anyone else could ever understand, and from whom we have a certain number of operas in which there is harmony, bits of song, disconnected ideas, fracas, lights, triumphs ... and who, after having buried the Florentine [Lully], will be buried by the Italian virtuosos ...[18]

The distance Diderot has travelled from Rameau becomes clear in the play's more prolonged discussion on music, where Diderot closely allies himself with the views of Rousseau, doing so through both Lui and Moi, who are in complete agreement on this subject. Moi, in fact, deliberately turns the conversation in a musical direction as he starts to feel the gap widening between himself and Lui in the moral domain: 'One could see that he had a better grasp of good music than of good morals ... I stayed, with the intent of turning the conversation to some subject that would chase the horror that was filling my soul.'[19] The focus of this musical discussion concerns the nature of musical expression or imitation. And here Diderot goes beyond his earlier efforts to show that music has special expressive powers, and tries to define more precisely what it is that music imitates and how it does so. Moi begins by asking: 'Every imitative art has its model in nature. What is the model for the musician when he composes a melody?'[20]

The response to this question draws very close to the views of Rousseau on musical expression, with melody taking a central role. Like Rousseau's, Diderot's underlying theme is that the model from nature must be the voice of passion, since of all the arts, music is 'the

---

[17] Dieckmann, 'Diderot's Conception of Genius', 175. For Dieckmann, the fact that Diderot was constantly responding to the changing views of his time helps to explain why Diderot seems to have several views on genius rather than a single concept. Dieckmann thus sees Diderot as engaged in a kind of communal process in the formation of ideas, which is a major point in the present study.

[18] *Le Neveu*; Hermann, xii. 73.   [19] Ibid. 156.   [20] Ibid. 157.

most violent'.[21] If the expressive content is energetic and strong, then the expressive means need only be a simple and direct expression of that content. He explains still further the language of passion by using the Rousseauian concept of 'accent'. It refers to the shape or inflections of expressive language—its rises and falls, its pauses, its division into short irregular phrases or single words: 'Passion disposes of prosody almost as it pleases ...'[22] And like Rousseau, Diderot considers this expressive state of language as a form of melody.[23] Diderot's emphasis on 'accent' points to recitative as a major vehicle for musical expression. At the same time, he makes it clear—as does Rousseau—that he is not advocating a slavish subservience of music to text. The accented line, far from being the same as text or libretto, is the natural and direct expression of feeling through the inflected voice. Diderot also includes arias, instrumental accompaniments, and symphonies in the imitative process, assigning them the same model from nature—and once again indicating that music is not completely dependent upon text. To emphasize the common bond between arias and recitatives, he makes the following point: 'There is no beautiful aria from which one could not make a beautiful recitative, and no beautiful recitative from which an able musician could not draw a beautiful aria.'[24] In similar fashion, Diderot reinforces the closeness between the symphony and vocal music by observing that the French fondness for Italian symphonies, in preference to their own, will also have an impact on their taste for vocal music. One cannot act as though 'the symphony is not to melody ... what melody is to actual declamation'.[25] The language of passion thus applies to all imitation in music, regardless of whether or not there is text.

Diderot's concern with natural accent also closely allies him with Rousseau's espousal of Italian music. And like Rousseau, his arguments tend to focus on language, even while recognizing untexted music as part of the imitative process. Using familiar arguments, Diderot views Italian as the language which is best suited for expression and for the derivation of melody. It lends itself to music through its 'roundness, harmony, prosody, ellipses, inversions'. French, on the other hand, is 'rigid, deaf, heavy, weighty, pedantic and monotone'.[26] Unlike Rousseau, however,

---

[21] Ibid. 168.   [22] Ibid. 171.

[23] The declamatory model, or accent of passion, is equated with a *type du chant* (ibid. 158).

[24] Ibid. 159. In his insistence, however, that strong passions need free and natural expression, he is mainly calling for recitative. He notes that arias almost always occur at the conclusion of a scene (ibid. 170).

[25] Ibid. 162. Diderot makes a similar point about the broad applicability of the natural accent for vocal and instrumental music in the 'Salon de 1767', published in Grimm's *Correspondance littéraire*: 'It is the language of nature; it is the model for the musician; it is the true source for the great symphonist.' (Quoted in Daniel Heartz, 'Diderot et Le Théâtre Lyrique', *Revue de musicologie*, 64 (1978), 243.)

[26] Ibid. 163.

Diderot does not preclude the possibility of expressive French music. Instead he makes a plea that the French become more aware of the obstacles of their language and try to overcome them through the direct use of more powerful emotions: 'The more monotone that our language is, the less accent that it has, the greater the need for simple discourses, the common voices of passion.'[27] Diderot's concern is directed at the French librettist: 'They don't know ... what suits the musician. Lyrical poetry has yet to be born.'[28]

Lui cites the music of the composer Duni (a Neopolitan, writing in France) as the model to be emulated by the French. His comic operas combine the operatic attractions of both nations, offering Italian-style arias and ensembles, with French text, plus French dances and popular tunes or *vaudevilles*. Lui predicts that if things continue on their present course, then Italian music will completely replace French music in a bloodless victory: 'The foreign god will humbly place himself on the altar beside the idol of our country; little by little ... the idol will fall.'[29] Duni's Franco-Italian operas in fact had an enormous success and exerted a strong influence on the genre of French comic opera.[30]

For Diderot, this projection of an Italian victory does not seem to yield the same total satisfaction as for Rousseau. Lui admits that not all

[27] *Le Neveu*; Hermann, xii. 170. We saw in the *Lettre sur les sourds* that while Diderot shared Rousseau's view that French was one of the more evolved languages that was far removed from the natural language of feelings and better suited to reason and ideas, he did not draw Rousseau's extreme conclusions about the French language and French music. Indeed, Lui cites a vocal selection by Jean-Philippe Rameau, 'Profonds abymes du Ténare', from the *Opéra-ballet Temple de la gloire*, as being particularly worthy of envy. For the identification of this last work, see Heartz, 'Diderot et Le Théatre Lyrique,' 232–3. (Heartz points out that this piece is sung by the allegorical figure 'Envie', which is a more than fitting choice for the envious nephew.) Heartz also observes that Diderot had a remarkably precise knowledge of the music and musical events of his day, which he incorporated into the play—further enhancing its quality of realism.

[28] *Le Neveu*; Hermann, xii. 168.

[29] Ibid. 163. Diderot's return to the issues of the 'Querelle' in *Le Neveu*, several years after the departure of the Bouffons, has prompted speculation among scholars. Jean-Luc Filoche's explanation invokes Diderot's synthesizing tendencies, which we have also emphasized in the present study. He suggests that far from presenting a mere repetition of 'Querelle' issues, *Le Neveu* transforms them and achieves a new level of synthesis through the use of pantomime and the invention of a new literary form. (Jean-Luc Filoche, '*Le Neveu de Rameau* et la Querelle des Bouffons: un son de cloche inédit', *Diderot Studies*, 21 (1983), 95–109.)

[30] Diderot's preference for the Italian style can also be seen in the large list of other Italian or Italianate opera composers who are praised in the play: Pergolesi, Traetta, Leo, Vinci, Terradoglia, Hasse, Jomelli, Alberti, Galuppi, plus the Italian-style French composers, Philidor and Dauvergne, among others. He also praises the Italian librettist Metastasio and the instrumental composers Locatelli and Tartini. As for Duni, Diderot cites the opera that launched his Parisian success, *Le Peintre amoureux de son model*, which was performed at the fair of Saint Laurent in 1757. Diderot's high praise for the lighter music of Duni has prompted observations by scholars about the incongruity of this choice in relation to Diderot's theoretical concept of powerful and even violent expression as a musical ideal. Daniel Heartz suggests that Diderot's ideal foreshadowed a number of important operatic works that had not yet reached the Parisian opera stage, but would do so in both the near and distant future (Heartz, 'Diderot et Le Théatre Lyrique'—in particular his discussion of Philidor's opera, *Ernelinde, princesse de Norvège*, pp. 244–51).

French music is to be scorned. He admires some passages by Lully (although Lully's librettist Quinault did not understand the new style), and some by Campra, and even singles out the dance music of his despised uncle for praise—'the airs for violin of my uncle, his gavottes, his entrées for soldiers, priests, sacrifices'.[31] Lui goes so far as to express some dismay at these 'cursed bouffons who have rudely given us a kick in the pants'.[32] He cannot help but wonder: 'Isn't it strange, that a foreigner, an Italian, a Duni comes to teach us how to add accent to our music . . .'[33] In the end, however, Lui simply shrugs his shoulders with pity, and suggests that while awaiting the outcome of all the dire projections for French music, 'let us drink a glass'.

After *Le Neveu*, Diderot maintained his belief in the importance of reflection and discipline for the creative artist. In the *Paradoxe sur le comédien*, written in 1773, he elaborates further on the means by which the artist can exercise control. This work focuses on a theory of acting, but includes all the arts in its concept of control.[34]

Going beyond *Le Neveu*, the *Paradoxe* makes explicit what was implied by the artistic failure of the nephew's pantomime—that in order for the actor to create a strong illusion of an emotion, he must be totally free of that emotion himself; otherwise he will give an uneven or unpredictable performance. In this doctrine, there is absolutely no room for sensibility for the actor or artist at work, as the following pronouncement makes clear: 'It is extreme sensibility which makes mediocre actors; it is mediocre sensibility which makes the multitude of bad actors; and it is the absolute absence of sensibility which prepares sublime actors.'[35]

Reflection alone does not hold the answer to controlling sensibility. The artist must be guided by an ideal or internal model that Diderot now considers an essential part of the creative process: 'The actor who performs on the basis of reflection, the study of human nature, the constant imitation of some ideal model, imagination, or memory, will always be consistently perfect.'[36]

With nature no longer the direct model to be imitated, there is an important role for the imagination, whose job it is to form the ideal

---

[31] *Le Neveu*; Hermann, xii. 167. Earlier in the dialogue Lui also praises the overture from Rameau's *Indes galantes* and, as noted, a vocal selection from Rameau's *Temple de la gloire*.

[32] Ibid. 160–1.   [33] Ibid. 171.

[34] *Paradoxe sur le comédien* (1773; Assézat, viii (1875), 361–423. The *Paradoxe* was originally drafted in 1769 as a review for the *Correspondance littéraire* of a pamphlet about the British actor Garrick, whom Diderot knew and greatly admired. Diderot then changed it to its present dialogue form.

[35] Ibid. viii. 370.

[36] Ibid. 365. Wilson observes that the presence of the concept of the *modèle idéal* in the *Paradoxe* links this work to Diderot's 'Salon de 1767', where it is also an important idea (Wilson, *Diderot*, 620).

model. Further light is shed on this process by Margaret Gilman in her study of the role of imagination in Diderot's aesthetics. She emphasizes that imitation is an active process for the artist, and offers the following description of the actions involved: 'In nearly all cases the word *imagination* as used by Diderot denotes the active faculty of combining, as well as recalling, concrete, and above all visual images.'[37] Gilman also emphasizes, as do other scholars, that the ideal model is not a Platonic concept. All the activities in the above description involve the senses and experience. She explains: 'The products of the imagination, though they have no direct models in nature, are composed of elements found in nature.'[38] Peter Gay aptly refers to this combination of the ideal and experience as 'empirical idealism'. He sees the artist as obeying an ideal model 'that he acquires—wrests ... from experience ... fully aware that even when he seems to be imitating nature he is really obeying art, for art and nature are not the same ...'.[39]

Taking these explanations of imitation and applying them to music, we could say that the genius as composer does not imitate the particular cry of passion of an individual, but an ideal model of the cry of passion—an amalgam formed by combining the many cries the composer may have heard or remembered, or in some other way experienced. In this manner, Diderot achieves a balance between a universal and rationalist doctrine of artistic creativity on the one hand, and a purely subjective aesthetics of sensibility on the other.

Scholars tend to agree that Diderot overstates his anti-sensibility position in the *Paradoxe*, and that he is more concerned with controlling the passions than excluding them in the creative process. Peter Gay makes this point by emphasizing Diderot's recognition of his own need for control: 'The creative artist cursed with extreme sensibility, he wrote, evidently and painfully using himself as an example, must make a real effort to dominate that sensibility and master his impulses. The unitarian priest of sensibility had become the trinitarian priest of sensibility, work, and intelligence.'[40] Dieckmann in discussing Diderot's concept of genius gives a similar warning against reading into

[37] Margaret Gilman, 'Imagination and Creation in Diderot', *Diderot Studies*, 2 (1952), 208.

[38] Ibid. 217. Elsewhere Gilman describes the ideal model as deriving from 'the images it has stored up' (p. 211). Yvon Belaval emphasizes empiricism in the concept, and sees an analogy between the formation of the ideal model and the discovery of scientific laws: 'The system of Diderot is an inversion of platonism: The point of departure is not a world of ideas which then descend into a world of the senses; the point of departure is the world of the senses in order to ascend by degrees to a world of ideas ... The artist thus discovers the ideal model by an analogous method ... to that employed by the scientist to discover laws.' (Yvon Belaval, *L'Esthétique sans paradoxe de Diderot* (Paris: Gallimard, 1956), 305.)

[39] Gay, *The Enlightenment*, ii. 285.

[40] Ibid. 282. Wilson makes the further observation that Diderot is unusually polemical and dogmatic in the *Paradoxe*, precisely because he strongly identifies himself with the doctrine that asserted a need for greater control (Wilson, *Diderot*, 626).

the change a complete repudiation of emotions: 'And though Diderot, in his polemic against "sensibilité" turns also against feeling itself, the genius is by no means reduced to rational faculties ... The highest function attributed to reason is to exert a control over the emotional faculties.'[41]

Gilman goes one step further and attempts to resolve the ambiguity over the role of sensibility in the creative process and in the concept of genius by specifying more precisely how Diderot conceives of its role. She explains that in addition to the imagination and its function of forming the ideal model, Diderot also recognizes that there are other faculties and steps involved in the creative process:

The imagination is ... a less comprehensive faculty than it was to be considered in the following century. It is 'la qualité dominante du poète'; it is not yet 'la reine des facultés' ... Diderot saw that the activity, when closely analysed, is rather the collaboration of several faculties, each of which has its special function. Imagination furnishes the model, technique translates it into art, enthusiasm [sensibility] arouses and inspires both. When all three are functioning with the greatest possible intensity, as in the genius, then, and only then, we have true creative activity.[42]

Diderot's position in the *Paradoxe*, then, may be viewed (using Peter Gay's apt description) as an effort 'to check passion without freezing it to death'.[43]

As a conclusion to this study of Diderot's changing aesthetic and scientific views as they apply to music, it is fitting to turn once again to harmony—where we began—and to examine the *Leçons de clavecin et principes d'harmonie, par M. Bemetzrieder*, published in 1771. In this work, Diderot not only continues the attack on Rameau as theorist which he launched in *Le Neveu*, but he proposes an alternative theory that is free of the defects of Rameau's.

Were we to be guided by its title, or by taking Diderot's Preface at face value, we would not include this work in the present discussion, since Diderot goes to great lengths to disclaim any authorship. He assures the reader in the strongest possible terms (too strong perhaps) that his only role in this treatise was to correct the teutonic French of M. Bemetzrieder, the young theorist from Alsace, a friend of Diderot and teacher of harpsichord to Diderot's daughter Angélique:

[41] Dieckmann, 'Diderot's Conception of Genius', 174–5.

[42] Gilman, 'Imagination and Creation in Diderot', 218. Dieckmann makes a similar observation about the combination of faculties in his examination of genius: 'The thought of explaining genius by a combination of different faculties which ordinarily do not work together in one individual ... is one of the most interesting attempts in the eighteenth century to solve the problem of genius.' (Dieckmann, 'Diderot's Conception of Genius', 172.)

[43] Gay, *The Enlightenment*, ii. 286.

There is nothing in this work, but nothing at all which belongs to me, neither for its foundation, its form, its method, its ideas. Everything is by the author, M. Bemetzrieder .... If any badly informed or badly intended people should pierce my heart and do harm to justice by attributing the least part of this work to another [other than Bemetzrieder], I would ... reserve for them the greatest scorn.[44]

Diderot scholars and editors, citing evidence in terms of both form and content, have long since concluded that this work does indeed belong in Diderot's œuvre.[45] Hence its inclusion here. As for the theoretical content, even if the work does contain ideas that originated with Bemetzrieder or were influenced by him (and it may well do so) they in any case have Diderot's strong endorsement.

The *Leçons* is essentially a dramatization of a series of harpsichord lessons. Diderot's skilled use of his favoured dialogue format serves well in this work, both as time-honoured pedagogical device, and as theatrical realism reminiscent of his use of dialogue in *Le Neveu* and other works. The principal characters are actual figures who in real life did have the roles assigned to them in the *Leçons*: the 'Master', Bemetzrieder, the 'Pupil', Diderot's daughter Angélique; and the 'Philosopher', Diderot, who attended his daughter's lessons and provided the following explanation of the origin of the *Leçons* in his report on it for the *Correspondance littéraire* (the full report, called a 'Compte rendu', appeared in the issues of 1 and 15 September 1771): 'As I often attended the lessons, I observed a progression, an order that could not fail to

---

[44] Diderot, *Leçons de clavecin et principes d'harmonie, par M. Bemetzrieder*; ed. Jean Mayer and Jean Citron, intro. Jean Varloot, Hermann, xix. (1983), 57. The late date of the *Leçons* might also preclude it from the present study, since its main objective is to reconstruct the dialogue on music that ended with Rameau's death in 1764. The *Leçons*, however, explicitly presents a harmonic theory that is meant to correct the failures of Rameau's, and in this sense it is very much a part of the dialogue with Rameau.

[45] Scholars have argued for Diderot's authorship of the *Leçons* both in terms of its close relationship to other works by Diderot, and its lack of resemblance to any other works of Bemetzrieder. Paul Henry Lang observes that nowhere in any of Bemetzrieder's other treatises are similar ideas to be found. (Lang, 'Diderot as Musician', 96). Robert Niklaus makes a similar observation, noting that Bemetzrieder's other works are 'in quite another class' (Robert Niklaus, 'Diderot and the *Leçons de clavecin*', in T. E. Lawrenson, F. E. Stucliffe, and G. F. A. Gadoffre (eds.) *Modern Miscellany Presented to Eugene Vinaver* (Manchester: Manchester University Press, 1969), 183.) Béatrice Didier, however, sees more of an affinity between Diderot and Bemetzrieder, especially in the area of pedagogical ideas, even while recognizing the clear sign of Diderot's hand in the dramatization of the lessons. She doubts that we will ever be able to resolve the exact nature of the collaboration between the two. (Béatrice Didier, *La musique des lumières* (Paris: Presses Universitaires de France, 1985), 310–11.) For a study of Bemetzrieder's personality and his relationship with Diderot, see Jean Gribenski, 'A propos des *Leçons de clavecin* (1771): Diderot et Bemetzrieder', *Revue de musicologie*, 66, no. 2 (1980) 127–78. Miscellaneous views on their relationship appear in Alocco-Bianco, *et al.*, *Diderot: Les Beaux-Arts et La Musique, Actes du Colloque International tenu à Aix-en Provence les 14, 15 et 16 Décembre 1984* (Aix-en-Provence: Université de Provence, 1986), 133–304.

reach its goal. I advised M. Bemetzrieder to write down these lessons for my daughter and myself. When they were written, I judged that they could be of general use. They were written in bad germanic French; I translated them into my language with the utmost simplicity and elegance. I preserved the dialogue form that the author had used ...' He then adds a remark that assigns an indeterminate role to Diderot as author, one of many such remarks made by Diderot in connection with this work: 'I hoped that in these dialogues the character of the interlocutors would be preserved.'[46]

The method and theory presented in this work, it should be emphasized, involves an explicit rejection of Rameau's theory, especially his use of mathematics and rational laws. The father explains why he has sought Bemetzrieder as harpsichord teacher for his daughter in the following terms: 'In the past, I tried to learn harmony. I knew Rameau; I went over his works; and I remained convinced that the true elements still remained to be done. These preliminary notions that fill your first lesson are unknown to my daughter ...'[47] The proposed system is a clear pedagogical method for teaching students to accompany and improvise preludes on the harpsichord. Starting with the preliminary elements, it proceeds in an orderly fashion, moving gradually to material of greater complexity, and seeking in this manner to be accessible to people with little or no training, as well as more advanced students. Diderot further emphasizes his result-orientated goals and his scepticism about theories that engage in too much abstract logic in the following comment from his report on the *Leçons* for the *Correspondance littéraire*:

The science of harmony is thus no longer an affair which is a long routine; it is rather a knowledge that one can acquire in a short time and a moderate amount of study and intelligence; it can become a part of education, and every

---

[46] Denis Diderot, 'Compte-rendu sure *Leçons de clavecin*', written for Grimm's *Correspondance littéraire* (1 and 15 Sept. 1771); Hermann, xix. 398. It is precisely this use of a quasi-historical dramatization, with its naturalistic and subtle treatment of dialogue and character, that is cited by scholars as clear evidence of Diderot's authorship. Roger Lewinter considers it an example of Diderot's 'bourgeois or domestic drama'. He calls attention to its realistic domestic setting and the inclusion of small details from Diderot's daily life. (D. Diderot, *Œuvres complètes, Edition chronologique* intro. Roger Lewinter, ix (Paris: Le Club français du livre, 1971), 116.) Even the authorship problem itself, especially the question as to whether or not Bemetzrieder actually contributed to any of the ideas in this work, is cited as typical of Diderot's technique of using historical figures in his works and masking the authorship of his own ideas. Certainly it injects a degree of complexity already familiar to us from *Le Neveu* and other works. As we shall see, the *Leçons* also includes many ideas on music that are unmistakably Diderot's.

[47] Diderot, Hermann, *Leçons*.; 159–60. Diderot's personal contact with the leading composers and theorists of his day was extensive. In addition to his study with Rameau, he cites study under Philidor and Blainville, whom he also includes in his condemnation of theory: 'these able masters have taught me nothing' (Diderot, 'Compte rendu'; Hermann, xix. 397).

child who will have received it for a year or more will be able to boast knowing it as much or more than any virtuoso.[48]

Despite the practical orientation of the method in the *Leçons*, it includes harmonic theory as well as practice (as announced in the title), but takes special care to relegate theory to its proper place. Diderot emphasizes in the Preface, and again in the text, that the Master deliberately refrains from presenting his theoretical speculations during the lessons themselves. Only during an after-dinner walk—to the Etoile—accompanied by father and pupil does the Master offer his theory of harmony. (In the text, Diderot places this presentation as the third and final postlude to the lessons.) 'My daughter remarked [during the after-dinner walk] that in the lessons there were many examples and little theory, and that it was less to principles than to method that she owed her progress. M. Bemetz . . . answered that the art of music had its own [principles] to which one more or less conformed, without knowing it.'[49] Proceeding without explicit theory, the lessons nevertheless emphasize reflective and intelligent playing, and this in turn means a manner of playing in which the student actually experiences the principles of harmony without consciously knowing them. The delay of explicit theory helps to safeguard the primacy of concrete experience.[50]

It is worth examining the theory closely, both because of its relevance to Diderot's changing epistemology, and because it further clarifies his distancing from Rameau.[51] The presentation of the theory begins, interestingly enough, with Rameau's principle of the *corps sonore*. The

---

[48] Diderot, 'Compte rendu'; Hermann xix. 403. According to contemporary testimony, Diderot's daughter was musically gifted, and reached an almost professional level in playing the harpsichord. She was already fairly advanced when she began her study with Bemetzrieder. The British musicologist Charles Burney, who met Diderot on his second trip to Paris in 1770, provides the following informative description of Angélique in his *Journal*: 'He presented me to his daughter, an amiable and pretty young person of seventeen years of age, who is a good harpsichordist and possesses a prodigious collection of the better German composers for this instrument. She played several pieces for me in very different styles; she is mistress in modulations, gifted with a good sense of fingering, but does not rigorously observe the beat.' (Cited in Gribenski, 'Diderot et Bemetzrieder', 137.) We also have ample testimony in Diderot's report for the *Correspondance* of his deep involvement in Angélique's musical training—he procured German harpsichord music of such composers as C. P. E. Bach, J. C. Bach, Eckardt, Schobert, and others, through the services of Grimm or through direct contact with the composers. Diderot himself gave Angélique her very first lessons, then selected her subsequent teachers—including Bemetzrieder, whom Diderot credits with having taught his daughter the 'art of prélude' and a knowledge of 'the science of chords' within eight months of lessons ('Compte rendu'; Hermann, xix. 398.)

[49] *Leçons*; Hermann, xix. 341.

[50] The importance of reflection in the *Leçons* forms a bond with Diderot's *Paradoxe sur le comédien*. For a study which emphasizes this link, see Guy Buchmann, 'Une Œuvre paradoxale de Bemetzrieder', *Diderot, les beaux-arts et la musique*, *Actes du colloque international tenu à Aix-en-Provence, Décembre 1984* (Université de Provence Press: Aix-en-Provence, 1984), 185–209.

[51] Buchmann (ibid.) includes an insightful but brief discussion of the theory, but to date there is no further elaboration elsewhere.

Master quickly credits Rameau, but assures us that there will be little else in common: 'That is Rameau's affair, and not mine.'[52]

Unlike Rameau, the Master uses the principle of the resonating string only to derive the perfect chord or tonic within a key, including its inverted forms as well as its 'natural order'. He does not make it the basis of his entire system. All other pitches within a key—and, indeed, all other harmonic phenomena—are assigned to the realm of art rather than nature. He describes the scale as being 'rigorously divided into two parts; on the one side that which nature has produced; on the other, that which art has imagined in order to make it [nature] valued and desired ...'.[53] Above all, since not all harmony comes from nature, the Master invokes the more flexible notion of music as art to a far greater extent than does Rameau, who attempts to place as many phenomena as possible within his rational system.

Of greatest significance, the Master does not view the principle of the fundamental bass as the determinant of chord progressions. Instead, he builds a system of progressions that is founded on a very broad principle of dissonance resolution, a principle that requires the un-natural to resolve to the natural. Since the members of the tonic harmony are the only products of nature within a key, all other pitches within that key must resolve to the natural pitches. He uses the term *appel* for each non-tonic pitch that 'calls' for resolution; and *appelé* for each member of the tonic harmony that is 'called' to provide resolution: 'I designate in melody and harmony the sounds *ut, mi, sol,* products of the resonating body, as *natural sounds* or *appelés*. I designate ... the sounds *si, ré, fa, la,* inserted between the natural sounds ... as *appels*.'[54] Music is defined as 'the art of shocking the sounds of nature in order to make the return more agreeable'.[55] He adds that the system applies not only to major, but to minor as well, although minor is a mode 'whose origin is not yet well known'.[56]

Diderot's admiration for this system also involves a negative comparison with the principle of the fundamental bass, as indicated in the following remark from his report on the *Leçons*: 'The theory of notes calling for resolution [*la théorie des appels*] satisfies all the phenomena of music; it is thus preferable to the fundamental bass.'[57] In the *Leçons*, the Philosopher acknowledges that his scepticism about the fundamental bass is a reversal of an earlier position, although he claims he always had some reservations: 'I was enchanted with a doctrine supported by a

---

[52] *Leçons*; Hermann, xix. 342. The Philosopher also acknowledges that he once admired Rameau, although he explains that it was mainly for his principle of the resonating body, which provided a solid base 'for an art which up to then had no other guides but routine and genius' (ibid. 378).

[53] Ibid. 366.　　[54] Ibid. 343.　　[55] Ibid. 358.　　[56] Ibid. 343.

[57] Diderot, 'Compte rendu'; Hermann, xix. 405.

natural phenomenon which presented a solid basis to an art which until
then had no guides other than habit or genius. I would have reproached
myself for even the least objection against a method that saved time and
study . . .'[58]

The Master offers still further elaboration of the theory and how
non-tonic pitches are treated. Since the *appels* occur as part of non-
tonic harmonies that must resolve to the tonic harmony, the principle
determines the behaviour of both individual pitches and chords. The
Master tells us it is a theory of melody and harmony in the following
description: 'Melody and harmony constantly offer us nothing but a
succession of more or less long departures, a succession of more or less
harsh little shocks, a repetition of more or less energetic appeals to
nature that we regret leaving, and that we leave only to return with
greater pleasure.'[59] However, despite this recognition of harmony's role
there is in general a greater emphasis on individual pitch resolution.
The Pupil, in fact, gives a warning against over-interpreting the importance of harmony: 'Ah . . . what great folly to pretend along with certain
authors that harmony inspires melody. It is genius, taste, sentiment,
passion, which inspire melody; it is study that makes a good harmon-
ist.'[60]

The importance of pitch resolution can be seen in the fact that non-
tonic pitches require resolution even if they occur in harmonies that are
internally consonant (*consonante en elle-même*)—and the Master cites,
for example, the harmony ACE in the key of C major, which must
resolve by having its non-tonic pitch—A—progress step-wise to a
member of the tonic harmony. The theory also includes harmonies that
are internally dissonant (*dissonante en elle-même*)—the more standard
meaning of dissonance—and these too must resolve according to the
same principle.[61] Resolution in all these cases may be delayed, since a
succession of *appels* can make the return to the tonic an even greater
source of pleasure:

Although each of these harmonies calls for the resonating body and makes
its return desired . . . this does not at all preclude that before this body
appears, there may be several successive sounds that make its return more
urgent.[62]

This interpretation of progression, with its emphasis on voice-
leading and the behaviour of individual pitches rather than chords,
differs dramatically from the system of chord progression as deter-

[58] Diderot, *Leçons*; Hermann, xix. 378.   [59] Ibid. 358.   [60] Ibid. 265–6.
[61] The distinction between the two kinds of dissonances appears in *Leçons*; Hermann, xix. 360.
The resolution of ACE appears on pp. 367–8.
[62] Ibid. 370.

mined by the fundamental bass. As noted, the proposed method, in general, relegates many more musical phenomena to the realm of art rather than nature, leading to a greater concern with individual details. It is precisely this tracking of individual details that is significantly reduced, if not eliminated, through Rameau's principle of the fundamental bass.

Diderot's espousal of a system that focuses on details of voice-leading and avoids a systematic use of general rules or laws is consistent with his growing scepticism about abstraction and his increasing concern with concrete experience. In the following observation, the Master expresses his antipathy to Rameau's rationalist approach: 'What does a good physicist do, when he encounters a phenomenon that contradicts his hypothesis? He renounces it [the hypothesis]. What does a meta-physicist do? He forces, twists the facts so well, that one way or another, he makes them fit his ideas; and that is what Rameau has done.'[63] The Philosopher adds a similar note of disdain for the use of rules or laws in the following comment: 'The imbecility of critics who do not understand the infinite variety of inspiration has restrained art through rules based on a small number of examples.'[64]

Given Diderot's emphasis on concrete experience, as well as his attacks on Rameau, it seems reasonable to ask how well the theory of dissonance resolution actually reflects practice. As it turns out, the results are mixed. On the negative side, the theory includes a number of progressions that are seldom found in eighteenth-century practice. A striking example is the theory's resolution of the non-tonic harmony ACE in the key of C major. The A is considered dissonant in relation to the natural sound G, and must progress to it, producing the unlikely progression of ACE to GCE.[65]

The theory also omits significant features found in tonal practice. For example, it gives little or no recognition to the distinctive roles of the dominant and sub-dominant, respectively, among the non-tonic chords within a key. Both these harmonies exist within the proposed system, but their prominence in actual practice over the other non-

---

[63] Ibid. 378. We have already noted that the proposed system relegates more musical phenomena to art rather than nature, and consciously seeks to avoid rationalist arguments and universal laws. However, the proposed theory still shows a use of nature that is not that sharply different from Rameau's. It assumes that the principle of resolving dissonances back to the natural harmony is universal. The action of the resonating string is assumed to have an automatic and even mechanical response, despite Diderot's shift to the biological sciences. In the proposed theory, there are no alternatives for the musician but to have melodies and harmonies return to the natural harmony; there are no alternatives for the listener, but to desire this goal. For a discussion of the role of nature in Diderot's musical thought, see Paul Chanier, 'L'Opposition majeur-mineur, est-elle dans la nature? (Physique, métaphysique et musique)', *Diderot, les beaux-arts et la musique*, 159–75.

[64] *Leçons*; Hermann, xix. 374.   [65] Ibid. 367–8.

tonic harmonies (especially the unique manner in which each progresses to the tonic and helps to define the tonic) becomes somewhat
lost in a system that views the tonic as the most natural resolution for all
non-tonic harmonies.[66]

The system's lack of recognition of fundamental bass progression by
fifths also fails to reflect common tonal practice.[67] And while its allow-
ance of delayed resolution to the tonic, which also allows progression by
fifths, does bring it closer to practice, nevertheless a theory that is more
accurate in the relaxation of its principle than in the application of it is
questionable at best in its claim to provide a comprehensive explanation
of practice.[68]

On the positive side, there are benefits to the system's avoidance of
deriving all harmonic principles from the single principle of the fundamental bass. By assigning more musical phenomena to the realm of
art, rather than nature, and by emphasizing voice-leading as well as
harmony, the system retains greater flexibility in its interpretations—
especially those concerning the use of dissonance. The suspension, for
example, is not forced to fit into a rigid harmonic model of chordal
construction by thirds from the bass, as it is in Rameau's system.
Bemetzrieder specifically recognizes a special kind of dissonance,
called the 'irregular dissonance', which occurs within harmonies that
cannot be reduced to 'the natural order'. The Master cites the 'harmonies' CFG or CDG, noting that the 'irregular dissonance' is best

---

[66] In Bemetzrieder's system, for example, the dominant GBDF in the key of C major would
resolve to the tonic CEG—just as in Rameau's system. However, the Master explicitly rejects an
interpretation that this is a fundamental bass progression from the dominant to the tonic (ibid.
377). In his system, this harmony would resolve to the tonic for the same reason as all other chords,
so that the non-tonic pitches BDF could resolve to the tonic pitches CEG. The dominant pitch G
in Bemetzrieder's system would be the one pitch that would not progress at all, whereas in
Rameau's system, it is the G as fundamental bass that progresses by fifth to the tonic, carrying the
other members of the dominant harmony along with it.

[67] Interestingly enough, the proposed system does recognize chord progression by fifths and the
closeness between the tonic and its fifths above and below, but only as recommended progressions
for moving from one key to another. Even these recommendations are based primarily on the
principle of moving to keys that are closest in terms of the number of sharps or flats in common.
For the discussion of recommended modulations, see ibid. 343–53.

[68] It should be noted that the principle in this system that all non-tonic harmonies should
resolve to the tonic is in fact not completely alien to Rameau's system. He too would subscribe to
the principle that the tonic is the only point of repose. It is the path to repose that differs in the two
systems. In Rameau's system, only the dominant and the sub-dominant progress to the tonic—
thereby performing the important role in actual practice of helping to define the tonic. The other
non-tonic harmonies in Rameau's system resolve in progressions of the fundamental bass by fifths.
An equally important difference is that in Rameau's system, non-tonic harmonies cannot be
internally consonant. They must carry a dissonance (normally a dissonant seventh) even if the
dissonance is only implied. Interestingly enough, non-tonic harmonies are dissonant in both
systems (although they resolve differently), and the tonic is the only internally consonant chord in
a key. For a more detailed discussion of Rameau's chordal syntax and the unique role of each
chord within a key, see Ch. 4 above, and also my article, 'Rameau's Views on Modulation'.

tolerated when it is built on the tonic. He adds that this is particularly the case because these structures often arise as the result of suspensions.[69]

All in all, it would appear that Rameau's theory, despite his rationalist framework and increasing metaphysical claims, is more successful in explaining the most crucial elements of tonal practice than is the alternative system proposed by Diderot. Rameau's success, as we observed in Chapter 4, stems from the fact that despite his many Cartesian arguments his theory is firmly grounded in experience. Rameau was more empirical than his rhetoric might lead others to believe.

In addition to Diderot's presentation of a new method and theory in the *Leçons*, he also interpolates into the dialogue some of his most important ideas about musical aesthetics—ideas that have already become familiar to us through his other works. In the *Leçons* he lends them an air of greater independence and objectivity by having them come, to a considerable extent, from the mouth of the Master rather than the Philosopher.

One of the most important ideas has to do with the less precise nature of imitation in music and the importance of the perception of the individual. Here it comes in the middle of a discussion of the potential richness of harmony, a theme which is important throughout the treatise. Bemetzrieder claims that a genius fully exploits all possible harmonies within a key, and all possible modulations to other keys—including all the major and minor keys, and all the sharp and flat keys, regardless of their distance from the original tonic.[70] Explaining still further how the soul is addressed in music, the Master emphasizes that music's indeterminate quality is an important part of its richness, allowing room for the individual imagination:

I cannot say that the image which is offered to my spirit will be the only one that can be attained by the same harmonic progression ... Such is the privilege and the richness of the indeterminate and vague expression of our art that each person disposes of our melodies according to the present state of his soul; and it

---

[69] Diderot, *Leçons*; Hermann xix. 382. Rameau, on the other hand, assigns the suspension to a 'chord by supposition'—a chord in which chordal construction by thirds is rigidly maintained. To do so he considers the lowest note or continuo bass as being outside the chord, placed or 'supposed' in a fixed position a third or a fifth beneath the fundamental bass and not participating in the inversions of the chord.

[70] The treatise is forward-looking in its emphasis on harmonic richness. Not only does he show all the modulations of Rameau's system, but also some to more distant keys. For example, the Master illustrates how to modulate from the key of C major to the key of C# major—involving a change in key signature from no sharps to seven sharps—with only three intervening keys. (The path is from C major to A minor; from A minor to its dominant, E major; from E major to C# minor; and from there to C# major; see *Leçons*; Hermann, xix. 350-1.)

is thus that the same cause becomes the source of an infinity of diverse pleasures or pains.[71]

The Philosopher injects something of a warning—also familiar—by saying that the vague expressive powers of music can be elusive, requiring a sensitive listener as well as a genius composer, both of which are rare: 'If excellent music has few composers, it has hardly any true listeners.'[72]

Closely related to the subject of imitation in music is the use of dissonance to enhance expression. The Master presents an analogy between the special role of dissonance in music and its role in the universe: 'It is the pain which makes pleasure more poignant; it is the shadow which makes light more desired; ... the ugliness which makes beauty more brilliant; it is through these oppositions that characteristics become more distinct ...'[73]

Diderot's inclusion of these important ideas on musical expression acquires greater significance if we keep in mind that this is a treatise focusing on practice and on the 'science of harmony'. That he found a way to integrate artistic themes is noteworthy. The form that he utilizes for the treatise, a dialogue set as a bourgeois drama, not only allows for this integration, but also conforms with his own artistic theory of drama.[74] There is a special irony in the fact that a work which contains so much of Diderot's own vision of art and life is one that he attempts so vehemently to attribute to someone else.

Finally, a rather touching observation in the *Leçons* reveals much about Diderot's own affair with music. He presents his vision of the role of music in life as part of the following fatherly advice to Angélique: 'Work, practice; occupy yourself seriously with an art where you are already quite advanced and which will one day become the most powerful consolation for the sorrows that await you; for no one under the heavens is exempt, and it is good to have a sure friend always at one's side.'[75] All

[71] Diderot, *Leçons*, 354.

[72] Ibid. 355. He cites the by-now familiar names of Pergolesi and Philidor as examples of properly gifted composers, adding the new name of Grétry, a popular composer of operas in the 1770s.

[73] Ibid. 196.

[74] The wide range of musical issues treated by Diderot is observed by Béatrice Didier, who also sees in them a wide range of types of discourse: 'Diderot, in order to talk of music, adopted several types of discourse, successively or in parallel—he tried all solutions, and it redounds to his credit that he even considerably extended the realm of possibilities, having truly created a new language.' (*La musique des lumières*, 331.) Didier cites the following types of discourse used by Diderot in his treatment of music: the technical language and style of physics and mathematics—including equations, formulas and theorems; the mixed language of music theory—with music treated as art and as science; the language of pedagogy; of philosophy; of criticism; of correspondence; of literary texts; of dialogues; of plays; of novels—with descriptions of music in the corresponding style for each of these genres. (ibid. 331-55.)

[75] Diderot, *Leçons*; Hermann, xix. 339.

Diderot's efforts to plumb the mysteries of musical expression, of harmony, of acoustics, are much more than a search for knowledge or a satisfaction of curiosity. These are pursuits that affect the very fibre of his being.

The appendix translations for this chapter are selections from the *Leçons de clavecin et principes d'harmonie, par M. Bemetzrieder.*

CONCLUSION

The ease with which Diderot travelled back and forth between the realms of music as art and music as science was by no means true of the other participants in the dialogue. Each, in fact, had a distinctive approach to music's duality, which helped to define the very nature of their musical thought.

D'Alembert was the most insistent that the boundary-line between music as art and as science be strictly observed. Music theory was to be treated with all the scientific rigour that was possible in a physical science. Aesthetic considerations did not lend themselves to this kind of rigour, and fell outside of the realm of theory or science. The inevitable result of d'Alembert's approach was that music theory was a highly limited and narrow subject.

Rameau, on the other hand, allowed music theory to encompass a wide range of issues, so wide in fact that there was little or nothing that was beyond its scope—just a few exceptional instances where he found it necessary to invoke the concepts of art, genius, or taste. The location of a boundary-line between music as art and as science for Rameau was virtually taken off the map; the overlap between the two was nearly complete.

Rousseau, the diametrical opposite of Rameau in almost all his views, created an analogous all-encompassing realm, only for him it was music as art rather than science that prevailed. In either approach, Rameau's or Rousseau's, the issue of the boundary-line lost most of its meaning; music was either art or science.

Looking back on this period from the perspective of our own time, we find many of the same boundary issues still with us today. D'Alembert's insistence on sharp dividing lines and Diderot's resistance to them are both pertinent. (Less so are the positions of either Rameau or Rousseau, since we tend to believe that boundaries do have some meaning.) We are just beginning to re-evaluate the compartmentalization that dominates so much of our musical thought. On the one hand, we feel a sense of methodological security through operating within clear disciplinary boundaries; and on the other, we are becoming increasingly aware of the artificiality of those boundaries and the narrowness imposed on our thinking. We feel a kindred spirit with the concerns of d'Alembert, but are strongly attracted to the freer explorations of Diderot. It is small wonder, then, that the Enlightenment figures never brought the issue of duality to a satisfactory close. The dialogue was destined to continue.

APPENDIX

Translations

We noted in the Introduction that the translations in this volume attempt to recapture the original tenor and tone of the arguments, and so the English follows the original French wording as closely as possible, except when alternative solutions are required in order to provide a clearer reading in English. This has been particularly necessary in the case of Rameau, whose well-known tendencies toward overly long and poorly organized sentences have required modifications in sentence structure and punctuation. Similarly, his almost constant use of emphasis italics has not been preserved. The translations also follow modern capitalization practice, rather than reproducing the frequent capitalizations that appear in the eighteenth-century texts.

The policy of staying close to the original wording, without sacrificing a clear reading in English, requires special treatment for a number of eighteenth-century French terms for which there is no exact equivalent in English, mainly because the meaning of terms has changed over time. In such cases, the translation seeks the closest approximation to the original meaning, guided by the context in which the expression is used, and accompanied by the original expression in square brackets.

Finally, there is the question of how to present a complete sense of the selected arguments, when, in most cases, they have been extracted from works of considerably greater length. We would emphasize once again that the appendix selections are meant to be read in close conjunction with the appropriate chapters in the main body of this volume, and that individual arguments only have their full meaning when viewed within the larger context of the dialogue that has been reconstructed. In addition, we have tried to select passages that form fairly discrete arguments, or even discrete formal subdivisions within the larger texts; and we have nearly always kept these passages intact. Occasionally, for the sake of economy, some sentences within passages have been omitted, but only when the omissions do not compromise the goal of conveying a clear sense of the tone or content of the arguments. Three ellipsis points indicate a brief omission; four ellipsis points on a line alone indicate that the excerpt is from a passage that continues. If whole pages have been omitted, page numbers precede the resumed translation. A solid line centered on the page indicates that a formal sub-division (such as a preface, or a complete dictionary article) is completed. Finally, text footnotes are placed within the text, but are identified as footnotes (FN) and enclosed within square brackets.

APPENDIX TO CHAPTER 2

Jean-Jacques Rousseau
Letter on French Music
Text: Jean-Jacques Rousseau, *Lettre sur la musique française* (Paris: np, 1753); facsimile edition in Launay, i. 767–826.

[*pp. 2–4*] Wouldn't it be appropriate, in order to judge it well, to put French music to the test of reason just this once, and to see if it passes the test.

It is not my intention here to make such a test in great depth. That's not the business of a letter, nor perhaps my affair. I would like simply to establish some principles on the basis of which artists, or rather philosophers, can direct their research, while awaiting better principles. As a wise man once said, it is up to the poet to make poetry, musicians to make music; but it is only the philosopher who can discuss both of them properly.

All music can only consist of three things: melody or song [mélodie ou chant; *Rousseau uses these two terms interchangeably to mean 'melody', hereafter to be translated as such*], harmony or accompaniment, rhythm or metre [mouvement ou mesure; *again, these terms are used almost interchangeably, with 'rhythm' as the closest English approximation in most instances, unless otherwise indicated*]. Although melody derives its principal character from rhythm, since it is generated directly from harmony, and always subjects the accompaniment to its progressions, I will unite these two parts in the same article; then I will speak of rhythm separately.

Since harmony has its principle in nature, it is the same for all nations. If it has some differences, they derive from differences in melody. Thus it is from melody alone that the particular character of a national music can be established. This is all the more the case since the character is primarily determined by language, and melody in turn feels its strongest influence.

. . . .

[*pp. 22–3*] The least experienced among us is content to say that Italian and French music are both good, each in its own way, each suiting its own language. But, aside from the fact that other nations don't agree on this parity, it remains to be seen which of the two languages can accommodate the best kind of music in its own right. This question produces much agitation in France, but nowhere else. It is a question which can only be decided by a perfectly neutral ear, and which consequently becomes more difficult to resolve daily in the only country where it is a problem.

. . . .

[*pp. 34–9*] When we begin to familiarize ourselves with Italian melody, at first we find only its charms and believe it only suitable for expressing agreeable feelings. However, with just a brief examination of its pathetic and tragic character, we are soon surprised by the power to which it lends itself in the hands of composers of great musical compositions. It is with the help of expert modulations, pure and simple harmony, lively and sparkling accompaniments, that these divine melodies ravish the soul, carry the spectator to a state of ecstasy, wrenching cries from him in this state which have never been elicited by our tranquil operas.

How does a musician manage to achieve these great effects? Is it through changes of metre, multiplication of chords, notes, voices? Is it through the piling up of theme upon theme, instrument upon instrument? All that fracas, which is only a poor substitute for genius, stifles melody rather than enlivening it, and deprives it of interest by dividing our attention. No matter what harmonies can be produced by several parts singing together, the melodies will lose their lovely effect when they occur at the same time. All that will remain is a succession of chords which, despite what anyone says, are always empty when not animated by melody. The more that one piles up melodies inappropriately, the less the music will be agreeable and singing, because it is impossible for the ear to follow several melodies at the same time; the effect of one cancels the effect of the other. The result is only confusion and noise. In order for music to arouse our interest and convey the sentiments it wishes to arouse in our soul, all the voices must work together to strengthen the expression of the subject. Harmony should serve only to make it more energetic; the accompaniment should embellish it without overshadowing or disfiguring it; the bass should guide the singer and the listener, in an unobtrusive manner, through a simple and steady pace. In sum, the ensemble as a whole should convey only one melody to the ear, and only one idea to the soul.

It seems to me that unity of melody is an indispensable rule, and equally as important in music as unity of action is in tragedy. They are founded on the same principle, and have the same goal. All the good Italian composers adhere to it so carefully that sometimes it degenerates into affectation. We need only reflect a little upon this, and it becomes obvious that it is from this unity that their music draws its principal effect. This great rule also explains the frequent unison accompaniments that we observe in Italian music. Such accompaniments strengthen the melodic idea, and at the same time produce a sonority which is more gentle, and which is less tiring for the voice. Unisons are not possible in our music, except perhaps in some types of arias expressly chosen and designed for that. They would never be possible as an accompaniment to a French pathetic aria, because there is such a difference between our vocal and instrumental parts, making it impossible to create a single line which would be suitable for both, without sinning against melody and taste. Furthermore, since our rhythm [mesure *is used here, which could as well refer to 'metre'*] is typically vague and indeterminate, especially in slow arias, the instruments and the voice would never be able to proceed simultaneously with enough co-ordination to produce an agreeable effect. Still another benefit which results from unisons is to make the melody more expressive—sometimes with a sudden reinforcement of instruments in a given passage, sometimes with a reduction, sometimes in having them treat the melody in a more salient and energetic fashion than the voice could do. The listener, cleverly deceived, will not attribute this effect to the orchestra, despite its role. This accounts for the perfect correspondence between orchestra and voice, in which admirable traits in one are no more than developments in the other. This accompaniment is so at one with the voice and with the words that often it seems to dictate the gestures and interpretation that the actor should use. An actor unable to play the role on the basis of the words alone will play it very well thanks to the interpretive function of the music.

. . . .

[*pp. 42–6*] Another violation of the unity rule that I have just established, and as problematic as is the multiplication of parts, is the abuse or rather the use of fugues, imitations, double fugues, and other arbitrary and purely conventional techniques. They have almost no merit, other than that of triumph over difficulty, and were invented in the nascent era of the art in order to demonstrate knowledge while waiting for genius to emerge. I am not saying that it is absolutely impossible to preserve unity of melody in a fugue, nor that it cannot be done by leading the attention of the listener with agility from one part to another as the subject moves. However, this work is so painful that hardly anyone succeeds, and so unrewarding that success can hardly compensate for the fatigue of it. Since it mainly results in making noise, which is the case in most of our admired choruses [*Text FN:* the Italians themselves have not completely given up this barbaric prejudice. They still pride themselves in having noisy church music . . . but the great masters only laugh at all this fracas . . . .], it is equally unworthy as an occupation for the man of genius as it is for the attention of the man of taste. In regard to retrograde fugues, double fugues, inverted fugues, ostinato basses, and other difficult foolery that the ear cannot absorb and reason cannot justify, they are evidently the remains of barbarity and bad taste which, like the portals of our Gothic churches, only survive as a testimony of shame for those who had the patience to make them.

There was a time when Italy was barbaric in its music, even after its renaissance in the other arts for which all Europe is indebted. Music, somewhat tardy, had not yet acquired that purity of taste which we admire today. Those who would say that France and Italy at one time had a common music and that their composers were close to one another merely convey an innaccurate picture [*Text FN:* The Abbé Du Bos torments himself to a great extent in order to give credit to the Low Countries for the renewal of music . . .], which reflects the seeds of jealousy and goes hand in hand with inferiority. Lully himself, alarmed by the success of Corelli, hastened to have him chased from France. This was made easier by the fact that Corelli was a great man, and consequently was less of a courtesan than Lully. In those days when music was barely of age, there was a ridiculous emphasis in Italy on harmonic science, those pedantic pretensions of doctrine which are still so dearly cherished in our country. These doctrines give rise to music which we recognize today as being methodical and formal, but without genius, without invention, without taste. It is music which in Paris is called 'written music' *par excellence*, and which in fact is only good to write but not to perform.

. . . .

[*pp. 69–71*] In regard to recitative, which I have yet to discuss, we should know once and for all precisely what it is, in order to judge it; for until now no one, among all those in dispute, has thought to define it. I do not know, Sir, what this word means to you; as for me, I define recitative as a harmonic declamation, that is to say, a declamation in which all the inflections are expressed through harmonic intervals. It follows from this that if each language has its own declamation, than each language must also have its own particular recitative. That doesn't mean that we can't compare one recitative with another, in order to know which is better or which achieves its goals more effectively.

Recitative is necessary in lyrical drama for the following reasons: 1. To link the action and to unify the spectacle. 2. To highlight the arias, whose continuous use would otherwise become unbearable. 3. To express a multitude of things which cannot or should not be expressed through singing and rhythmic music. Spoken dialogue cannot fulfil those needs in a lyrical drama, because the transition from speech to singing and above all from singing to speech would have a harshness which would be difficult for the ear to absorb. It would also form a shocking contrast which would destroy all illusion and consequently all interest. There is a kind of verisimilitude which must be maintained, even at the Opera, by making the discourse so uniform that the whole can be considered at least a hypothetical language. Add to that the fact that the use of chords enhances the vitality of the harmonic declamation. At the same time it compensates advantageously for any unnaturalness in the intonations.

It is evident from these ideas that the best recitative, in no matter what language, as long as it otherwise has the necessary conditions, is that which is closest to speech; if there were one which were thus close, while maintaining the appropriate harmony, then we would have to readily confirm that it had attained all the perfection of which recitative is capable—unless our ear or mind was mistaken.

. . . .

Jean-Philippe Rameau
Observations on our instinct for music

Text: Jean-Philippe Rameau, *Observations sur notre instinct pour la musique* (Paris: Prault Fils, Lambert, Duchesne, 1754); facsimile edition in *CTW* iii. 255–330.

Preface

[*in its entirety; pp. ii–xvi*] In order fully to enjoy the effects of music, we must be in a state of pure abandon; and in order to judge these effects, we must refer to the principle which causes them. This principle is nature itself; it is the source of the sentiment which moves us in all our musical activities. We have received a gift [*from nature*] which is called instinct: let us consult it in our judgements, and see how its mysteries evolve in us before we make pronouncements; and if there are still some men who are so immodest that they dare to decide on their own authority, we may hope that others won't be so weak as to listen to them.

A person whose mind is preoccupied while listening to music is never free enough to judge it. For example, if in his opinion he finds that the essential beauty of this art lies in the changes from low to high, from soft to loud, from fast to slow, which are the means for varying non-harmonic sounds [*the term* bruit *is used here, but 'noise' does not convey Rameau's distinction between harmonic and non-harmonic sounds*], he will judge everything by these criteria without reflecting on their weakness or how little merit there is in using them, and he will fail to notice that they are distinguished from harmony, which is the unique basis of music and the principle of its greatest effects.

A truly sensitive soul cannot judge otherwise. It won't be absolutely satisfied unless it is pierced by the force of expression, or by those vivid images of which harmony alone is capable. Not that such a soul is unable to give itself to all that might amuse it; but rather, that it appreciates things in proportion to the effects which it experiences.

Harmony alone can move the passions. Melody only derives its force from this source, from which it emanates directly. As for the differences between high and low pitches, etc., which are only superficial modifications of melody, they add almost nothing—as we will demonstrate with some striking examples during the course of this work. We will show that the principle is verified by our instinct, and this instinct by its principle. In this fashion the cause is verified by the effect that we experience, and this effect by its cause.

If the imitation of noises and movements is used less in our music than in the Italian, that is because the main object of our's is feeling, which has no fixed movements, and which consequently cannot be reflected by a regular rhythm [mesure régulière *is used here, and it could refer to 'regular metre'*], without losing that naturalness which is its charm. The expression of physical things resides in metre and rhythm [la mesure & le mouvement]; the pathetic, on the other hand, is expressed through harmony and through inflections. All this should be weighed before deciding which element is of primary importance.

Since sentiment is almost never the object of the comic genre, it is consequently the sole genre which lends itself to that regular rhythmic phrasing [ces mouvemens cadencés] for which Italian music has been praised. At the same time, it has gone unnoticed that our musicians have employed it quite successfully in the small number of cases where it was tried, and in which the delicateness of French taste would allow the risk of using it. We have shown in such pieces how easy it was for us to excel in this genre. [*Text FN: Les Troqueurs* presented at the last Fair of S. Laurent and S. Germain, and *La Coquette trompée* presented at Fontainbleau in 1753.]

This small work can be regarded as the result of all the others which I have presented on the same subject, and I hope that I will be pardoned some repetitions necessary for the comprehension of new material. If my discussion is a little too extended on certain items which perhaps won't be of equal interest to all readers, at least some experts may be able to recognize their own mistakes.

While I was working on this treatise, which originally was intended to deal only with our instinct for music and its principle, several works appeared on the theory of art. [*Text FN:* Perhaps these authors will be grateful if I refrain from naming them.] I believed that the best way to respond to these theories was to present my original ideas, so that each person might not only judge them for himself, but could also comprehend the different effects of harmony, all without straining either mind or memory.

To achieve an understanding of material which may have appeared incomprehensible until now is simply a matter of focusing solely on the products of a sounding body. These products can be divided into two genres, based on the order in which their sounds are generated—an order which is distinguished in its own way by two very significant elements of the art; that is, the dominant, which is a fifth above, and the sub-dominant, which is a fifth below [*the principal sound*]. The former indicates that the voice must rise, the latter that it must descend; the former is always accompanied by a new sharp or natural sign, the latter by a new flat. The former generally partakes in energy and joy, the latter in weakness, gentleness, tenderness, sadness. The one and the other ultimately serve as interpreters of expression—as, for example, when we cite the sharp or the natural as a sign of force, of vigour, and indicate that the voice should ascend, and when the voice descends, and we cite the flat as a sign of softness or weakness, all in such a way that the whole, when considered with just a little reflection, can be reduced to the greatest simplicity.

The examples contained in my *Observations* confirm the truth of the precepts which I give to arrive at a knowledge of causes, and go so far as to justify this nation's taste and the musical compositions that we favour.

In order to give these precepts their necessary strength, it was necessary to present a proof of instinct through its principle, and of this principle through that same instinct. Both are the works of nature: let us not abandon her, the mother of the arts and sciences. We must examine her well, and henceforth try to be led by her alone.

The principle in question not only applies to all the tasteful arts—as has already been confirmed in the *Treatise of essential beauty in the arts, applied principally to architecture* [*Text FN:* by M. Briseux]—it also applies to all the sciences involving calculations. We cannot deny this without denying that all these sciences are founded on the proportions and progressions which nature indicates to us through the phenomenon of the sounding body. The evidence is so pronounced that it is impossible to deny it. How could we deny it! If there were no proportions, there would be no geometry.

All other hypotheses or arbitrary systems must fade beside such a principle. No other can claim to be as illuminating. If we already find therein the germ of all the elements of geometry, of all the rules of music and of architecture, how much more would we rightfully expect by founding it more scrupulously on this principle?

[*pp. 1–12*] Music is natural to us; the agreeable feeling which we feel through it is due purely to instinct. This same instinct can affect us through several other sources which are related to music. That is why people who cultivate the arts and sciences should not be indifferent to knowing the principle behind instinct.

This principle is now known: it exists, as we must acknowledge, in the harmony which results from the resonance of all sounding bodies, such as the sound of our voice, a string, a pipe, a bell, etc. To be further convinced, we need only examine for ourselves all the ways in which we make music.

For example, a man without musical experience, as well as one who is more experienced, will ordinarily, in improvising, place the first note that he sings in the middle of his vocal range, and then always ascend, even though his vocal range is almost equal below and above the first sound. And this conforms completely with the resonance of the sounding body, where all sounds that emanate from it are above that of the totality that we think we are hearing alone.

In another instance, no matter how little experience we have, we hardly fail, when we make a prelude of our own, always in ascending, to then play the perfect chord, composed of the harmony of the sounding body, whose genre, which is major, is always preferred to minor, unless the latter is suggested by some reminiscences.

If we ordinarily play a third first in a perfect chord, in ascending order, even though the sounding body only produces that interval two octaves higher—making it the interval of a seventeenth, and that is above the octave of the fifth, which is the twelfth—that is because the ear appreciates intervals more promptly, and the voice produces them more readily, when we naturally reduce them to their smallest degrees. [*Text FN:* See my response to M. Euler on the identity of octaves, p. 13.] This would not be true, however, for someone without experience, who would never have heard music, or who would never have listened to it, for there is a difference between hearing and listening. If such a person hears a low pitch which is clear and distinct, and then promptly lets his voice go where it wishes—purely mechanically, without any premeditated destination—he would certainly sound the fifth first, in preference to all other intervals. This is according to an experiment which we have made several times. [*Text FN:* R. P. Castel has discussed this experiment in the *Journal de Trévoux.*]

We well know that the fifth is the most perfect of all the consonances. The rest of these observations will only serve to confirm it.

The smaller natural degrees, which are called diatonic degrees, and which are in the scale of *ut re mi fa*, etc., are only suggested by the consonances to which they move, and that the successive intervals form. It is the consonances which always present themselves first to any person without experience. After that, if we wish to follow the order of these smaller degrees, without any preconditions, we will always ascend by a whole step and descend by a half-step, especially if we wish to return to the original pitch on which we began. For example, let us call the original pitch *ut*, which represents a sounding body; and call the fifth *sol*, which resonates with the original. If we wish to depart immediately and move from *ut* to the next degree, then *sol* would become a new sounding body with all its harmony—consisting of its major third *si* and its fifth *re*. That in turn would force us to ascend by a tone from *ut* to *re*, and to descend by a semi-tone from *ut* to *si*. [*Text FN:* We will say fifth instead of twelfth, and third instead of seventeenth, because of octave equivalence.]

Furthermore, following this first rising whole step, we will naturally be carried to sound another. A half-step would only present itself through reminiscence, since two whole steps form a major third which resonates in the sounding body, while a whole step and a half-step form only a minor third which doesn't resonate in it. After the two whole steps, we will feel ourselves forced to sound a half-step, which would bring us to the interval of a fourth. A third whole step in this case would give a dissonance. It is precisely for this reason that it has become a matter of common knowledge, because it is something that we feel, that three consecutive whole tones are not natural. After this last half-step, another one would never present itself again; a whole step would prevail in everyone's ears, in order to arrive at the consonance of a fifth.

Such is the power of consonances on the ear, which is only preoccupied, as it happens, with the degrees which form consonances or which lead to consonances. These consonances in turn are the product of the resonance of a sounding body. We have no choice but to recognize that the principle which has been demonstrated applies to all those faculties which we consider natural to us.

Furthermore, no matter how little experience we have, we can identify by ourselves the fundamental bass of every cadence in a melody, according to the explanation given in *Nouveau système,* page 54. This proves still further the power of the principle in everything that it produces, since in this case the progression of its products recalls to the ear that of the principle which determined it, and consequently suggested it to the composer.

This last experiment, as well as the preceding ones, where instinct alone comes into play, proves fully that melody has no other principle than the harmony produced by the sounding body. The ear is so preoccupied with this principle without our realizing it, that it alone suffices for enabling us to identify immediately the harmonic foundation on which a given melody depends. This is true not only of the present author who conceived of it, but even of people with only moderate experience. Also, we find a number of musicians who can accompany by ear a melody which they hear for the first time.

Furthermore, what is the driving force behind those preludes or delightful capriccios which are performed as quickly as they are imagined, especially on the organ? The fingers, in a state of readiness to obey instantaneously the imagination guided by ear, would move in vain through every possible melody, if the guide were not of the simplest order.

This guidance of the ear is none other than the harmony of a sounding body. As soon as it is struck it activates all those pitches which can follow this harmony, or lead to it. That means the fifth for the less experienced, and also the third for those whose experience has led them to make the greatest progress.

. . . .

[*pp. 16–17*] Instead of consulting nature about music, the philosophic mind in earlier times turned to geometry, following Pythagoras in that without first examining the basis for his ideas. They attributed speeches and actions to him as they imagined he might have made them. They imagined with him, or according to him, a hypothesis for taking the square of the proportions which he had assigned to pitches, in different orders suggested by experience. Each person said whatever he thought, and everyone was equally in error.

Who is the philosopher or man who would not recognize with a little common sense that the agreeable feeling which he experiences in hearing certain relationships between sounds, is due to nature and pure instinct? And, in that case, who wouldn't benefit from what he could learn from this mother of the sciences and the arts and behave accordingly?

. . . .

[*pp. 21–2*]) In music, the ear obeys only nature; it takes no heed of measures and compasses; instinct alone leads it along. Our modern thinkers were therefore wrong to conclude, based on the falsity of the Pythagorean system, that the ancients did not practice harmony. In this error, we have placed too much confidence in those who have advised us on this subject; and if it were not for the chimeras on music that come forth each day, we would not have missed such a simple and sound reflection. In music, the ear only obeys nature. We repeat it once again, and all the false systems which have been promulgated until now, the false proportions which are found, even in the perfect system [*Text FN: Démonstration* etc., pp. 54–9], have not prevented our musicians from singing with correct intonation, and from practising their art with the highest degree of perfection.

. . . .

[*pp. 43–5*]) If we first see in the resonance of sounding bodies the source of our natural feeling for harmony, we will also see in the sounds that are common to that harmony a series of different fundamental sounds which immediately succeed one another, which is also the source of the succession, called melody, [*that occurs*] in each particular part. Here is the explanation.

When *ut* resonates, the fifth *sol* resonates with *ut*; this *sol* thus is present for us in hearing *ut*. And the moment that our ear fixes on it, this harmony is naturally implied. Accordingly, everything prompts us to progress from *ut* to *sol*, or to one of its harmonic sounds. The return from *sol* to *ut* is quite simple. We feel the implication of the fifth below, just as we feel the fifth above. Thus, in hearing *ut*, we are equally inclined to *fa*, of which it is the fifth. There is a common sound from either side, the fifth above or below. And it is through such means that the ear is guided from one sound to another. Since the resonance of a fundamental sound always includes its harmony, there is a natural freedom of choice among all the harmonic sounds that follow one another from there. It is on the basis of this choice, dictated by good taste, that the most agreeable melody is formed.

. . . .

[*pp. 52–3*] If it were a question here of comparisons, wouldn't we naturally assign to joy that group of offspring produced by the multiples, whose resonance indicates its existence? It is here in fact that the major third, the major mode, the sharps, the ascending melody which grows in strength, and the dominant, a fifth above, find their source. For the opposite reason, wouldn't we assign to regrets, tears, etc. those multiples of which the mournful silence is only awakened at the same divisions as the principal body that makes them vibrate, and which we identify as representing them? Well, it is from this side, accordingly, that the minor third, the minor mode, the flat keys, the melody which becomes weaker in descending, the lower fifth of the sub-dominant, and what's more, the chromatic and enharmonic genres which will be discussed presently.

. . . .

[*p. 58*] When we wish to experience the effect of a melody, we must sustain it with all the harmony which is its source. The cause of the effect lies completely in harmony and not at all in melody which is only a product of harmony: this is a truth that will be recognized in a moment when we discuss the subject of chromatics. Furthermore, it is important to sing the opening measures to a given melody, because it is the impression that we receive from the starting key [mode] that determines the feeling we experience in the key which follows.

. . . .

[*pp. 61–3*] Often we attribute to music that which is only due to words. Or when we wish to lend expression [*to words*], we try to impose forced inflections on them, and that is not the means that enables us to judge them. Instead, we must abandon ourselves to the feeling that this music inspires, without our thinking about it, without thinking at all. This feeling in turn will become the organ of our judgement. As for the reason why this is so, it is there for all the world to know; we have just extracted it from the very heart of nature. We have even proven that instinct reminds us of it at every moment, in our actions, in our words. Now, when reason and feeling are in agreement, there will be no other recourse possible.

. . . .

[*pp. 66–9*] We often hear it said that a piece of music is chromatic—sometimes as a form of criticism, sometimes as praise. Often, however, the real issue is not a matter of chromatics. On the other hand, sometimes we don't suspect the presence of chromatics in music where they exist in abundance. This is so because we still only think of chromatics as being represented by the interval, when in reality the interval is only the accident caused by the products of a fundamental succession, which is the source of the feeling that we experience. Let us examine, for this effect, the rondeau from the monologue 'Tristes apprêts', etc., in the opera *Castor and Pollux.* The feeling of mournful sadness and lament which prevails is completely due to the chromatics provided by the fundamental succession. However, there is not a single chromatic interval in any of the parts. [*Text FN:* The feeling that we experience from the chromatics, which do not formally exist in this monologue, proves the necessity to attach to melody all the harmonic foundations on which it depends . . .] This feeling is not the same as in the preceding chorus where descending chromatic intervals abound, painting a picture of tears and trembling caused by strong regrets.

We cite this use of chromatics—and it also applies to enharmonics—primarily to show that the feeling that we experience from it always relates to sadness, sometimes to weakness, tenderness, and that its source lies in the minor mode [*Text FN: Démonstration,* etc. pp. 28 and 92.], the direction of the multiples as we have already stated—as does the source of enharmonics. This is just one more proof of the influence of the totality of the sounding body. From it we derive the arithmetic proportion which is the basis of the minor mode, and also of the minor third, the sub-dominant, the flat keys—all of which we can't repeat too often. But perhaps we can make a stronger case through examples rather than reasons. That will also give us an opportunity to render the justice that is owed to Lully, and that he was robbed of by a critique that is as ill-founded as it is contradictory to the principles which the author himself has set forth in the *Encyclopédie.* Let us examine what he has to say:

. . . .

[*pp. 104–6*] There is a play of chromatic tones which don't appear in the figures of Lully, but which nevertheless appear to be the basis of the different expressions in the music. We need only accompany it on a harpsichord to become absolutely convinced. No matter what the figure, we must judge it on the basis of the various feelings that the actor and audience experience. The author can only have been guided by the foundations of harmony which we have described.

Isn't it a virtue to be able to conceal art through art itself? Let us assume that his music is only the work of instinct, as it appears to be. His accomplishment is perhaps even greater, since he was able to convey the impetuosity of so many different emotions with such a simple harmonic foundation. But let us not be deceived. In this simplicity there are all the harmonic departures that are required. In truth, they are not the usual harmonic departures which we might imagine, which are always abrupt and harsh, and normally the work of limited talent, which can only be aroused by forcing nature. Instead, these are gentle departures, of which the connection, although agreeable, allows us to feel only the different emotions that they paint. As long as we allow ourselves to be guided by feeling alone, without any outside interference, we will continue to experience in music what we have often felt before.

. . . .

[*p. 110*] Some readers will judge a piece without profound reflection, and be seduced by its style. They will say that a piece is well written and take it as a matter of faith; whether it is true or not is a matter of no importance. Such folly! What we really must look for in music is imagination, genius, discernment, judgement, taste, feeling, and, finally, a good ear. We might also amuse ourselves with the character of the composer, since he automatically expresses himself in his music. However, we should only concern ourselves with the truth.

. . . .

APPENDIX TO CHAPTER 3

Jean-Philippe Rameau
Errors on Music in the Encyclopédie

Text: Jean-Philippe Rameau, *Erreurs sur la musique dans l'Encyclopédie* (Paris: Chez Sebastien Jorry, 1755); facsimile edition in *CTW*, v. 195–262.

[*pp. 16–36. In the midst of Rameau's critique of the* Encyclopédie *article 'Accompagnement', he turns abruptly to Rousseau's* Lettre sur la musique française. *This occurs just at the point where Rameau starts to address the issue of Rousseau's preference for Italian accompaniments and his specific praise for the Italian use of incomplete harmonies.*]

M. Rousseau goes even further in his *Lettre sur la musique française*, pp. 51–6, where he claims to offer as an example of good taste a harmony stripped of all its fullness: this is due quite simply to the ignorance common to all who have only their ear as a guide to accompaniment.

That which presents itself gropingly to the ear, does not present itself in the same way to our judgement, nor to our fingers at the moment of performance, where we do not have time to reflect. In this situation, being unable to perform the [*appropriate*] harmonic foundation instantaneously, we grasp at a few notes from the score, or else we follow the bass line at the octave. This is that so-called 'refinement', this choice so readily practised and conceived, which is common to nearly all accompanists lacking method.

If the choice of intervals and their placement is all that matters, and also making the resonance of some [*intervals*] more pronounced than that of others, then that becomes the principal object of a concert, which alone must occupy the listener. But, in an accompaniment that is not supposed to distract from this principal object, and which is only used at all to represent the sounding body, the choice [*of intervals*] becomes not only useless, but pernicious, especially if it is made to the detriment of the full complement of harmony ordered by nature itself, and confirmed by the given definition. Lacking this complement, the succession is interrupted by the missing elements, so much so that it is precisely in this case that the accompanist may err, since the ear will no longer find in the music that harmonic nourishment which the sounding body's resonance offers it.

With a little reflection, we will see how necessary it is for players to have the fullness of harmony in the accompaniment, to avoid being deceived by the eye or the ear, or by the error of a copyist, or, above all, when they wish to add some tasteful ornamentations to a song. In their score they may see only a single note of a harmony which could have as many as five different notes. No matter how well organized they may be, they will often fall into error, avoiding a very natural modulation, from which the composer has deliberately made a detour in order to create a surprise, unless the accompanist is careful in this uncertain situation to provide the complete harmony, which will contain the very interval that is capable of guiding the ear.

The greatest musicians, that is to say only those who show the greatest talent in their art, at times avoid certain intervals because of a lack of reflection. Italians, for example, for a long time had the affectation of never using an augmented fifth in their harmony, even though it contains the leading tone itself, and consequently the one most capable of guiding the ear on the path of modulations. I don't know whether this is still true. It's apparently on the basis of similar prejudices that the so-called retrenchment [*from full harmonies*] was founded, as well as the imaginary notion of choice that was absolutely contrary to the definition [*of accompaniment*].

Italians have little interest in noise. [*Rameau is quoting here from the* Encylopédie *article on accompaniment; he uses such quotations as subheadings for organising his discussion.*] I recall this statement to call attention to the fact that the word 'noise', all too familiar to the author [*Rousseau*], in the context of harmony, can in fact only be used to refer to a bad harmony. Otherwise, we can only object to the ear of the person using such a label.

When it comes to resolving a musical question, we must consult nature, and not our own opinion.

If the harmony of the accompaniment requires a certain restraint, our only model, in this case, is the sounding body which it represents. The fundamental sound of this sounding body dominates to such an extant over its harmonics that they are barely distinguishable from it. Therefore, we could never overdo the bass notes, nor diminish the force of the members of its harmony. It is for this reason that we not only double the bass note with its octaves, but other instruments also play it along with the harpsichord. As to the chords, if the effect dominates too much, it is the loudness of the instrument that we should diminish, and not that which we erroneously assume to be in the harmony, which one could never truncate without violating the law of nature itself, both in the fullness of harmony which it prescribes to us, and in the most perfect succession which it indicates to us by the fundamental routes which we receive from it.

Self-love is a great seducer, above all when it reinforces our passions, preventing us from imagining that there are limits beyond our own point of view.

If rhythm is natural to all animals, it is also the first effect which strikes us in music. We only notice the relationships between sounds after having heard a piece of music for a certain time. Our sensitivity at first has only melody as its object, and it is only after a certain number of years, according to whether we are more or less well constituted, and whether we listen to music frequently or not, and whether we pay more or less attention to it, that finally harmony begins to gain the upper hand. Now you can tell, following this author's line of reasoning, that he is still sensitive to rhythm alone, since he was able to subscribe to a retrenchment of the parts in chords, which interrupts the succession of these parts, and consequently [*interrupts*] the melody which must emerge from them, above all when there is a dissonance before or after the missing part. It is true that this fault is easily overlooked in the accompaniment. But nothing should be overlooked when we wish to understand an art, where each part of a successive harmony has its natural melody, and where [*the harmony*], in fact, must rule over all else. Furthermore, it [*the rule of harmony*] is generally followed in the most agreeable melodies. [*Text FN:* It is the order of the smallest natural degrees for the voice, called 'diatonic'.]

It is therefore only rhythm which has seduced M. Rousseau, which is to be expected since it is of primary importance in Italian arias. He speaks a great deal on this subject in the *Lettre* which I have already cited, to the point of reproaching our music for not being susceptible to it, when this is only true in recitative, including that of the Italians. And what's more, the rhythm of the poetry makes up for it. This was, on the contrary, the occasion for praise, since the heart's emotions and passions could only be well expressed by altering the rhythm.

A person who needs to be excited and animated by movement, because he is still only sensitive to the difference between high and low, soft and loud, may be forgiven; but a musician, or at least someone claiming to be one, who wishes to dogmatize— — —

It is easy to see, then, that giving his complete attention to rhythm, everything else escapes him. Lacking an ear, he saw the Italians using sometimes more, sometimes less fingers in playing chords, from which he concluded that they did not always complete these chords. Biased in favour of such an accompaniment, he was so impressed by it that he wished to offer it as a model in his *Lettre*, and the better to convince us on this subject, he applies to it that which has no relevance, and that M. Rameau only claimed was applicable to the principal parts of a composition. Here are his actual words in the *Lettre*.

[*Text FN:* Lettre sur la Musique Française, p. 54 to 58.]] *I remember having read in some work by M. Rameau, that each consonance has its own particular character, a way of affecting the soul belonging to it alone; that the effect of the third is not at all the same as that of the fifth etc.* Further along, p. 57. *It is therefore a certain and well-founded principle in nature, that all music whose harmony is scrupulously filled, all accompaniment whose chords are complete, must make a great deal of noise, but have very little expression etc.*

We can only praise the consequences drawn from these principles, except that they do not at all apply to the harpsichord's accompaniment, for which they are invoked. This entire accompaniment represents the sounding body, whose harmony is always complete, and I'm repeating this again, in addition to the other reasons I have offered in favour of this fullness.

Lack of knowledge and an ear thus caused such beautiful principles to be applied so inappropriately to an object which is not at all susceptible to them. In this way, he felt authorized to cite as a perfect insight what was in fact only a manifestation of ignorance, without seeing or feeling that it was derived from an essential error, against melody itself, in favour of which so many beautiful arguments have been imagined.

Let us remember those words cited only a moment ago; *they,* that is to say the Italians, *wish to hear nothing in the accompaniment, in the bass, which can distract the ear from the principal object, and they are of the opinion that attention falters when it is divided.* If this is true, of what use is that notion of choice which was so readily conceived, since we should not focus our attention on it.

To surprise a musical legislator showing an insensitivity to melody, that is to say, to the natural and indispensable progression which the parts of several successive chords must have amongst themselves, is already quite a lot; but what are we to conclude from this surprising contradiction that exists between the entire subject and its definition? Isn't good judgement just as necessary as is the ear?

It's really spiteful for a partisan of melody to come out against the fullness of harmony in general.

Although the effect of the third is different from that of the fifth, that doesn't mean we should eliminate a consonance in favour of the one whose effect must dominate. Most often it is a lack of balance between the voices, between the instruments, which causes the part which should dominate to be overwhelmed by one which should barely be heard, just as with the harmonic tones of the sounding body. Think of the effect produced upon all sensitive souls by 'l'Amour triomphe', in a chorus from *Pigmalion* [*written by Rameau*], where the actor repeats alone those same words on the seventeenth, the double octave of the third, while the fundamental sound is many times multiplied by unisons and octaves, and while the twelfth, the octave of the fifth of this same fundamental sound, is also multiplied, but less so. It is here that harmony triumphs, without help from a melody which has its own effect, nor with any of the accessories which this melody needs in order to be pleasing, that is, rhythm, contrast between high and low, soft and loud, the sound of voice and instrument, the situation and the actor; all of which we often attribute to melody alone. We leave aside harmony, which controls modulation and the intervals proper to a given effect, and whose absolute dominion reigns everywhere, like a mother over her children.

This single example necessarily destroys the beautiful argument used in the *Lettre* to create a chimera, the 'unity of melody', words which are striking to the ear in a discourse, but whose effect has only minimal attraction in music without the help of harmony. Moreover, this word 'unity' doesn't stop each part of a duo, of a trio, of a quartet, from having its own particular melody: what then does it signify? Here, if I'm not mistaken, M. Rousseau counted on his readers' lack of knowledge, and on ears still little versed in the ways of this art. Who, however, would believe that he himself undermines his whole edifice, after having built it to the heavens, by saying, pp. 48–49 of the *Lettre*, *we must keep the harshness of dissonances, sounds that are strong and piercing, the fortissimo of the orchestra, for those moments of disorder and disarray, where the actors seem to forget themselves, and to carry their distraction into the soul of every sensitive spectator, causing him to feel the power of harmony that is seriously arranged.* What power! The truth slips out here, despite one's self: what a confession for an exaggerated partisan of melody! What is left, then, to this melody? The Italians' use of it will soon give us the answer.

. . . .

Jean-Jacques Rousseau
'Opera', from the *Dictionary of Music*

Text: Jean-Jacques Rousseau, 'Opéra' (the article in its entirety), from the *Dictionnaire de musique* (Paris: Duchesne, 1768; facsimile edition, Hildesheim: Olms, 1969).

OPERA. masc. noun. Dramatic and lyrical spectacle which attempts to unite all the charms of the fine arts in the representation of a passionate action in order to excite interest and illusion, with the help of agreeable sensations.

The parts which constitute an opera are: the poem, the music, and the decor. Through poetry, we speak to the mind, through music, to the ear, through painting, to the eyes. These all must unite to move the heart and bring to it the same impression through diverse organs, all at the same time. Of these three parts, my subject only allows me to consider the first and last as they may relate to the second; thus I will pass immediately to that second subject.

The art of agreeably combining sounds can be thought of in two very different ways. Considered as an element of nature, music's effect is limited to the sensation and the pleasure which results from melody, harmony, and rhythm. Ordinarily, church music can be thought of in this way, as can dance airs and songs. But as an essential part of the lyrical stage, whose principal object is imitation, music becomes one of the fine arts, capable of painting all pictures, of arousing all feelings, of struggling with poetry, of giving it a renewed force, of embellishing it with renewed charms, and of triumphing over it by crowning it.

The sounds of the speaking voice, being neither sustained nor harmonic, are inappreciable, and consequently cannot agreeably be allied with those of the singing voice and instruments, at least in our languages, which are too distant from the character of music. We need only hear the passages of the Greeks and their manner of reciting, in order to assume that their language was as melodic [accentuée *is Rousseau's term, which refers to melodic inflections, rather than to what we normally mean by 'accent'*] as the inflections of a discourse delivered in sustained declamation, forming appreciable musical intervals. In this way we could say that their plays were a kind of opera; it is for this same reason that there could be no opera *per se* amongst them.

Considering the difficulty of uniting melody [chant] and discourse in our languages, we can easily appreciate how the intervention of music as an essential part must give the lyrical poem a different character from that of tragedy and comedy [*referring to the spoken genres*], and make of it a third type of drama, which has its own particular rules. These differences, however, can only be determined with a perfect knowledge of the added part, of the means of joining it with speech, and of its natural relations with the human heart. These details are known less by the artist than by the philosopher, and we must leave it to a pen that is capable of explaining all the arts, in order to show to those who declare them [*the details*] to be the principles of their rules, and also to men of taste, the sources of their pleasure.

Limiting myself, then, to a few observations which are more historical than analytical, I will begin by noting that the Greeks did not have in their theatre a lyrical genre like ours, and that what they called by this name did not at all resemble ours. Since their language was highly inflected and their music had little fracas, all their poetry was musical and all their music declamatory. In this way their melody was almost a sustained discourse, and they truly sang their verses, as they announce at the beginning of their poems. The Romans imitated this, and then we did, which resulted in the ridiculous practice of saying 'I am singing', when we are not singing at all. As for what they called the lyrical genre in particular, this was a heroic poetry whose style was pompous and ornamented, and which was accompanied by the lyre or cithara in preference to all other instruments. It is certain that the Greek tragedies were recited in a manner very similar to melody, that they were accompanied by instruments, and that choruses were involved.

But if we claim for all that that these were operas similar to our own, we would have to imagine operas without arias: for it seems to me to be proven that Greek music, including even instrumental music, was actually only a recitative. It is true that this recitative, which combined the charms of musical sounds with all the harmony of poetry and all the force of declamation, must have had much more energy than modern recitative, which can barely manage to use one of these attributes without weakening the others. In our living languages, which reflect, for the most part, the harshness of the climates from which they arose, the application of music to speech is far less natural. An uncertain prosody is poorly suited to the regularity of rhythm; silent syllables, harsh articulations, weak and unvarying sounds, lend themselves with difficulty to melody. A poetry whose rhythm is articulated solely by [une poésie cadencée uniquement par] the number of syllables is set with a harmony that is insensitive to musical rhythm, and it conflicts incessantly with any diversity of expression and feeling. These were the difficulties which it was necessary to overcome or bypass in the invention of the lyrical poem. Through choice of words, phrases, and verses, the creation of an appropriate language was attempted. This language, called lyrical, was rich or poor in proportion to the softness or harshness of the one from which it was drawn.

Having, in a way, prepared speech for music, it was then a question of applying music to speech, and of making it so suitable for the lyrical stage that the whole could be taken for a single and identical idiom. This produced the necessity for always singing in order to appear to be always speaking; the necessity for this grows according to a language's lack of musicality. For the less a language is soft and inflected, the more the alternative passage from speech to song and from song to speech becomes harsh and shocking to the ear. From this came the need to substitute for recited discourse a sung discourse, which could imitate it so closely that it was only the harmony of chords that distinguished it from speech.

This way of combining music and poetry in the theatre, which, in the case of the Greeks, sustained interest and illusion, because it was natural, for the opposite reason, was insufficient in our case when applied to the same goal. When listening to a hypothetical and constrained language, we hardly conceive of what we are being told; with a lot of noise, we are given little emotion: from this arises the necessity of bringing physical pleasure to the rescue of moral pleasure, and of supplementing through the use of harmony the energy of expression. Thus, the less we touch the heart the more we must be able to flatter the ear; we are forced to seek in sensation the pleasure which emotion denies us. This, then, is the origin of arias, of choruses, of the symphony, and of that enchanting melody with which modern music is often embellished to the detriment of poetry, but which repulses the man of taste at the theatre, when one tries to flatter him without moving him.

At the birth of opera, its inventors, wishing to avoid the unnatural quality of uniting music with discourse in the imitation of human life, ventured to transport the stage to the heavens and to hell; and not knowing how to make men talk, they preferred to make the gods and devils sing, rather than heroes and shepherds. Soon magic and the supernatural became the foundations of the lyrical theatre. Content with the enrichment of a new genre, we never even thought of inquiring whether it was for the good that we made this choice. To sustain so great an illusion, it was necessary to exhaust all that human art could imagine that was most seductive in a nation whose prevailing taste for pleasure and the fine arts was enviable. This famous nation, which only retains of its past glory its ideas concerning the fine arts, lavished its taste, its enlightenment, to give to this new spectacle all the splendour it required. Across all of Italy we saw theatres arise that were equal in size to the Palais des Rois, and equal in elegance to the monuments of antiquity with which that country was filled. They invented, to decorate them, the art of perspective and decoration. The artists of each genre let their talents shine to the envy of others. The most ingenious machines, the most daring flights, tempests, thunder, lightning, and all the power of the magic wands, were employed to fascinate our eyes, while multitudes of voices and instruments astonished our ears.

None the less, the action always remained lifeless, and the situations lacked interest. Since there was no plot that couldn't easily be resolved with the help of some god, the spectator, who knew the poet's power, calmly relied on him to take care of his heroes and to save them from the greatest of dangers. Thus the apparatus was immense and produced little effect, because the imitation was always imperfect and crude, and the action which was taken from other than nature was without interest to us; also the senses have difficulty in accepting illusion when the heart is not involved. All in all, it would have been difficult to bore an audience at greater expense.

This spectacle, as imperfect as it was, was long admired by contemporaries, who knew nothing better. They even congratulated themselves on having discovered such a beautiful genre: 'Look at that', they said, 'a new principle joined to those of Aristotle, here we have admiration joined to terror and pity'. They failed to see that this apparent richness was at heart only a sign of sterility, like flowers which cover a field before the harvest. It was because of a lack of knowing how to touch the emotions that they [*the spectacles*] sought to surprise, and this so-called admiration was in effect only a childish astonishment which should have embarrassed them. A false air of magnificence, of celebration, and of enchantment was so imposing for them that they spoke only with enthusiasm and respect of a theatre which deserved no more than boos; they had, with the best faith in the world, as much veneration for the scenery itself as for the chimerical objects which one attempted to represent within it: as if there were more merit in making the king of the gods speak banally than the last of the mortals, and as if Molière's footmen weren't preferable to Prado's heroes.

Although the authors of these first operas had no other goal than to dazzle the eyes and stun the ears, it would have been difficult for the musicians never to be tempted to use their art to bring out the emotions present in the poem. The songs of the nymphs, the hymns of the priests, the cries of the warriors, the infernal roars—all these did not fill the crude dramas so completely that there were not at least some moments of interest and some situations where the spectator would expect to feel some tenderness. Soon one came to feel that, while the language, independently of the musical declamation, was often ill-suited, the choice of rhythm, of harmony and of melodies was not indifferent to the things that were being said, and that consequently the effect of music alone, until then only limited to the senses, could touch the heart. Melody, which was at first separated from poetry only by necessity, took advantage of this independence to give itself absolute and purely musical beauties; harmony, which was discovered and perfected, opened new paths to please and move the listener; and rhythm, freed from the encumbrance of poetic rhythm, also acquired a kind of independent movement [cadence] which it possessed from itself alone.

Music, having thus become a third imitative art, soon had its own language, expression, and tableaux, completely independent of poetry. The symphony itself learned to speak without the aid of words, and there often arose from the orchestra feelings that were no less animated than those from the mouths of the actors. At this time, growing disgusted with all the gaudiness of fairies, the infantile fracas of the machinery, and the fantastic image of things that had never been seen, one sought in the imitation of nature more interesting and truthful tableaux. Until that point, opera had been constituted as best as it could be; for what better use could one make in the theatre of a music that was unable to paint anything, than to use it to represent things that could never exist, and of which no one could possibly be in a position to compare the image to the object? It is impossible to know if we are affected by the depiction of the supernatural in the same way as we would be by its presence. However, since each man is able to judge for himself whether the artist well knows how to make his language speak to the passions, and whether the objects of nature are well imitated, as soon as music had learned to paint and to speak, the charms of feelings replaced the charms of magic wands, and the theatre was purged of mythological jargon, interest was substituted for the supernatural, the machines of the poets and the carpenters were destroyed, and lyrical drama took on a more noble and less gigantic form. All that could move the heart was successfully employed; one no longer needed to impose upon it creatures of reason, or rather, of folly, and the gods were banished from the stage when men were represented there. This more reasonable and regular form is still the most appropriate for illusion. It was felt that the masterpiece stroke of music was to make itself unnoticed, that by provoking disorder and distress in the spectator's soul the music would make it impossible to distinguish the tender and pathetic melodies of a lamenting heroine, and the true accents of grief; and that a furious Achilles would freeze us with terror using the same language that would have shocked us from his mouth at another time.

These observations caused a second reform no less important than the first. It was felt that opera had no need for anything cold and reasoned, nothing that the spectator could listen to calmly enough to reflect on the absurdity of what he was hearing; it was above all this which constituted the essential difference between lyrical drama and simple tragedy. All political deliberations, conspiratorial projects, expositions, recitations, tendentious maxims; in a word, all that spoke to reason alone was banished from the language of the heart, along with the witty phrases, the madrigals, and all that is no more than thoughts. Even the tone of simple *galanterie*, which is at odds with the great passions, was barely admitted in the context of tragic situations, since it almost always ruins the effect: for one never has a stronger impression that the actor is singing than when he is given a song.

The energy of all the emotions, the violence of all the passions are therefore the principal object of the lyrical drama; the illusion, which is its charm, is always destroyed as soon as the author and actor leave the spectator to himself for a moment. Such are the principles upon which modern opera is established. Apostolo-Zeno, the Corneille of Italy; his gentle student, who is that country's Racine, began and perfected this new enterprise. They dared to show the story's hero on a stage which seemed suitable only for the phantoms of a fairy tale. Cyrus, Caesar, even Cato, successfully appeared on the stage, and the spectators who were the most repelled to hear such men sing, soon forgot they were singing, overwhelmed and enraptured by the spirit of a music that was as filled with nobility and dignity as with enthusiasm and fire. We can easily believe that emotions so different from our own must also be expressed in a different tone.

These new poems which genius has created, and which it alone can sustain, readily excluded bad musicians who knew only the mechanics of their art, and who, deprived of the fire of invention and the gift of imitation, created operas as if they were making shoes. As soon as the bacchantes' cries and the sorcerers' conjurations (whose songs were truly only noise) had been banished from the theatre; as soon as one tried to substitute for this barbarous fracas the inflections of anger, pain, threats, tenderness, tears, laments, and all the impulses of a troubled soul, then the Vinci's, the Leo's, the Pergolesi's, forced to give feelings to heroes and a language to the human heart, and disdaining a servile imitation of their predecessors, getting off to a new start, approached it on the wing of genius, and found themselves at their goal almost from their first steps. But one cannot walk along the path of good taste for long without climbing and descending, and perfection is a point where it is difficult to remain for long. After testing and feeling its forces, music, being strong enough to walk alone, begins to disdain the poetry which it must accompany, and believes it would be better for it to draw from itself the beauties which it was sharing with its companion. Music still proposes, it is true, to render the ideas and feelings of the poet; but it takes on, in a certain sense, another language, and, although the object may still be the same, the poet and the musician, too far apart in their work, produce at once two similar but distinct images, which undermine one another. The mind, forced to divide itself, chooses and focuses on one image rather than the other. In this case, the musician, if he is more artful than the poet, effaces the latter and causes him to be forgotten: the actor, seeing that the spectator sacrifices the words for the music, sacrifices in turn the gesture and the theatrical action for the song and the brilliance of the voice; all this causes the play to be forgotten, and changes the spectacle into an actual concert. If, on the other hand, the advantage is with the poet, the music, in turn, will become almost a matter of indifference, and the spectator, fooled by the noise, will be misled into attributing to a bad musician the merit of an excellent poet, and into thinking he is admiring masterpieces of harmony while he is in fact admiring poems that are well composed.

Such are the faults which the absolute perfection of music and its faulty application to language can introduce into operas in proportion to the competition between these two factors. About which it must be noted that the languages most suited to adapting to the laws of rhythm and melody are those where the duplicity of which I just spoke is the least apparent, because if music gives itself only to the ideas of poetry, poetry in turn gives itself to the inflections of melody; and because when music ceases to observe the rhythm, the inflections, and the harmony of the verse, the verse is adapted and follows the movement of the rhythm and the musical inflections. But when the language has neither gentleness nor flexibility, the poetry's harshness prevents it from serving the melody, even the gentleness of the melody prevents it from serving the proper recitation of the verses, and we notice in the forced union of these two arts a perpetual constraint which shocks the ear and destroys both the attraction of the melody and the effect of the declamation. This weakness is without remedy, and to try at any length to apply music to a language which is not musical is to give that language even more harshness than it had to begin with.

Following what I have said to this point, we can see that there is a closer relation between the objective for the eyes or the decoration, and music or the objective for the ears, than was previously apparent between the two senses that seemed to have nothing in common; and in certain regards, opera, constituted as it is, is not an entity as monstrous as it appeared to be. We have seen that, wishing to offer to the eye the interest and movements lacking in music, one had imagined the vulgar attractions of the machines and flights, and that until it was discovered how to move us, one was content to surprise us. It is therefore only natural that music, having become passionate and filled with pathos, would have sent back to the theatres of the Fair [*where comic operas were performed*] these bad supplements which it no longer needed for itself. Then opera, purged of all those supernatural elements which merely debased it, became a spectacle equally touching and majestic, worthy of pleasing people of taste and of arousing the interest of sensitive hearts.

It is certain that one could subtract the pomp of the spectacle to the same extent that one added to the interest of the action; because the more we pay attention to the characters, the less we are occupied by the objects surrounding them. However, it is necessary that the place where the action takes place must be suitable for the actors who are speaking there; and the imitation of nature, often more difficult and always more pleasing than that of imaginary beings, becomes only more interesting as it becomes more believable. A beautiful palace, delightful gardens, mysterious ruins please the eye more than the fantastic image of Tartarus, Olympia, the sun's chariot; these images, moreover, are all the more inferior to those which each person sketches for himself, since with chimerical objects, it costs the mind nothing to go beyond the realm of possibility, and to create models beyond all imitation. From this it follows that the supernatural, which, although out of place in tragedy, is not at all misplaced in the epic poem, where an always industrious and bountiful imagination takes charge, and draws from it a completely different component than the talent of the best machinist in our theatre can, or even the magnificence of the most powerful king would be unable to accomplish.

Music as an imitative art has a still closer relationship with poetry than with painting; the latter is employed in the theatre in such a manner that it is not as likely as poetry to create with music a double representation of the same object, because the one portrays man's feelings, and the other only the image of the place where they are to be found, an image which reinforces the illusion and transports the spectator to any place that the actor is supposed to be. But this movement from one place to another must have rules and limits: it is only permitted if it takes advantage, in this regard, of the agility of the imagination in consultation with the law of verisimilitude, and although the spectator seeks no more than to abandon himself to the fictions from which he derives all his pleasure, one must never abuse his credulity to a point where it is shameful. In a word, one must imagine that one is speaking to sensitive hearts without forgetting that one is speaking to reasonable beings. It's not that I wish to impose on opera that rigorous unity of place that is required in tragedy, which one can hardly obey except at the expense of the action, since one is only correct in this regard by being absurd in a thousand other ways. Moreover, this would eliminate the advantage of changes of scene, which mutually enhance one another: a pernicious uniformity would result in ill-conceived oppositions between the scene which remains unchanged and the situations which change; this would spoil, each for the other, the music's effect along with that of the decor, like presenting voluptuous symphonies amongst boulders, or gay airs in the *Palais des Rois*.

Thus it was right to have allowed changes of scene from act to act, and in order for them to be orderly and admissible, it suffices that one could pass naturally from the place that one is leaving to the place that one is going, in the interval of time which elapses or which the action presupposes between the two acts: in this way, as the unity of time must remain within the span of about twenty-four hours, the unity of place must remain within the space of about a day's travel. Regarding changes of scene which are practised sometimes within a single act, they seem to me equally contrary to both illusion and reason, and should be absolutely banished from the theatre.

That is how the combination of acoustics and perspective can perfect the force of illusion, flatter the senses by diverse but analogous impressions, and carry to the soul a single interest with a double pleasure. It would thus be a great error to think that the law of the theatre has nothing in common with that of music, aside from the general agreement that they draw from the poem. It's up to the imagination of the two artists to determine between them what the poet has left to their discretion, and to be in such agreement on this that the spectator always feels perfect harmony between what he sees and what he hears. We must admit, though, that the musician's task is the greater of the two. The imitation of painting always remains cold, because it lacks that succession of ideas and impressions which fires the soul by degrees, since everything is revealed with the first glance of an eye. The imitative power of this art, though having many apparent objectives, is in effect limited to very weak representations. It is one of the musician's great advantages that he can paint things which we cannot hear, while it is impossible for the painter to paint those things which we cannot see; and the greatest wonder of an art which has no other activity than movements, is to be able to form even the image of repose. Sleep, the night's calm, solitude, and silence itself are among the number of music's tableaux. At times, noise produces the effect of silence, and silence the effect of noise; as when a man falls asleep during an unvaried and monotonous lecture, and wakes up the minute the speaker finishes; there are other effects which are similar. But art has substitutions that are more fertile and even more refined than those; it can excite through one sense emotions that are similar to those that can be aroused through another; and since the relation cannot be perceptible unless the impression is strong, painting, devoid of this force, has difficulty in providing music with the imitations that the latter can draw from it. Even if all of nature were asleep, he who contemplates it is not sleeping, and the musician's art consists of substituting for the imperceptible image of the object, that of the movements which its presence excites in the spectator's soul: he doesn't represent the object directly; but he awakes in our soul the same sentiment that we experience in seeing it.

In this way, while the painter has nothing to draw from the musician's score, a talented musician will never leave the painter's studio without having gained something. Not only will he stir the ocean as he wishes, excite the flames of a fire, make the streams flow, make the rain fall, and swell the torrential downpours; but he will augment the horror of a frightening desert, darken the walls of a subterranean prison, calm the storm, make the air grow quiet, the sky serene, and spread, with the help of the orchestra, a new freshness in the groves.

We have just seen how the union of the three arts which constitute the lyrical stage form amongst themselves a well-united whole. Some have tried to introduce a fourth art therein, of which it remains for me to speak.

All the body's movements, that are ordered according to certain laws in order to have a visual effect through some action, generally go under the name of gestures. Gesture is divided into two sorts, of which one serves as an accompaniment to speech and the other serves as its supplement. The first, natural for any man who speaks, has different adaptations, depending on the persons, the languages, and the characters. The second is the art of speaking to the eyes without the aid of the written word, through movements of the body which have become conventional signs. Since this gesture is more difficult, less natural for us than the use of speech, and which the latter makes unnecessary, it excludes speech and even presupposes its absence; this is what is known as the art of pantomime. If you add to this art a choice of agreeable attitudes and rhythmic movements [mouvements cadencés], you will have what we call dance, which hardly deserves the name of art when it says nothing to our soul.

This stated, it remains to discover if dance, being a language, and consequently being able to be an imitative art, can join the three others in moving the lyrical action forward, or, indeed, if it can interrupt and suspend the action without spoiling the effect and the unity of the piece.

Now, I don't see how this last case can even be a question. Everyone feels that the interest of an action that we are following depends on the continuous and reinforced impression that its representation has upon us; that all objects that suspend or divide our attention are counterforces that destroy interest; that in dividing the spectacle by other spectacles that are foreign to it, we divide the principal subject into independent parts which have nothing in common beyond the general relationship of the subject-matter of which they are composed; and finally that the more the inserted spectacles are agreeable, the greater is the mutilation and deformity of the whole. In such a way that if we imagine an opera that is divided by whatever *divertissements* one can invent, if they let the principal subject be forgotten, the spectator, at the end of each festivity, would find himself as little moved as at the beginning of the piece; and in order to move him again and revive his interest, this process would have to begin all over again. This is why the Italians finally banished from the intermissions [entr'actes] of their opera those comic interludes [intermèdes] which they had formerly inserted; a pleasant type of spectacle, witty and well studied from nature, but so out of place in the middle of a tragic action, that the two plays each weakened the other, and one could never be interesting except at the expense of the other.

It remains to be seen whether, dance being unable to be part of the lyrical genre when it is an alien embellishment, might not be able to enter therein as a constituent part, and to contribute to the action with an art that does not suspend the action. But how to admit at the same time two mutually exclusive languages, and join the art of pantomime to the speech which makes it superfluous? The language of gestures, being the resource of mutes or people who cannot hear, becomes ridiculous amongst those who speak. We never respond to words by prancing about, nor to gestures by discourse; I see no reason why someone who understands the other's language wouldn't respond to him in the same way. Therefore suppress speech if you want to use dance: as soon as you introduce pantomime into opera, you should banish poetry from it; because of all the unities, the most necessary is that of language, and it is absurd and ridiculous to say the same thing to the same person at the same time, both by word and by writing.

The two reasons I have just given are joined in all their strength to banish from lyrical drama the festivities and *divertissements* which not only suspend the action, but either say nothing, or brusquely substitute for the language that has been adopted another that is opposed to it, whose contrast destroys all verisimilitude, weakens interest, and—whether it is part of the principal action, or in an inserted episode—it affronts our reason as well. It would be even worse if these festivities offered the spectator only interludes with no connection to the action, or dances with no purpose, a gothic and barbarous fabric in a genre where everything should be painting and imitation.

We must admit, however, that dance is so advantageously placed in the theatre, that to take it away completely would be to deprive the theatre of one of its greatest charms. Also, although one should never debase a tragic action with interludes and capers, the spectacle could end very nicely if a ballet were given after the opera, as with a short play after a tragedy. In this new spectacle, which is completely separate from the first, one could also choose to use another language; it is another nation which is appearing on stage. The art of pantomime or dance thus becomes the language of convention, and speech in turn must be banished, while music, remaining the means of connection, is applied to dance in the short piece, as it was to poetry in the main piece. But before using this new language, it must be created. To begin by giving action ballets, without having first established conventions governing gestures, would be to speak a language to people who have no dictionary, and who, consequently, would be unable to understand it.

———

APPENDIX TO CHAPTER 4

Jean le Rond d'Alembert
from the *Elements of Theoretical and Practical Music following the
Principles of M. Rameau*
New Edition
Reviewed, corrected and considerably augmented
Preliminary Discourse

Text: Jean le Rond d'Alembert, *Elémens de musique théorique et pratique, suivant
les principes de M. Rameau. Nouvelle Edition, Revue, corrigée, & considerablement
augmentée* (Lyon: Bruyset, 1762), 'Discours préliminaire', pp. i–xxxvi;
facsimile in *CTW* vi. 457–77.

We can consider music, either as an art which has for its object one of the
principal pleasures of the senses, or as a science through which this art is
reduced to its principles. It is the double point of view that I propose to treat in
this work.

There were [*principles*] of music as in all the other arts invented by man.
Chance at first revealed some facts; soon observation and reflection have
revealed some others; and from these different facts, joined and united, the
philosophers have not delayed to form a scientific corpus, which then grew by
degrees.

The first theories of music go back almost to the first known age of philosophy, to the century of Pythagoras; and history leaves us no room to doubt that
since the time of this philosopher, the ancients have strongly cultivated music,
both as art and as science. But there remains much uncertainty as to the degree
of perfection to which they carried it. Almost all the questions that they proposed concerning ancient music have divided scholars, and evidently still
divide them, due to a lack of sufficient and incontestable documents which
would allow us to substitute evidence for suppositions and conjectures ... We
would very much wish that in order to become as enlightened as possible on
this important point in the history of science, that some man of letters, equally
versed in the Greek language and in music, would undertake to reunite and
discuss in a single work the most plausible opinions established or proposed by
scholars on a curious and difficult matter. This analytic history of ancient
music is a work that is missing in our literature.

In awaiting someone sufficiently instructed in this part of the arts and history
to undertake this work, we will take music in the state that it is today; and we
will confine ourselves to exposing in this work the additions that theory has
received in recent times.

Music has two parts, melody and harmony. Melody is the art of making
several sounds succeed one another in an agreeable manner to the ear; harmony is the art of flattering the organ through the union of several sounds that
are heard at the same time. Melody has existed forever; it is not the same for
harmony; we do not know if the ancients used it, and when it began to be used.

It isn't that the ancients did not use in their music some of the simplest and
most perfect chords, such as the octave, the fifth, and the third; but it is

doubtful that they were familiar with others, and if they even drew from the simple chords that they knew the same advantages that experience and combination have drawn since then.

If harmony, such as we practise it, is due to the experiences and reflections of the moderns, it is likely that this art had, like almost all the others, some weak and almost imperceptible beginnings; and then augmented gradually through the successive efforts of several men of genius, it became elevated to the point that we see it ... Thus the arts that we enjoy do not belong for the most part to any man in particular, to any nation exclusively; they belong to all of humanity; they are the fruits of united and continuous reflections of all men, of all nations, of all centuries ....

The first works that we know on the laws of harmony only go back around two centuries; and they were followed by many others. But none of these works were capable of satisfying the mind on the principle of harmony. We were limited almost exclusively to assembling rules, without giving reasons. We had not seen any analogies and common sources. Blind experience was the sole compass for artists.

M. Rameau was the first to begin to unravel this chaos. He found in the resonance of the sounding body the most probable origin of harmony, and of the pleasure that it causes. He developed this principle, and showed how the phenomena of music are born. He has reduced all chords to a small number of simple and fundamental chords, of which the others are only combinations and inversions. He has known at last how to perceive and make us feel the mutual dependence of melody and harmony.

Although these different things are contained in the writings of this famous artist, and can be understood by philosphers versed in the art of music, the musicians who are not philosophers, and the philosophers who are not musicians, have wished for a long time that someone would make them accessible to them. That is the object of the treatise that I present to the public. I first wrote it for the use of some friends. The work having struck them as clear and methodic, they have engaged me to bring it out, persuaded (perhaps too easily) that it would serve to facilitate the study of harmony for beginners. That is the sole motivation that made me decide to publish a book, in which I would not hesitate to take pride, where the foundations are not mine, but for which I have no other credit than to have clarified, developed, and perhaps perfected in certain ways the ideas of others. [*Text FN:* See the letter of M. Rameau on this subject, *Merc. de Mai 1752* ....]

The first edition of this work, published in 1752, having been favourably received by the public, and having been sold out, I have tried to add in this one some new degrees of perfection. The exposé that I am going to do in my work will give to the reader a general idea of the principle of M. Rameau, some consequences that one can draw from it, the manner in which I presented this principle and its consequences; finally that which remains to be done in the theory of the art of music; that which scholars must do in order to perfect this theory; the pitfalls that they must avoid in this research, and which will only result in delaying their progress.

All sounding bodies produce, in addition to the principal sound, the twelfth and the major seventeenth of this sound. This multiple resonance, known for a long time, is the basis of the entire theory of M. Rameau, and the foundation on which he builds his whole musical system. We will see in our *Elémens* how we can draw from this experience, through an easy deduction, the principal points of melody and harmony; the perfect chord—both major and minor; the two tetrachords of ancient music; the formation of our diatonic scale; the difference in value that the same sound can have, depending on the progression that we give to the bass; the alteration that we observe in this scale, and the reason for the ear's total lack of perception of this alteration [*d'Alembert is referring to tuning and temperament*]; the rules of the major mode; the difficulty in striking up three consecutive keys; the reason why two successive perfect chords are forbidden in a diatonic progression; the origin of the minor mode; its subordination to the major and its varieties; the use of dissonance; the cause of the effects produced by the different genres of music—the diatonic, chromatic, and enharmonic; the principle and the laws of temperament. We can only give some indication here of the different subjects; they will be developed in this work with the detail and precision that they require.

We have had as a goal in this treatise, not only to present the researches of M. Rameau in the clearest light, but also to simplify them in certain respects. For example, in addition to the fundamental experience of which we have spoken above, this famous musician, in order to provide an explanation of certain phenomena, employed still another experience; that is, that a sounding body, once struck and set into vibration, forces its lower twelfth and major seventeenth to vibrate and to divide itself. M. Rameau seized mainly on this second experience in order to derive the origin of the minor mode, and to provide a rationale for some other rules of harmony; and we have followed him in this regard in our first edition [*d'Alembert's first edition was based heavily on Rameau's* Génération harmonique, *in which Rameau derived the minor mode, and also the sub-dominant, from assumptions that he made about undertones*]: in this work we have found the means to draw from the first experience all alone the formation of the minor mode, and to isolate moreover this formation from all the questions which are alien to it.

There are also some other points (like the origin of the sub-dominant chord, and the explanation of certain seventh chords) which we believe to have simplified further, and perhaps have extended a little the principles of the famous artist.

We have also banished from this edition, as we have done from the first, all considerations of proportions and geometric, arithmetic, and harmonic progressions, that were sought in the resonance of the sounding body, persuaded as we are that M. Rameau could have dispensed with having any regard for these proportions, the use of which we believe to be completely useless, and even, if we dare say it, completely illusory in the theory of music. Indeed, if the proportions of the octave, the fifth and the third, etc. were completely other than what they are; if we did not observe any progression or any law; if they were incapable of being measured with one another; the resonance of the sounding body, and the multiple sounds that we derive from it, would suffice to found the whole system of harmony.

For the rest, in aiming this work to clarify the theory of music, and to reduce it to a scientific corpus that is more complete and illuminating than we have accomplished until now, we must warn those who will read this treatise not to have any illusions about the nature of our goal, and about that of our work.

We must not seek here that striking evidence, which is characteristic only of works of geometry, and which is encountered so rarely in those where physics is mingled. There always enters into the theory of musical phenomena a kind of metaphysics, that these phenomena implicitly impose, and that lend to it its natural obscurity; we must not expect in this matter that which we call *demonstration*; it is much to have reduced the principal facts in a system that is well linked and orderly, to have deduced them from a single experience, and to have established on this simple foundation the most well-known rules of the art of music. But on the other hand it is unjust to require here that tight and unshakeable persuasion, which is only the product of the most powerful light; at the same time, we doubt that it is possible to bring to these matters a greater light.

We will not at all be surprised after this confession, that among the facts that are deduced from the fundamental experience, there are some which seem to depend immediately on this experience, and others which are deduced in a more distant and less direct manner. In matters of physics, where it is hardly permitted to employ anything but reasoning by analogy and agreement, it is natural that the analogy is sometimes more, sometimes less perceptible: and, we dare to say, it would be the character of a mind that is very unphilosophic, not to be able to recognize and distinguish this gradation and these different nuances ....

Thus, although most of the phenomena of the art of music seem to be deduced in a simple and easy manner from the resonance of the sounding body, we must not perhaps rush further to affirm that this resonance is *demonstrably* the unique principle of harmony. [*Text FN:* The *Demonstration of the principle of harmony* by M. Rameau, did not carry this title in the Memoire that he presented in 1749 to the Academy of Sciences ...] But at the same time we would be no less unjust by rejecting this principle, because certain phenomena do not appear to be derived from it as readily as others do. It is only necessary to conclude, either that we will succeed perhaps through new researches to reduce these phenomena to the principle; or that harmony has perhaps some other unknown, more general principle than that of the resonance of the sounding body, and of which that is only a branch; or finally, that we should not try to reduce all the science of music to a single and same principle—a natural tendency of that impatience so common to philosophers, that makes them partial to the whole, and to judge the entire object by the greatest number of its appearances.

In the sciences that one calls *physico-mathematic* (and the science of sounds can perhaps be counted in this number), there are some which depend on a single experience, a single principle; there are some which necessarily assume several, of which the combination is indispensable in order to form an exact and complete system; and music is perhaps in this last category. That is why, in applauding the efforts and the discoveries of M. Rameau, we must not neglect to urge scholars to perfect them further, in adding to them, if it is possible, the last traits that may be lacking.

Whatever the fruits of their efforts would be, the glory of this learned artist has nothing to fear; he will always have the advantage of having been the first to make music a science worthy of occupying the philosophers; to have simplified and facilitated practice; and to have taught musicians to carry the flame of reason and analogy in this matter.

We invite all the more willingly scholars and artists to follow and perfect the views of their famous precursor, since several of them have already made some laudable and even satisfactory attempts, in certain respects, to throw some new lights on the theory of the art of music. It is in this view that the famous Tartini has given us in 1754 a *Treatise of harmony*, based on a different principle than that of M. Rameau

. . . .

[*D'Alembert's somewhat vague description of Tartini's rival principle is omitted here. It focuses on the acoustical phenomenon of a combination tone that results from the resonance of two different fundamental sounds.*]

Whatever it may be, it is in this experience that M. Tartini tries to find the origin of harmony; but his book is written in such an obscure manner that it is impossible for us to judge it; and we know that famous scientists feel the same way. It would be desirable if the author would engage some man of letters who is well versed in music and the art of writing to develop the ideas that he has not presented clearly, and from which the art [*of music*] can perhaps draw great benefit, if they were presented in a more suitable light. I am all the more persuaded that even if we would not join M. Tartini in regarding the experience in question as the foundation of the art of music, it is nevertheless probable that we could make some strongly advantageous use of it to clarify and facilitate the practice of harmony. [*Text FN:* See in the article FONDAMENTAL in the *Encyclopédie*, vol. 7, p. 63, the views that we have proposed on this subject . . . .]

In urging philosophers and artists to make new efforts to perfect the theory of music, we must warn them at the same time not to misunderstand what the true goal of their researches must be. Experience alone must be the basis; it is uniquely in observing facts, in relating them to one another, in making them depend either on a single fact if possible or at least on a very small number of principal facts, that they will be able to reach the goal that is so desired, of establishing a theory for music that is exact, complete, and illuminating. The philosophers will dispense with the effort of explaining the facts, because they know the limitations of most of these types of explanations. If we want to appreciate how little they are worth, it suffices to glance at the attempts made by very able physicists, to explain, for example, the multiple resonance of the sounding body. After having observed that the total vibration of a musical string is a mixture of several particular vibrations (which is not difficult to conceive), they conclude that the sound produced by the resonating body must be multiple, as indeed it is. But why does the multiple sound appear to contain only three, and why these three preferably to others? They claim that in the air there are some particles that are pitched to different tones, and that these differently activated particles are the cause of the multiple resonance. What do we know of all that? Even assuming the claimed diversity of tension in the particles of air, how does this diversity of tension prevent [*the particles*] from being activated thoroughly indistinctly by the movements of the sounding body? What therefore would be the result for the ear, from a multiple and confused noise, where we could not distinguish any particular sound? [*Text FN:* For greater details on this subject, see in the *Encyclopédie* under FONDA-MENTAL.]

If the musician-philosophers must not waste their time in seeking physical explanations of musical phenomena, explanations that are always vague and insufficient, they must consume themselves even less with efforts to climb to a region that is further from their sights, or to lose themselves in a labyrinth of metaphysical speculations on the causes of the pleasure that harmony makes us experience. In vain will they pile up hypotheses on hypotheses, in order to explain why certain chords please us more than others. In excavating these hypotheses they will soon recognize their weakness. Let us judge this [*the weakness of speculation about musical pleasure*] through the most probable that we have imagined for this effect until now. Some attribute the different degrees of pleasure that chords make us experience to the more or less frequent con-currence of vibrations; others to the greater or less degree of simplicity of the proportion that these vibrations have between them. But why the concurrence of vibrations, that is to say, their same direction, and the property of frequently beginning together, why is this such a great source of pleasure? On what is this gratuitous assumption based? And if we admit it, wouldn't it follow from there that the same chord would make us experience very contradictory sensations successively and rapidly, since the vibrations would be alternatively concur-rent and opposite? On the other hand, how is the simplicity of proportions so perceptible to the ear, when most often these proportions are unknown to those for whom the organ is otherwise most strongly affected by good music? We can conceive without difficulty how the eye judges proportions; but how can the ear judge them? Why furthermore do certain very agreeable chords, such as the fifth, lose almost nothing of their agreeability when they are altered, and conse-quently where the simplicity of their proportion is destroyed; while other chords, also very agreeable, such as the third, become harsher by just a weak alteration; while finally the most perfect and agreeable of all the chords, the octave, cannot withstand even the smallest alteration? Let us confess with good faith our ignorance on the first reasons for all these facts. It is clearly in the metaphysics of hearing, if we can speak of such a thing, as in that of vision, that the philosophers have made so little progress until now, and in all probability will hardly be surpassed by their successors. [*Text FN:* To these reasons one can add still others, that one will find in the article CONSONANCE in the *Ency-clopédie*, where this question has been discussed very well by M. Rousseau.]

Since the theory of music (even for those who wish to limit themselves to it), contains questions on which every wise musician must abstain, there is even greater reason for avoiding rushing beyond the limits of this theory, and to try to find chimeric relationships between music and the other sciences. The odd opinions advanced on this subject by some of the most famous musicians do not deserve to be raised, and should only be regarded as new proof of the traps into which men of genius can fall, when they speak about things where they are ignorant.

. . . .

[*The remainder of the Discourse is mainly an outline of the contents of the work.*]

APPENDIX TO CHAPTER 5

Denis Diderot
from *Conversations on The Natural Son*

Text: Denis Diderot, *Entretiens sur 'Le Fils naturel'* (1757; the three *Entretiens* appear with the play under the overall title *Dorval et Moi*); ed. Jacques Chouillet and Anne-Marie Chouillet, Hermann, x. 83–162.

from the Third Conversation

[*In this passage (Hermann, pp. 155–9) Dorval, a sensitive artistic genius, presents his views on reforming drama, and especially lyrical drama. It follows Dorval's discussion of reforming dance through the use of pantomime, and his scene-by-scene illustration of how to set a pantomime to music, referred to as* pantomime mesurée.]

DORVAL. Well! Do you think that the century just past has left nothing to be done in this one?

There is the domestic and bourgeois tragedy to create.

The serious genre to perfect.

The conditions of human beings to substitute for characters, perhaps in all genres.

Pantomime to be closely linked with the dramatic action.

Having scene changes, and tableaux instead of theatrical gestures. [*Diderot is calling for greater realism than the traditional classical unities and artificial conventions allowed.*] That would provide a new source of invention for the poet, and of study for the actor. For what use is it for the poet to imagine tableaux, if the actor remains attached to his symmetrical positions and his formal action.

To introduce real tragedy in lyrical drama.

Finally to reduce the dance to the form of a true poem, to write and to distinguish it from all other art of imitation.

ME. What tragedy would you like to establish on the lyrical stage?

DORVAL. Ancient.

ME. Why not domestic tragedy?

DORVAL. Because tragedy, and in general all composition destined for the lyrical stage, must be in metre, and it seems to me that domestic tragedy precludes versification.

ME. But do you think that this genre furnishes the musician with all the resources suitable to his art? Each art has its advantages; it seems that [in this regard] they are something like the senses. The senses are not all just a single feeling; all the arts are not just a single imitation. But each sense touches, and each art imitates in a manner that is appropriate to it.

DORVAL. There are two styles in music, the simple, and the ornate [figuré]. What would you say, if I show you, without leaving my dramatic poets, some pieces on which the musician could freely deploy all the energy of the one [*the drama*] or all the richness of the other [*the music*]? When I say *musician*, I mean the man who has the genius of his art; that is different from someone who only knows how to connect modulations and combine notes.

ME. Dorval, one of these pieces, please?

DORVAL. Gladly. They say that even Lully had noted the one that I am going to cite. Which proves perhaps that this artist was only lacking poems from another genre, and that he felt himself to be a genius capable of the greatest things.

Clytemnestre, whose daughter has just been torn from her for sacrifice, sees the knife of the sacrificer raised on her breast, her blood which flows, a priest who consults the gods with palpitating heart. Troubled by these images, she cries:

> Oh wretched mother!
> My daughter crowned with odious garlands,
> Offers her throat to the knives prepared by her father.
> Chalk flows in his blood. Barbarians, stop;
> It is the pure blood of the god who hurls down thunder.
> I hear the thunderbolt roar and feel the earth tremble.
> A vengeful god restrains these blows.

[*Editor's FN: It is thus to Racine that Diderot goes finally to ask for rhythmic models susceptible to rejuvenate opera* (Iphigénie, *act V, scene 4*).]

I do not know, either in Quinault, or in any other poet, any verses that are more lyrical, or any situation more suitable for musical imitation. The condition of Clytemnestre must tear the cry of nature from her entrails; and the musician will carry it to my ears with all its nuances.

If he composes this piece in the simple style, it will be filled with the pain, the despair of Clytemnestre; he will only begin to work when he feels himself gripped by the terrible images that obsess Clytemnestre. [*Diderot at this stage subscribes to the highly emotive view of artistic creation.*] What a beautiful subject, those first lines, for a recitative with orchestral ritornello [récitatif obligé]! How well one can separate the different phrases with a plaintive ritornello! 'Oh heaven! Oh wretched mother!' first occasion for a ritornello. 'My daughter crowned with odious wreathes', second occasion. 'Offers her throat to the knives prepared by her father', third occasion. 'By her father!' fourth occasion. 'Chalk flows in his blood', fifth occasion. What characteristics could one give to this symphony? It seems to me that I hear it. It paints the lament, the grief, the fright, the horror, the fury.

The aria begins with 'Barbarians, stop'. The musician can set this 'Barbarians', this 'stop', in as many ways as he likes; it would show an astonishing sterility, if these words are not an inexhaustible source of melodies.

Lively, 'Barbarians, barbarians, stop, stop; it is the pure blood of the god that hurls down thunder; it is the blood, it is the pure blood of the god that hurls down thunder. This god sees you, hears you, threatens you, barbarians, stop! I hear the thunderbolt roar, I feel the earth tremble, stop. A god, a vengeful god restrains these blows, stop, barbarians. But nothing stops them. Ah my daughter! Ah wretched mother! I see her, I see her blood flow, she dies. Ah, barbarians! Oh Heaven!' What a variety of feelings and images!

If we were to deliver these verses to mademoiselle Dumeni [*Editor's FN: Marie Françoise Marchand, called Dumesnil (1711–1803). She played at the Comédie française from 1735 to 1775. Her first role was Clytemnestre.*]; what turmoil she would unleash, if I am not mistaken; what feelings would follow one another in her soul. That is what her genius would suggest to her, and it is her declamation that the musician must imagine and write. If we were to try an experiment, we would see nature lead the actress and the musician to the same ideas.

But does the musician use the ornate style? Different declamation; different ideas, different melody. He will make the voice perform what another has reserved for instruments. He will make the thunder-bolt roar. He will hurl it down. He will make it fall in bursts. He will show me Clytemnestre frightening the murderers of her daughter, through the image of the god whose blood they are going to spread. He will carry this image to my imagination which is already aroused by the pathos of the poetry and the situation, with as much truth and force as possible. The first [*the simple style*] was completely concerned with the accents of Clytemnestre; the latter [*the ornate style*] is concerned somewhat with her expression. It is no longer the mother of Iphigénie that I hear. It is the thunder-bolt which howls; it is the earth which trembles; it is the air which contains these terrifying noises.

A third [*musician*] will try to unite the advantages of both styles. He will seize the cry of nature, when it is violent and inarticulate, and he will make it the basis of his melody. It is on the tones of this melody that he will make the thunder-bolt roar, and hurl down the thunder. He will try to show perhaps the vengeful god; but he will make the cries of a distressed mother emerge through the different characteristics of this painting.

But whatever prodigious genius this artist has, he will not attain one of these goals without detouring from the other. Everything that he will devote to [*painting*] tableaux will be deflected from the pathos. The whole will produce more of an effect on the ears, less on the soul. This composer will be more admired by artists [*painters*], less by people of taste.

And do not think for one moment that it is the parasitic words of the lyrical style that creates the pathos in this piece, *hurl down* [lancer], *roar* [gronder], *tremble*, [trembler]: it is rather the passion with which it is animated. And if the musician, neglecting the cry of passion, amuses himself by combining sounds instead of words, the poet will have created a cruel trap for him.

. . . .

[*After these remarks, the discussion turns away from lyrical theatre and soon concludes.*]

APPENDIX TO CHAPTER 6

Denis Diderot
from the *Lessons for harpsichord and principles of harmony, by M. Bemetzrieder*

Text: Denis Diderot, *Leçons de clavecin et principes d'harmonie, par M. Bemetzrieder* (1771), ed. Jean Mayer and Pierre Citron, intro. Jean Varloot, Hermann, ixx. 59–391.

from the Second Suite of the Twelfth Dialogue and of the Seventh Lesson of Harmony

[*This passage (Hermann, pp. 337–40) follows the Pupil's performance of the prelude that she has composed for the birthday celebration of her father, the Philosopher in the dialogue. (The real-life figures are Angélique and her father Diderot.)*]

THE PHILOSOPHER. I would not say that that was bad, nor even that the effect was bad. Is that your first endeavour?

THE MASTER. No, sir. The piece that you have just heard is one of the twelve bass progressions that Mademoiselle has composed, written and figured in all the keys [*referring to the continuo bass practice of using figures or numbers to give the intervallic configuration of the chord above the bass note*]; among these progressions, there is one where every chord is used, and almost every related modulation, even very skilfully, and at each instant [*there are*] truly expressive departures, and completely new turns.

THE PHILOSOPHER. And these preludes, where are they?

THE PUPIL. Here they are.

THE PHILOSOPHER. What? But this is considerable work.

THE PUPIL. And necessary. Imagine, Papa, that this was the only way to fix in my memory the sharps and flats in each key [modulation], the connection and the succession of harmonies, the variety of transitions from one to the other, the nature of chords, the manner of figuring them, in a word, the multitude of things that it is necessary to have presented, if we propose to make a prelude [préluder].

THE MASTER. I advise my pupils to do as many as you have done, and to you, Mademoiselle, to overcome your reluctance to take up the pen and to return to an exercise that will give you facility.

THE PHILOSOPHER. And ideas. There are some [*preludes*] that are born under the fingers by chance, that come from who knows where, and that are no less precious for that.

THE PUPIL. I will never write music, perhaps even when I would be able to promise myself to write excellently.

THE PHILOSOPHER. And why?

THE PUPIL. Because I prefer to read and to think than to combine sounds.

THE PHILOSOPHER. You are going to say that I never let go; but I would really like to hear you make a prelude from your head.

THE PUPIL. That is what I once wished.

THE PHILOSOPHER. One moment. (*to a servant*) No; no tea, it is too late.

THE MASTER. Mademoiselle, start in a key, it does not matter which. Strike the chords; arpeggiate them; make a melody above, for the bass. Do not subordinate yourself to any rhythmic metre; listen only to your heart, your imagination and your ear; and nevertheless play in strict time [de mesure].

THE PUPIL. Papa, give the key.

THE PHILOSOPHER. B major.

THE PUPIL. (*She plays a prelude.*)

THE PHILOSOPHER. Very good. Very good. It only remains for you to hear good music.

THE PUPIL. That is the affair of monsieur the Baron of B ... [*Editor's FN: The Baron de Bagge ... organized ... concerts which were among the best in Paris. He is cited in* Le Neveu de Rameau.]

THE PHILOSOPHER. And accompanying? Where are we?

THE MASTER. The accompaniment is a kind of reading that a knowledge of harmony illuminates and facilitates, but which demands practice and time. M. Grimm sends us works of the first masters; we have already done several; and that is coming nicely.

THE PHILOSOPHER. I understand that the use of modulations, the continual practice of chords, the facility of relating them to certain notes of the scale to which they belong, the exercise of the ear, can sometimes dispense with figures; but always? To accompany well and without figures?

THE MASTER. No matter how versed one is in the theory and practice of the art, do not imagine that among so many different combinations with which the bass can be accompanied, that it is easy to encounter immediately the one that suits the pure harmony and the spirit of the piece, and you will be right. However, one can accompany very well, without figures, a bass for which one sees the melody. I have even noticed that my pupils are more securely guided by the melody than by ambiguous figures. The melody and bass suffice in order to indicate the chain of modulations, the harmonies and chords, and nothing more is necessary. Taste does the rest, and taste comes with time.

THE PHILOSOPHER. My daughter, since you have enough regard for men to strive for their praise, a disposition of which I approve and that I advise you to maintain, and that the praise of those whom you esteem and that you love is pleasurable to you, accept mine. Work, practice; occupy yourself seriously with an art where you are already well advanced and which will one day become the most powerful consolation of the sorrows which await you; for no one on earth is exempt from them, and it is fortunate to have a sure friend always near you.

THE PUPIL. It will be all the easier to obey you, since I prefer infinitely more to follow my ideas than to read the ideas of others. Papa, the science of harmony makes pieces considerably less tasteful.

THE PHILOSOPHER. I am not surprised. However, one talent must not harm another. Few are in a condition to appreciate a beautiful prelude, well planned, varied, well thought-out; everyone feels the merit of a piece that is well done and well played.

THE PUPIL. Because there are more ears than souls.

THE PHILOSOPHER. That is the opposite of what you mean.

THE PUPIL. No, no; I understand myself well, and some day I will explain myself to you on this matter. Whenever that may be, if I were a long time without going near my instrument, I could lose the facility that I have in reading and performing. As for the science of harmony, I believe that I would never forget it, and that it is a very sure means, Monsieur, of making me remember you, as long as I live.

A SERVANT. The tea is ...

THE PHILOSOPHER. No more tea, I have told you. I hope, Monsieur, that you will accord me a small quarter of an hour of your time, tomorrow morning.

THE MASTER. Gladly, Monsieur.

THE PUPIL. Papa,

THE PHILOSOPHER. What do you want?

THE PUPIL. That you tell Mama that you are content with me a little, tomorrow morning.

THE PHILOSOPHER. I love you to distraction. (*To the Master*) You will spend the rest of the day with us, won't you? The weather is gentle, we will go out after dinner. A little air will do all three of us good. [*end of the Second Suite*]

Third Suite of the Twelfth Dialogue
and of the Seventh Lesson of Harmony
Elementary and General Principles of Theory
              The Master, the Pupil, the Philosopher

[*Hermann, pp. 340–43.*] We dined gaily, because we were all satisfied with one another; the Master with his Pupil; me [*the Philosopher*] with both of them. The day was quite nice for the season. We left the table early. I proposed a long walk. They accepted the proposition, and we went to the Etoile. Arrived there, we withdrew to the end of one of the alleys which open to the south, where the eye wanders over quite a large expanse of countryside, and where there is sun to enjoy from the moment when it rises above the buildings of the city until it sets. The shadow of the dome of the Invalides was not yet very long. Its lighted hemisphere was approximately south-west. Monsieur Bemetz sat down, his back leaning against a tree. We placed ourselves casually on the ground, my daughter and I; and we continued the conversation that we had begun on our walk. It was a matter of the different systems of music, of the fundamental bass of Rameau, the resonance of the intermediary sound of Tartini, and of the ancient rule of the octave [*in continuo bass practice, the rule for how to harmonize each note of the diatonic scale*]. My daughter remarked that there were many examples in her lessons and very little theory, and it was less to principles than to the method that she owed her progress. Monsieur Bemetz, her Master, answered her that the art of music also had its own [*principles*] to which one conformed approximately, without knowing them well. And who does not know the fundamental bass, I asked? And who told you that this system was true or false, he answered? Monsieur Bemetz had some reluctance to explain himself. 'We came here to take the air, and not to dispute. The thing did not yet have all the clarity and thoroughness in his head of which it was susceptible. It was better to be silent than to rush out incoherent and undigested ideas, above all to those who were not people who would be satisfied with that.' To these pretexts he added others. We insisted; and it was not without pain that he drew from his pocket three small notebooks that he read to us, on one condition which was agreed to; that we would listen without interrupting him, unless he expressly permitted it.

Number 1

THE MASTER. It is a beautiful discovery, the resonance of the sounding body. How many consequences one could draw from it! Every sounding body, in addition to a principal and fundamental sound, produces its major third and fifth, or the overtones at the point of the harmonics.

THE PUPIL. But is this phenomenon well proven?

THE MASTER. Mademoiselle, you are not keeping your word.

THE PUPIL. Speak, Monsieur, I am quiet.

THE MASTER. A sounding body *ut*, produces *ut*, *mi*, *sol* [*in C major, CEG*]; but the fifth *sol*, with which the ear is preoccupied, produces *sol*, *si*, *re* [*GBD*]; a third *re*, gives *re*, *fa* sharp, *la* [*DF#A*]; a fourth *la*, *la*, *ut* sharp, *mi* [*AC#E*]; and from sounding body to sounding body a fifth apart from one another, one can form the diatonic and chromatic octaves; and that is perhaps the reason why the scales, more or less complete in the past and in every nation, were universally ordered by intervals which indicate some law of nature that guides the organ.

If that is the case, the scale would be a common product of nature and of art; of nature which has furnished the three sounds of the sounding body, *ut*, [*C, in C major*] for example; of art which has used different sounding bodies and their harmonics, *si*, *re*, *fa*, *la*, [*B,D,F,A*], and which has inserted them among the three sounds of a first [sound], in order to form the scale *ut*, *re*, *mi*, *fa*, *sol*, *la*, *si*, *ut*.

Whatever it may be; it is the affair of Rameau, and not mine. I came; I found seven sounds ordered like that; and that is sufficient for me.

THE PUPIL. The chromatic octave, *ut*, *ut* sharp ...

THE MASTER. Yes, Mademoiselle, it is neither more nor less natural than the diatonic octave; and after that ... I am gathering my papers.

THE PUPIL. Pardon, Monsieur; no more interruptions; no more; I promise.

Number 2

THE MASTER. The ear barely accommodates itself to thirteen sounds of this chromatic octave; and I doubt that their succession has ever been established and will ever establish a musical genre. In waiting, I confine myself to the octave *ut*, *re*, *mi*, *fa*, *sol*, *la*, *si*, *ut* [*C,D,E,F,G,A,B,C*]. Or *la*, *si*, *ut*, *re*, *mi*, *fa*, *sol*, *la* [*A,B,C,D,E,F,G,A*]. Except for my recourse to the five other sounds [*the chromatic tones*], when it pleases me to move from a diatonic interval to another, through shades or nuances.

I call the major mode the succession of eight sounds, *ut*, *re*, *mi*, *fa*, *sol*, *la*, *si*, *ut*, or the succession of all other sounds ordered in the same manner.

I call the minor mode the succession of eight sounds, *la*, *si*, *ut*, *re*, *mi*, *fa*, *sol*, *la*, or the succession of all other sounds ordered in the same manner.

I call in melody and harmony the sounds *ut*, *mi*, *sol*, [*CEG*], products of the sounding body, *natural sounds* or *appelés* [*the closest translation would be 'consonances'; however, since it is not completely satisfactory, we leave the term in the original*].

I call in melody and harmony, the sounds *si*, *re*, *fa*, *la*, [*B,D,F,A*], inserted among the natural sounds *ut*, *mi*, *sol*, *appels* [*the closest translation would be 'dissonances'*].

Thus, in *ut* sharp major, the natural sounds are *ut* sharp, *mi* sharp, *sol* sharp [*C#,E#,G#*]; and the *appels* are *si* sharp, *re* sharp, *fa* sharp, *la* sharp [*B#,D#,F#,A#*].

. . . .

[*The rest of section* 2 *continues in similar fashion.*]

Number 8

[*The section begins with a discussion of various modulation sequences through a wide range of sharp and flat keys, both major and minor (Hermann, pp. 351–3). Our translation begins on p. 353.*]

THE MASTER. Have I employed anything other than the simplest resources of musical magic?

THE PUPIL. No.

THE MASTER. However, if you have a little imagination; if you can feel; if the sounds capture your soul; if you are born with a volatile disposition; if nature has chosen you to experience ecstasy [enthusiasm] for yourself and to transmit it to others, what will have happened to you [*during these modulations*]? [You will have seen] a man who awakens at the centre of a labyrinth. There he is searching left and right for an exit; one moment he believed that he was reaching the end of his errors; he stops, he follows with an uncertain and trembling step, the route, deceptive perhaps, that opens before him; there he is once again gone astray; he walks, and after some turns and returns, the place from which he left, is where he finds himself. There, he turns his eyes around him; he notices a straighter route; he throws himself into it; he imagines a free place beyond a forest that he proposes to cross; he runs; he rests; he runs again; he climbs, he climbs; he has attained the summit of a hill; he descends; he falls; he rises, bruised from falls and refalls, he goes; he arrives, he looks, and he recognizes the very place of his awakening.

Unease and pain seize his soul; he complains; his complaint echoes in the surrounding places; what will become of him? He does not know; he abandons himself to his destiny which promises him an exit and which deceives him. Hardly has he made some steps than he has returned to the place of his departure.

THE PHILOSOPHER. And that is what we mean by linking sounds in a succession that gives us pause; to know how to speak to the soul and to the ear, and to know the sources of song and of melody whose true type is at the core of our heart; do you understand, my daughter? Immerse yourself in a first idea; follow it, until it calls forth a second, which [*calls forth*] a third, and take as a given that your successions, [*although*] interpreted differently by each of your listeners, will not be devoid of meaning for anyone.

THE MASTER. I do not say that the image that suggests itself to my soul is the only one that we can associate with the same succession of harmony. It is [*the same*] with sounds as [*it is*] with abstract words of which the definition is determined ultimately in an infinity of different examples which touch one another through some common points. Such is the privilege and the richness of the indeterminate and vague expression of our art that each of us disposes of our songs according to the present state of our soul; and that is why a single cause becomes the source of an infinity of pleasures or diverse pains.

What an astonishing variety of momentary and fleeting sensations I would have aroused, if I had mingled dissonant harmonies with consonant harmonies and put to work all the power of the art? Ask your father what happens inside himself when he is seated, with eyes closed, at the far end of the harpsichord, and he gives himself up to the discretion of the sensitive artist who knows how to link a series of chords. A musical genius has colours on his palette for every phenomenon of nature and all the passions of man; he knows how to paint both the sunrise and the end of the day; and the sadness of wickedness, and the serenity of innocence; but this trait is so elusive that if there are few composers of excellent music, there are hardly any true listeners.

After having led you astray through the detours of a labyrinth, with the aid only of the principal harmonies of the twenty-four keys; if it had pleased me to call forth silence and darkness; there would have been silence and darkness. If it had pleased me to pierce the silence and gloom with cries; a wail and reinforced cries were beneath my hand. If I had proposed to augment the sadness of solitude with the horror of the night, to open tombs, to invoke spirits, and to frighten you with their murmur, you would have heard them yourself; you would have trembled, you would have cried out, souls of my fathers, speak; souls in pain, what do you wish of me? Then suddenly, rearranging a single finger, the day would have returned, all the sad phantoms would have disappeared; and if the fantasy came to me, I would have been the master of having them [*the sad phantoms*] succeeded by a cortege of pleasure, laughs, games, loves, tenderness and voluptuousness. What a crowd of diverse tableaux are piled up sometimes in a recitative with orchestral ritornellos [récitatif obligé]! The heart is moved, the touch is urgent, and the feeling is created.

And there it is, what Mademoiselle has called a combination; that's what it undoubtedly is, but who has succeeded in doing it?

THE PHILOSOPHER. Hasse and Pergolesi; Philidor and Grétry, and some others who have taught me that the musician, with his lyre in his hand, could advance himself along the lines of a Puget, Le Sueur, Voltaire, and Bossuet, and to say, me too, I know how to master people's souls.

THE PUPIL. But a fault that is quite common is to scorn the talents that one despairs of ever acquiring; I have committed this small foolishness, and I would not know how to repent for it; except that you have made it the occasion for raising the excellence of your art so well.

THE MASTER. With the diatonic keys known and their connections demonstrated, the art proceeds to the question of what can be obtained from each one.

Let us retrace our steps for a moment. We will form some successions of sounds or melody. We will strike the sounds together, and we will produce harmony. [*end of section 8 of the Third Suite*]

————————

SELECT BIBLIOGRAPHY

THIS bibliography consists of works that are central to the arguments in this study; it does not include works mentioned incidentally in footnotes. When 'complete works' editions are given, these appear before individual titles by that author. Individual titles are accompanied by original dates of appearance of works—either in manuscript or in published form. Modern editions are identified as facsimilies if they present photocopies of the original. Square brackets are used for names or dates where the information has been established by means other than the title page. For abbreviations used in this bibliography see the list at the front of the work.

Alembert, Jean le Rond d', 'Discours préliminaire des éditeurs', *Encyclopédie, ou dictionnaire raisonné des sciences, des arts et des métiers par une société de gens de lettres. Mis en ordre et publié par M. Diderot, quant à la parties mathématique, par M. d'Alembert*, vol. i (Paris: Briasson, David l'aîné, Le Breton, Durand, 1751), pp. xi–xii.

——'Avertissement des editeurs', *Encyclopédie, ou dictionnaire raisonné* ... , vol. vi (Paris: Briasson, David l'aîné, Le Breton, Durand, 1756), i; facsimile edn. in *CTW* v (1969), 288–90.

——'De la liberté de la musique', *Mélanges de littérature, d'histoire, et de philosophie* (Amsterdam: Zacharie Chatelain et Fils, *1759)*, vol. iv. 377–454.

——*Elémens de musique théorique et pratique, suivant les principes de M. Rameau* (Paris: David, 1752); facsimile edn. New York: Broude, 1966. 2nd edn. *Revue, corrigée, & considérablement augmentée* (Lyon: Bruyset, 1762); facsimile edn. of 'Discours préliminaire' (1762) in *CTW*, vi (1972), 457–77.

Alocco-Bianco, *et al.*, *Diderot, les beaux-arts et la musique, actes du colloque international tenu à Aix-en-Provence, décembre 1984* (Aix-en-Provence: Université de Provence Press, 1984).

Anthony, James, *French Baroque Music* (New York: W. W. Norton & Co., 1974).

Batteux, Charles, *Les Beaux-arts réduits à un même principe* (1743; 2nd edn. 1747); facsimilie edn. of 1747 edn. New York: Johnson Reprint Corp., 1970.

Beleval, Yvon, *L'Esthétique sans paradoxe de Diderot* (Paris: Gallimard, 1956).

Bernard, Jonathan, 'The Principle and the Elements: Rameau's Controversy with d'Alembert', *Journal of Music Theory*, 24 (1980), 37–62.

Boileau-Despréaux, Nicolas, *L'Art poétique* (1674); ed. Guy Riegert, Paris: Larousse, 1972.

Buchmann, Guy, 'Une Œuvre paradoxale de Bemetzrieder', *Diderot, les beaux-arts et la musique, actes du colloque international tenu à Aix-en-Provence, décembre 1984* (Aix-en-Provence: Université de Provence Press, 1984), 185–209.

Buelow, George, 'Rhetoric and Music', in *The New Grove Dictionary of Music and Musicians*, ed. Stanley Sadie, 20 vols. (London: Macmillan, 1980).

Cassirer, Ernst, *The Philosophy of the Enlightenment*, trans. Fritz C. A. Koelln and James Pettegrove (Boston: Beacon Press, 1955).

Chailley, Jacques, 'Rameau et la théorie musicale', *La Revue musicale*, 260 (1964), 65–95.

Chanier, Paul, 'L'Opposition majeur-mineur, est-elle dans la nature? (Physique, métaphysique et musique)', in Alocco-Bianco *et al.*, *Diderot, les beaux-arts et la musique, actes du colloque international tenu à Aix-en-Provence, décembre 1984* (Aix-en-Provence: Université de Provence Press, 1984), 159–75.

Chouillet, Anne-Marie, 'Présupposés, contours et prolongements de la polémique autour des écrits théoriques de Jean-Philippe Rameau', in Jerome de La Gorce (ed.), *Jean-Philippe Rameau: Colloque international organisé par la Société Rameau: Dijon 21–24 septembre 1983* (Paris: Champion-Slatkine, 1987), 425–43.

Chouillet, Jacques, *Diderot poète de l'énergie* (Paris: Presses Universitaires de France, 1984).

Christensen, Thomas, 'Science and Music Theory in the Enlightenment: D'Alembert's Critique of Rameau' (Ph.D. diss., Yale University, 1985).

——'Eighteenth-Century Science and the *Corps Sonore*: The Scientific Background to Rameau's Principle of Harmony', *Journal of Music Theory* 31 (1987), 23–50.

——'Rameau's "L'Art de la basse fondamentale"', *Music Theory Spectrum*, 9 (1987), 18–41.

——'Music Theory as Scientific Propaganda: The Case of d'Alembert's *Elémens de Musique*', *Journal of the History of Ideas*, 50 (1989), 409–27.

Condillac, Etienne Bonnet de, *Essai sur l'origine des connaissances humaines* (Paris, 1746); Paris: Galilee, 1973.

——*Jean-Philippe Rameau: The Science of Music Theory in the Enlightenment* (Cambridge: Cambridge University Press, forthcoming).

Cowart, Georgia, *The Origins of Modern Musical Criticism: French and Italian Music, 1600–1750* (Ann Arbor, Mich.: University Microfilms International, 1981).

Crocker, Lester, *Diderot's Chaotic Order: Approach to Synthesis* (Princeton, NJ: Princeton University Press, 1974).

——'The Idea of a "Neutral" Universe', *Diderot Studies*, 21 (1983), 45–76.

Darnton, Robert, *The Literary Underground of the Old Regime* (Cambridge, Mass.: Harvard University Press, 1982).

de Man, Paul, 'The Rhetoric of Blindness: Jacques Derrida's Reading of Rousseau', *Blindness and Insight: Essays in the Rhetoric of Contemporary Criticism* (New York: Oxford University Press, 1971), 102–41.

Derrida, Jacques, *De la Grammatologie* (Paris: Minuit, 1967).

——*Of Grammatology*, trans. Gayatri C. Spivak (Baltimore: Johns Hopkins University Press, 1976).

Descartes, René, *Compendium musicae* (pub. *1650*; MS 1618); facsimile edn. New York: Broude, 1968. English trans. of 1618 by Walter Robert (np: American Institute of Musicology, 1961).

Diderot, Denis, *Œuvres complètes de Diderot*, ed. Jules Assézat and Maurice Tourneux, 10 vols. (Paris: Garnier, 1875–7).

——*Œuvres complètes, Edition chronologique*, intro. Roger Lewinter, 15 vols. (Paris: Le Club français du livre, 1969–73).

——*Denis Diderot: Œuvres complètes, édition critique et annotée*, secretary-general Jean Varloot, 23 vols. to date (Paris: Hermann, 1975–).

——*Les Bijoux indiscrets* (1748); ed. Jean Macary, intro. Aram Vartanian, Hermann, iii (1978), 35–281.

——*Mémoires sur différens sujets de mathématiques* (1748); ed. Jean Mayer, Hermann, ii (1975), 231–338.

——*Lettre sur les aveugles* (1749); ed. Robert Niklaus, with commentary by Yvon Belaval and Robert Niklaus, Hermann, iv (1978), 15–107.

—— *Lettre sur les sourds et muets* (1751); ed. Jacques Chouillet, Hermann, vol. iv (1978), 129–233.

——'Beau' in the *Encyclopédie* (1751); ed. John Lough and Jacques Proust, Hermann, vol. vi (1976), 135–71.

——*Pensées sur l'interprétation de la nature* (1754); ed. Jean Varloot, with commentary by Herbert Dieckmann and Jean Varloot, Hermann, ix (1981), 25–111.

——*Entretiens sur 'le Fils naturel'* (1757); ed. Jacques Chouillet and Anne-Marie Chouillet, Hermann, x (1980), 83–162.

——*De la Poésie dramatique* (1758); ed. Jacques Chouillet and Anne-Marie Chouillet, Herman, x (1980), 323–427.

——*Le Neveu de Rameau* (1761); ed. Henri Coulet, Hermann, xii (1989), 69–196.

——'Salon de 1767', ed. Else Marie Bukdahl, Hermann, xvi (1990), 55–519.

——*Paradoxe sur le comédien* [original version, 1769; revision, 1773], Assézat, viii (1875), 361–423.

——*Le Rêve de d'Alembert* (1769); ed. Georges Dulac, with intro. by Jean Varloot, Hermann, xvii (1987), 89–207.

——'Compte rendu sur *Leçons de clavecin*', written for Grimm's *Correspondance littéraire* (Sept. 1771); ed. Jean Mayer and Pierre Citron, intro. Jean Varloot, Hermann, xix (1983), 397–407.

—— *Leçons de clavecin et principes d'harmonie, par M. Bemetzrieder* (1771), ed. Jean Mayer and Pierre Citron, intro. Jean Varloot, Hermann, xix (1983), 59–391.

—— *Observations sur un ouvrage intitulé 'Traité du mélodrame'* (1771; ed. Roger Lewinter, *Œuvres complètes, Edition chronologique* (Paris: Le Club français du livre, 1969–73), ix (1971), 934–41.

—— *Denis Diderot: Ecrits sur la musique*, ed. and intro. Béatrice Durand-Sendrail (Paris: Editions Lattès, 1987).

Diderot, Denis (ed.), *Encyclopédie, ou dictionnaire raisonné des sciences, des arts et des métiers par une société de gens de lettres. Mis en ordre et publié par M. Diderot, quant à la parties mathématique, par M. d'Alembert*, 17 vols (Paris: Briasson, David l'aîné, Le Breton, Durand, 1751–65).

Didier, Béatrice, *La musique des lumières* (Paris: Presses Universitaires de France, 1985).

Dieckmann, Herbert, 'Diderot's Conception of Genius', *Journal of the History of Ideas*, 2, no.2 (1941), 151–82.

Dubos, Jean-Baptiste, *Réflexions critiques sur la poésie et la peinture* (Paris: Mariette, 1719).

Duchez, Marie-Elisabeth, '"Principe de la mélodie" et "Origine des langues": Un brouillon inedit de Jean-Jacques Rousseau sur l'origine de la melodie', *Revue de musicologie*, 60 (1974), 33–86.

—— 'Valeur épistémologique de la théorie de la basse fondamentale de Jean-Philippe Rameau: connaissance scientifique et représentation de la musique', *Studies on Voltaire and the Eighteenth Century*, 245 (1986), 91–130.

—— 'D'Alembert diffuseur de la théorie harmonique de Rameau: déduction scientifique et simplification musical', in Monique Emery and Pierre Monzani (eds.), *Jean d'Alembert, savant et phillosophe: Portrait à plusieurs voix, actes du colloque organisé par le Centre International de Synthèse-Fondation pour la Science, Paris, 15–8 juin 1983* (Paris: Archives contemporaines, 1989), 475–96.

Escal, Françoise, 'Musique et science', *International Review of the Aesthetics and Sociology of Music*, 14 (1983), 167–90.

Fellows, Otis, 'The Theme of Genius in Diderot's Neveu de Rameau', *Diderot Studies*, 2 (1952), 168–99.

——*Diderot* (Boston: Twayne Publishers, 1977).

Ferris, Joan, 'The Evolution of Rameau's Harmonic Theories', *Journal of Music Theory*, 3, no. 1 (1959), 231–55.

Filoche, Jean-Luc, '*Le Neveu de Rameau* et la Querelle des Bouffons: Un Son de cloche inédit', *Diderot Studies*, 21 (1983), 95–109.

Gay, Peter, *The Enlightenment: An Interpretation*, vol. ii, *The Science of Freedom* (New York: Alfred A. Knopf, 1969).

Gilman, Margaret, 'Imagination and Creation in Diderot', *Diderot Studies*, 2 (1952), 200–20.

Gossman, Lionel, 'Time and History in Rousseau', *Studies on Voltaire*, 30 (1964), 311–49.

Gribenski, Jean, 'A propos des *Leçons de clavecin* (1771): Diderot et Bemetzrieder', *Revue de musicologie*, 66, no. 2 (1980), 127–78.

Grimm, Friedrich Melchior, *Lettre de M. Grimm sur Omphale* (Paris: np, 1752); facsimile edn. in Launay, i. 3–54.

Guerlac, Henry, 'Where the Statue Stood: Divergent Loyalties to Newton in the Eighteenth Century', in Earl R. Wasserman (ed.), *Aspects of the Eighteenth Century*, (Baltimore: Johns Hopkins University Press, 1965).

Hankins, Thomas, *Jean d'Alembert: Science and the Enlightenment* (Oxford: Clarendon Press, 1970).

Heartz, Daniel, 'Diderot et Le Théatre lyrique', *Revue de musicologie*, 64 (1978), 229–41.

Hunt, Thomas Webb, 'The *Dictionnaire de musique* of Jean-Jacques Rousseau' (Ph.D. diss., North Texas State University, 1967).

Jansen, Albert, *Jean-Jacques Rousseau als Musiker* (Berlin: G. Reimer, 1884).

Kabelac, Sharon L., 'Irony as a Metaphysics in *Le Neveu de Rameau*', *Diderot Studies*, 14 (1971), 97–112.

Kiernan, Colm, 'Diderot and Science', *Diderot Studies*, 14 (1971), 113–19.

Kintzler, Catherine, *Jean-Philippe Rameau: Splendeur et naufrage de l'esthétique du plaisir à l'âge classique*, 2nd edn. (Paris: Minerve, 1988).

Kisch, Eve, 'Rameau and Rousseau', *Music and Letters*, 22, no.2 (1941), 97–115.

La Gorce, Jean de (ed.), *Jean-Philippe Rameau: Colloque international organisé par la Société Rameau, Dijon, 21–24 septembre 1983* (Paris, Geneva: Champion-Slatkine, 1987).

Lang, Paul Henry, 'Diderot as Musician', *Diderot Studies*, 10 (1968), 95–107.

Launay, Denise (ed.), *La Querelle des Bouffons: texte des pamphlets avec introduction, commentaires et index*, 3 vols. (Geneva: Minkoff, 1973).

Le Huray, Peter, and Day, James (eds.), *Music and Aesthetics in the Eighteenth and Early Nineteenth Centuries*, abridged edn. (Cambridge: Cambridge University Press, 1988).

Lecerf de la Viéville, Jean Laurent, *Comparison de la musique italienne et de la musique française* (Paris, 1704); facsimile edn. Geneva: Minkoff, 1972.

Lescat, Philippe, 'Conclusion sur l'origine des sciences', in Jerome de La Gorce (ed.), *Jean-Philippe Rameau Colloque International*, 409–24.

Masson, Paul-Marie, 'La "Lettre sur Omphale"', *Revue de musicologie*, 27 (1945), 1–19.

Meyer, Paul, 'Diderot: *Lettre sur les sourds et muets*, Edition commentée et présentée par Paul Hugo Meyer', *Diderot Studies*, 7 (1965).

Neubauer, John, *The Emancipation of Music from Language* (New Haven, Conn.: Yale University Press, 1986).

Niklaus, Robert, 'Diderot and the *Leçons de clavecin*', in T. E. Lawrenson, F. E. Stucliffe, and G. F. A. Gadoffre (eds.), *Modern Miscellany Presented to Eugene Vinaver* (Manchester: Manchester University Press, 1969), 180–94.

Oliver, Alfred, *The encyclopédistes as Critics of Music* (New York: Columbia University Press, 1947; reprinted New York: American Musicological Society Press, Inc., 1966).

Palisca, Claude, 'Scientific Empiricism in Musical Thought', in Hedley Howell Rhys (ed.), *Seventeenth Century Science and the Arts*, (Princeton, NJ: Princeton University Press, 1961), 91–137.

Pappas, John, 'Diderot, d'Alembert, et l'Encyclopédie', *Diderot Studies*, 4 (1963), 191–208.

——'D'Alembert et la querelle des Bouffons d'après des documents inédits', *Revue d'Histoire littéraire de la France*, 65 (1965), 479–84.

Paul, Charles B., 'Jean-Philippe Rameau (1683–1764), the Musician as Philosophe', *Proceedings of the American Philosophical Society*, 114, no. 2 (1970), 140–54.

Perrault, Charles, *Parallèle des anciens et des modernes en ce qui regarde les arts et les sciences* (Paris, 1688); facsimile edn. in *Theorie und Geschichte der Literatur und der schoenen Kuenste*, vol. ii, Munich: Eidos Verlag, 1974.

Proust, Jacques, *Diderot et l'Encyclopédie* (Paris: Armand Colin, 1962).

Raguenet, François, *Parallèle des Italiens et des Français en ce qui regarde la musique et les opéras* (Paris, 1702); facsimile edn. Geneva: Minkoff, 1976.

Rameau, Jean-Philippe, *Jean-Philippe Rameau: Complete Theoretical Writings* ed.

Erwin R. Jacobi, 6 vols. (Rome: American Institute of Musicology, 1967–72).

—— *Traité de l'harmonie* (Paris: Ballard, 1722); facsimile edn. in *CTW* i (1967).

—— *Nouveau système de musique théorique* ... *pour servir d'introduction au traité de l'harmonie* (Paris: Ballard, 1726); facsimile edn. in *CTW* ii (1967).

—— *Génération harmonique, ou Traité de musique théorique et pratique* (Paris: Prault Fils, 1737); facsimile edn. in *CTW* iii (1968), 1–150.

—— *Démonstration du principe de l'harmonie, servant de base à tout l'art musical théorique et pratique* (Paris: Durand, Pissot, 1750); facsimile edn. in *CTW* iii (1968), 151–254.

—— *Nouvelles réflexions de M. Rameau sur sa démonstration du principe de l'harmonie* (Paris: Durand, Pissot, 1752); facsimile edn. in *CTW* v (1969), 95–142.

Rameau, Jean-Philippe, *Extrait d'une réponse de M. Rameau à M. Euler sur l'identité des octaves* (1753); facsimile edn. in *CTW* v (1969), 167–88.

—— *Observations sur notre instinct pour la musique* (Paris: Prault Fils, Lambert, Duchesne, 1754); facsimile edn. in *CTW* iii (1968), 255–330.

[Rameau, Jean-Philippe], *Erreurs sur la musique dans l'Encyclopédie* (Paris: Chez Sebastien Jorry, 1755); facsimile edn. in *CTW* v (1969), 195–262.

Rameau, Jean-Philippe, *Code de musique pratique* ... *avec de nouvelles réflexions sur le principe sonore* (Paris: L'Imprimerie Royale, 1761); facsimile edn. in *CTW* iv (1969), 1–264.

—— 'Lettre de M. Rameau aux philosophes' (Paris: *Journal de Trévoux*, August 1762); facsimile edn. in *CTW* vi (1972), 507–14.

—— 'Vérités également ignorées et intéressantes tirées du sein de la nature', MS (*c.*1764); published in Herbert Schneider, *Jean-Philippe Rameaus Letzter Musiktraktat* (Stuttgart: Franz Steiner Verlag, 1986).

Rex, Walter, 'A Propos of the Figure of Music in the Frontispiece of the Encyclopédie: Theories of Musical Imitation in d'Alembert, Rousseau, and Diderot', *International Musicology Society: Report of the Twelfth Congress, Berkeley, 1977* (Kassel: Barenreiter, 1981).

Richebourg, Louisette, *Contribution à l'histoire de la querelle des Bouffons* (Paris: Nizet & Bastard, 1937).

Rousseau, Jean-Jacques, *Œuvres complètes de J.-J. Rousseau*, ed. Bernard Gagnebin and Marcel Raymond, 4 vols. (Paris: Bibliothèque de la Pléiade, Editions Gallimard, 1959–).

—— *Confessions* (1764–70), Pléiade, i (1959), 5–656.

—— *Ecrits sur la musique par J.-J. Rousseau*, ed. and intro. Catherine Kintzler (Paris: Editions Stock, 1979).

—— 'Projet concernant de nouveaux signes pour la musique' (1742); in *Ecrits sur la musique par J.-J. Rousseau*, ed. and intro. Catherine Kintzler (Paris: Editions Stock, 1979), 3–19.

—— *Lettre à M. Grimm au sujet des remarques ajoutées à sa lettre sur Omphale* (Paris: np, 1752); facsimile edn. in Launay, i. 89–117.

—— *Lettre sur la musique française* (Paris: np, 1753); facsimile edn. in Launay, i. 767–826.

—— 'Du principe de la mélodie ou réponse aux erreurs sur la musique', MS (*c.*1755); published in Duchez, '"Principe de la melodie"', and Wokler, 'Rameau, Rousseau, and *Essai*'.

Rousseau, Jean-Jacques, *Lettre à d'Alembert sur les spectacles* (1758); ed. Leon Fontain, Paris: Garnier, 1926.

——*Dictionnaire de musique* (Paris: Duchesne, 1768); facsimile edn. Hildesheim: Olms, 1969; reprint, New York: Johnson Reprint Corp., 1969.

——*Essai sur l'origine des langues* (pub. 1781; MS draft *c.*1755), ed. and intro. Jean Starobinski, Folio/Essais Series 135 (Paris: Gallimard, 1990).

——*Examen de deux principes avancés par M. Rameau* (pub. 1781; MS draft *c.*1755), in *Ecrits sur la musique par J.-J. Rousseau*, ed. and intro. Catherine Kintzler (Paris: Editions Stock, 1979), 337–370.

Sadowsky, Rosalie, 'Jean-Baptiste Abbé Dubos: The Influence of Cartesian and Neo-Aristotelian Ideas on Music Theory and Practice' (Ph.D. diss., Yale University, 1960).

Schneider, Herbert, *Jean-Philippe Rameaus letzter Musiktraktat* (Stuttgart: Franz Steiner Verlag, 1986).

Shirlau, Matthew, *The Theory of Harmony* (London: Novello, 1917).

Snyders, Georges, *Le Goût musical en France aux XVIIe et XVIIIe siècles* (Paris: Librairie Philosophique J. Vrin, 1968).

Tonelli, Giorgio, 'The "Weakness" of Reason', *Diderot Studies*, 14 (1971), 217–43.

Verba, Cynthia, 'The Development of Rameau's Thoughts on Modulation and Chromatics', *JAMS* 26, no.1 (1973), 69–91.

——'Rameau's Views on Modulation and their Background in French Theory', *JAMS* 31, no. 3 (1978), 467–79.

——'A Hierarchic Interpretation of the Theories and Music of Jean-Philippe Rameau' (Ph.D. diss., University of Chicago, 1979).

——review of Catherine Kintzler's *Jean-Philippe Rameau: Splendeur et naufrage de l'esthétique du plaisir à l'âge classique*, *JAMS* 38, no.1 (1985), 169–78.

Voltaire, François, *Elémens de la philosophie de Neuton* (Amsterdam: Jacques Desbordes, 1738).

Weber, William, 'Musical Taste in Eighteenth-Century France', *Past and Present*, 89 (1985), 58–85.

Wellek, René, *A History of Modern Criticism: 1750–1950*, vol. i, *The Late Eighteenth Century* (5 vols. to date; New Haven, Conn.: Yale University Press, 1955).

Wilson, Arthur M., *Diderot* (New York: Oxford University Press, 1972).

Wokler, Robert, 'Rameau, Rousseau, and *Essai sur l'origine des langues*', *Studies on Voltaire and the Eighteenth Century*, 127 (1974), 179–238.

——'Rousseau on Rameau and Revolution', *Studies in the Eighteenth Century*, 4 (1978), 251–83.

INDEX